Innovative Approaches to Reducing Global Poverty

To:
Andy Ryskamp
I hope you'll find
this book useful and
stimulating.
Best regards
Charles Wankel 7/8/07
WANKELC@STJOHNS.EDU
Jim (JAMES AF) Steven

Innovative Approaches to Reducing Global Poverty

edited by

James A. F. Stoner
Fordham University

and

Charles Wankel
St. John's University, New York

Information Age Publishing, Inc.
Charlotte, North Carolina • www.infoagepub.com

Library of Congress Cataloging-in-Publication Data

Innovative approaches to reducing global poverty / edited by James A. F.
Stoner and Charles Wankel.
      p. cm.
    Includes bibliographical references.
      ISBN-13: 978-1-59311-752-8 (pbk.)   ISBN-13: 978-1-59311-753-5 (hardcover)
 1. Economic development projects—Developing countries--Case studies.
 2. Industries—Social aspects. 3. International business enterprises—Social
 aspects. 4. Human capital. 5. Poor—Employment--Developing countries.
 6. People with social disabilities--Employment—Developed countries.
 7. Economic development—Social aspects. I. Stoner, James Arthur Finch, 1935-
 II. Wankel, Charles.
    HC59.72.E44I465 2007
    362.5'57091724—dc22

                                                                2007027015

Copyright © 2007 IAP–Information Age Publishing, Inc.

Printed in the United States of America

ISBN 13: 978-1-59311-752-8 (pbk.)
ISBN 13: 978-1-59311-753-5 (hardcover)
ISBN 10:   1-59311-000-0 (pbk.)
ISBN 10:   1-59311-000-0 (hardcover)

CONTENTS

INTRODUCTION

"a privilege and an honor ...
that gives us hope for the future"

James A. F. Stoner and Charles Wankel

We all know that poverty comes in many guises and is found in many places. It seems as though it will always be with us and perhaps it always will be. However, in a sense maybe it is more accurate to say that for us—the various authors, and you, the readers, of this book—it is barely with us, no matter how sensitive we might be as individuals, how empathic, sympathetic and caring our inherent nature's may be, and no matter how much of our time is devoted to "fighting," researching, and writing about poverty. Almost all of us who touch this volume have a relationship with poverty that is very different from the relationship that billions of others have. Poverty is "really with" those billions of people who may never hold in their hands a book as expensive and sophisticated as this one, or perhaps any book of any type over the course of a lifetime ... perhaps a very short lifetime for many millions of those billions.

The authors of the chapters in this book—maybe especially the authors of this chapter—have the good fortune and the blessed lives that allow them to seek ways to relieve the poverty that is such a burden for so many

Innovative Approaches to Reducing Global Poverty
pp. vii–xiii

but that does not impact us in the same ways. Yet, as one of the investing "sponsors" (sponsors is our word not theirs) in the social venture described in Chapter 4 says: *"It is an honour and a privilege for our foundation to work with Southwest Creations Collaborative ..."*, we suspect that for all of the authors in this book, it is an honor and a privilege to be able to make whatever contribution we can to reducing poverty wherever it exists. For the authors of this chapter it has certainly been an honor and a privilege to have the opportunity to *start* to *begin* to learn about the many varied approaches being taken in the many varied places discussed in the 10 chapters that follow.

We were reminded of many things as we edited these chapters. We were reminded that poverty is everywhere; that there are endless opportunities to contribute to its reduction; that productivity is a key—sometimes "the" key—to reducing poverty; that the number, scope, and variety of experiments with new types of social enterprises hold special promise for reducing poverty and perhaps for transforming all of society; that attempting to bring many of these innovative approaches into reality requires exceptional levels of commitment and energy; and that traditional for-profit companies have always been key contributors—perhaps "the" key contributors—to reducing poverty and that they may always be "the" key contributors even if so far they have only barely begun to make the contributions to reducing poverty that they are capable of making.

EVERYWHERE

Poverty is everywhere. One thing we were reminded of is that poverty is everywhere—not just in Bangladesh (chapter 6), India (chapter 3), and Kenya (chapter 5), but also in countries among the richest and most developed in the world—the United Kingdom (chapters 9 and 10) and the United States (chapter 4). In India the poverty is of the most severe kind, the poverty of Indian children who are HIV positive with active AIDs and the poverty of the 200-250 million "untouchable" Dalits," 75-80% of (whom) subsist below the poverty line" (chapter 3). In New Mexico, poverty may take the form of women with children to support whose life situations yield "traditional metrics of education, English-language skills, and family obligations (that would normally make) them unemployable or unable to run their own business." And whose "social status would normally limit their ability to provide for their dependents and lead to the cycle of poverty and societal isolation" that is often the face of poverty in more developed countries (chapter 4). In all of these places poverty is very real—very much "with" those who experience it day after day after day. And if poverty is everywhere, there are endless opportunities to contribute to reducing it.

ENDLESS OPPORTUNITIES

The possibilities for creating and taking innovative approaches to reduce poverty are seemingly endless. The innovations for reducing poverty described in this book come in more sizes and shapes than there are chapters in the book (if the reader is generous enough with this chapter's authors to be willing to add sizes and shapes together to get up to and beyond the number 10).

In terms of "sizes," one set of innovations focuses on multinational companies (MNCs) and addresses the ways they can contribute to reducing poverty at a level that exceeds the nation state—reaching beyond national borders to see groupings of LDCs in terms that unconceal otherwise "hidden" regional markets they might otherwise be blind to—markets that are large enough to justify their making the investments and conducting the operations that can contribute jobs—and perhaps education and maybe even some social transformation—that reduce poverty (chapter 7).

At the other extreme, another innovation involves a very small not-for-profit factory whose purpose is to train otherwise unemployable women to the point where they can move on to a small for-profit factory which in turn gives 30% of its profits to support a small orphanage. The numbers involved are quite small. The orphanage cares for five HIV-positive children and the training factory has assisted less than a dozen untouchable women to trade the degradation and dangers of careers in sex work for the greater self-esteem, work/life opportunities, and physical security that occur in a transition from prostitution to working in a for-profit manufacturing company (chapter 3).

In between these two examples in terms of size lie two other innovative organizations. One is the Kenya Women's Finance Trust (KWFT)—a Kenyan microcredit and business support institution, whose 80,000 small loans every year may impact moderately directly the lives of well over a million individuals (chapter 5). The other, the Bangladesh Extension Education Services (BEES) in chapter 6, provides similar fianancial and managerial/agricultural-expertise support mainly to small farmers and may have very similar levels of impact on poverty and on the lives of those farmers, their families, and their communities.

In the terms of "shapes," the innovations include such things as changing the ways MNCs see their own worlds (chapter 7), providing financial assistance and technical/managerial support to farmers and nascent businesswomen and men (chapters 5 and 10), and experimenting with new and perhaps evolving organizational purposes, forms, structures and processes (chapters 2, 3, 4 5, and 6). Sometimes well-known public figures are key players, like Bono, Ali Hewson, and Rogan Gregory who are involved in creating jobs in Sub-Saharan Africa (chapter 2). Sometimes things as seemingly ordinary and traditional as small businesses and retail stores are the focus and are seen as often making significant contributions to the reduction of poverty, with—perhaps—the potential to make even greater contributions in the future (chapters 9 and 10).

POVERTY AND PRODUCTIVITY

We do not recall when we first heard a saying we attribute to Peter Drucker along the lines of *the task of reducing poverty is not about making people rich, but—instead—about making them productive.* (One of this chapter's authors thinks he may have first heard it in East Africa in the very early 1960s.) The theme of enabling people to escape poverty by becoming more productive recurs in many of these chapters. Southwest Creative Collaborations (SCC) has developed an innovative and very inexpensive set of social support systems that combine with other activities and a powerful social/business philosophy to enable unemployable women to become very productive and very reliable workers (chapter 4). Edun (chapter 2) seeks to create new products and brands so it can increase its ability to offer jobs in impoverished parts of Africa and it exists in the first place only because the founders wanted to develop a vehicle to create such jobs—a social mission that was in search of a business to be involved in. That same theme of creating jobs so people can be productive to escape poverty is heard in the candle factory-manufacturing company-orphanage in Pune, India (chapter 3). And, to some extent, it is easy to hear that message in the Bangledesh (chapter 6) and Kenya (chapter 5) institutions. That theme—the theme of "missions seeking businesses"—is, perhaps, the defining nature of social enterprises.

SOCIAL ENTERPRISES

The authors of at least 4 of the 10 chapters have found social enterprises or social ventures particularly exciting vehicles for reducing poverty. All four of the chapters have at least some elements of organizational experimentation with new ways to conceptualize and bring social enterprises into being. In some of the chapters the innovation in organizational form is a very major theme, in some it is more muted. However, all of those chapters communicate the message that today much of the "social enterprise action" is about seeking to create bold new models that can become "scalable"—that can be used many times over in many different situations. And that "action" often seems to include the willingness to fail in hopes that the "failures" are really experiments that can create learning steps for future experiments in organizational form—steps that will eventually lead to organizational innovations that can be replicated in many many, many locations and industries.

In chapter 1, Easterly and Miesing provide a thorough discussion of the nature of, possibilities offered by, and challenges facing social ventures. Their views are echoed by Smith and Barr in chapter 2 when they discuss the roles of social entrepreneurship in reducing poverty, and then introduce Edun—the social enterprise founded by Bono, his wife Ali Hewson, and the New York fashion designer Rogan Gregory to bring employment to impoverished parts of Sub-Saharan Africa. An unusual aspect of that chapter is the fact that Edun and Smith and Barr's university are actively collaborating on a brand extension of Edun's product line for university students and their campuses.

In chapter 3, Cycyota and Volkland describe an experiment in organizational innovation involving three "intertwined" institutions committed to lifting disadvantaged women out of poverty and caring for children wth AIDS. In chapter 4, Raman presents the philanthropy/for-profit business SCC whose raison d'etre is also to provide jobs for women who would otherwise be unemployable. SCC's second purpose is to demonstrate that its way of doing business and creating social capital can make money. Making money is necessary for scalability in the large—for attracting purely or primarily profit-minded investors to these types of nontraditional "business enterprise." It is clear from Raman's writing that the social investors involved with SCC are seeking models that can be replicated—and that those investor's goals are to find organizational forms and processes that will create social capital. As the SCC investor cited above said: *The model they are developing is one that gives us hope for the future.*

Although the terms social enterprises and social ventures do not appear in chapters 5 and 6, the institutions they present fit comfortably under that umbrella (if we are not too nit-picky in our definitions of social ventures/enterprises)—both of the poverty-reducing institutions described in those chapters are organizations whose purpose is to make a social contribution—to create social capital. They generate revenues not enrich shareholders but to sustain and grow the institutions' contributions to reducing poverty and to serving society. KWFT in Kenya and BEES in Bangledesh demonstrate how social enterprises influence other social enterprises. Both institutions have been influenced greatly by the ideas and work of BEES' neighbor Muhammad Yunus. Their institutions are very similar in many ways, and deeply influenced by the Grameen Bank microcredit movement that emerged from his pioneering work.

COMMITMENT, ENERGY AND PERSISTENCE

Bringing these innovative approaches into being requires exceptional levels of commitment, energy, and persistence. All of the organizations described in this book have required exceptional levels of commitment from many individuals, and sometimes institutions, to survive. The two institutions presented in part II of this book are placed there to create a section of the book emphasizing "bumps in the road" because their survival stories are particularly rich. The Bangladesh Extension Education Services (BEES) survived the withdrawal of the financial and expert/managerial support of it's initial founder when the founder's own strategy and overseas mission changed. BEES survived only because of the personal and financial sacrifices of some of its Bengladeshi members and their ability to innovate the organization into a new persona (chapter 6).

When the new leader of the Kenya Women's Finance Trust came into the organization's office, what she saw *"was shocking, papers strewn everywhere on the floor and dust on the walls. The worst sight was that of the employees. Everybody in the office hung their heads and looked at me like 'just another passing MD (Managing Director)!' The dusty records ... revealed that the institution was in great debt."* Just as she was "coming to terms with the shock" a major donor institution demanded (and received) the transfer of the KHSH 840,000 remainder of its grant to another institution because it had given up on KWFT, as had all but two of the sponsoring organizations (chapter 4.) The survival of both of these institutions, and all of the other ones presented in this book, have required exceptional commitments and "stick-to-it-ness" from their key members and supporters.

NOT JUST SOCIAL ENTERPRISES

As enthusiastic as some of the authors are about the roles social ventures can learn to play in reducing poverty, companies in the for-profit private sector—seeking to achieve traditional economic success—are also seen as major contributors to the reduction of poverty. The final set of chapters, composing part III of this book, opens with a compelling engagement by Heslam in chapter 7 with the role commercial businesses can, should, and perhaps even "must" play in reducing poverty. Their business interest can be served, Heslam argues, by their social interest, and visa versa. Such businesses should therefore be considered part of the solution to poverty, rather than merely as part of the problem. Lyon and Bertotti and Whysall in chapters 9 and 10 remind us that poverty also exists in disadvantaged parts of developed countries and argue for the roles that are being played or can be played by small businesses and by the retail sector in the United Kingdom. Lyon and Bertotti present and test out a method for determining how much or how little contribution to reducing poverty private businesses of various types and under various conditions make. In offering a framework for predicting and evaluating the kinds and amounts of impact various businesses will have under various conditions, the provide the opportunity for a much more comprehensive analysis of the impact of businesses on disadvantaged on impoverished areas.

Hipsher, in chapter 8, emphasizes the positive roles MNCs can play in reducing poverty by rethinking what constitutes appropriate markets, especially markets in small developing countries, again emphasing the self interest—selfless interest combination. In these chapters on business, the reader may well be reminded of a major theme of many business and academic conferences in 2006-2007. Just two examples: The theme of the August 2007 annual meeting of the Academy of Management in Philadephia is "Doing Well by Doing Good." In coordination with that academy annual meeting, the Business as an Agent of World Benefit conference was held in Cleveland in October 2006.

Together, social enterprises and traditional businesses commited to reducing global poverty together can *give us hope for the future.*

PART I

**SOCIAL VENTURES FOR REDUCING POVERTY—
CREATING SKILLS AND JOBS ...
AND PERHAPS MODELS**

CHAPTER 1

SOCIAL VENTURE BUSINESS STRATEGIES FOR REDUCING POVERTY

Lisa Easterly and Paul Miesing

ABSTRACT

Social ventures are innovative businesses that operate with social purposes to provide services to disadvantaged individuals or the community that the market does not. While typically established as not-for-profit organizations, they compete with for-profit businesses that produce similar goods or services. They have been used to reduce poverty through job creation for the chronically unemployed, help impoverished communities produce their own products rather than importing them, create markets for products produced by impoverished communities, and provide job training to help the chronically unemployed acquire employable skills. The operation of social ventures is fraught with challenges that constrain their viability. This chapter describes diverse types of social venture models that contribute to poverty reduction and explores various innovative business strategies used to improve their business performance.

Innovative Approaches to Reducing Global Poverty
pp. 3–25
Copyright © 2007 by Information Age Publishing

INTRODUCTION

Social venturing is an expanding sector of entrepreneurship. Worldwide issues of persistent poverty and unemployment in the face of decreasing governmental and philanthropic support have led many not-for-profit organizations to establish social ventures to address these growing concerns (Brinkerhoff, 2000; Seelos & Mair, 2005). An increasing body of research confirms that the number of organizations that operate a sustainable business venture with a social mission is growing in many countries (Paton, 2003; Thompson & Doherty, 2006). Seed funding for such poverty-fighting ventures has become available from various international organizations and development institutions including the World Bank (Seelos & Mair, 2005). Social ventures have been used to reduce poverty through job creation for the chronically unemployed, help impoverished communities produce their own products rather than importing them, create markets for products produced by impoverished communities, and provide job training to help the chronically unemployed acquire employable skills (Brennan & Ackers, 2004; Easterly-Klaas, 2005; Emerson & Twersky, 1996; Thompson & Doherty, 2006).

Many poverty reduction programs operate as charities that foster dependence rather than rebuild communities (Peredo & Chrisman, 2006). Through enterprise development that creates local value and builds self-reliance among the chronically unemployed, social ventures have often succeeded in reducing poverty in areas where charities have failed (Brennan & Ackers, 2004; Thompson & Doherty, 2006). Although social ventures are businesses similar to for-profit companies, they operate with a strong social purpose mission. They often seek to employ disadvantaged groups of people or start businesses in impoverished communities that lack customers who can afford the products sold by for-profit companies, neither of which are attractive investments to for-profit companies that are trying to maximize profits (Seelos & Mair, 2005). By choosing to enter less viable markets or employing a lower-skilled workforce, social ventures operate at a competitive disadvantage as compared to their for-profit competitors. In the past, social ventures were able to rely on public funds and donations to help sustain their operations but decreasing public funds and growing competition for charitable donations has made it more difficult for these ventures to remain in operation (Brinkerhoff, 2000). Faced with the challenge to become more competitive, many social ventures have adopted for-profit business practices including strategic management to remain viable while fulfilling their social purpose mission (Brinkerhoff, 2000; Dees, 2001; Easterly-Klaas, 2005; Viravaidya & Hayssen, 2001).

In this chapter, we examine several successfully operated social ventures and the management strategies their organizations have employed to operate as a viable business while achieving their mission to reduce poverty and chronic unemployment. We conclude with a list of innovative business strategies and strategic management practices social ventures have successfully used to help them achieve their mission to reduce poverty.

WHAT IS A SOCIAL VENTURE?

Social ventures are often described as businesses that operate with a social purpose to provide a service to disadvantaged individuals or the community (Darby & Jenkins, 2006; Paton, 2003). What distinguishes social ventures from private sector businesses is the use of conventional business practices not just to generate a profit but also to achieve a social purpose or mission. Since social venturing, sometimes called social entrepreneurship, is still an emerging field, a clear definition of what constitutes such a venture has not been fully established. Many writers on the topic focus solely on the visionary entrepreneur and the management of their venture (Maitland, 2006; Spear, 2006). However, several authors have noted that the operation of a successful social venture involves the collective achievements of multiple constituents both inside and outside the organization (Dees, 1998; Easterly-Klaas, 2005; Emerson & Twersky, 1996; Paton, 2003; Spear, 2006). Since this chapter is concerned with social venture business strategies, we will consider a wide range of individual, contextual, and institutional elements that contribute to the sustainable operation of these ventures.

We do not want to confuse social ventures with for-profit businesses that operate with a strong focus on corporate citizenship and ethics. Corporate citizenship theory has been recognized as a framework under which private corporations should operate to ensure they behave in a socially responsible manner toward their stakeholders (Carroll, 1998; Meehan, Meehan, & Richards, 2006; Waddock, 2004). Businesses such as Ben & Jerry's, The Body Shop, and Tom's of Maine each sell decent products, seek to maintain reasonably responsible labor and environmental practices, and make substantial donations to charity (Shuman & Fuller, 2005). However, they do so with the goal of generating profits that can be distributed back to shareholders. In contrast, social ventures generate excess revenue to support the social purpose mission rather than distribute profits to shareholders (Dees, 1998; Maitland, 2006).

Although social ventures are often incorporated as not-for-profit charities, they are distinctly different from charities, foundations, and trusts.

Charities operate under a social-purpose mission to deliver services and are primarily supported by donations, grants, and governmental funding. Foundations and trusts, which exist with the mission to support charitable causes, frequently support causes that offer some social benefit to the community. In contrast to social ventures, these types of organizations typically do not use the sales of goods and services with the intent of generating excess revenue as their primary income source to support their social purpose mission (Brinckerhoff, 2000; Maitland, 2006).

Despite being different from charities, foundations and trusts in their approach to revenue generation, social ventures are similar to them in legal structure and their adherence to a social purpose mission. Since both legal structure and mission can create competitive advantages and disadvantages for social ventures in the competitive market, we examine them in the following sections.

Structure of Social Ventures

Social ventures can take numerous forms and have been established under varying legal and operating structures (Dees, 1998; Viravaidya & Hayssen, 2001). While a thorough discussion of these organizations is beyond the scope of this chapter, some distinctions are important to make. Many social ventures are legally structured as a not-for-profit organization (Dees, 1998; Easterly-Klaas, 2005; Emerson & Twersky, 1996). Still others have been established as for-profits, mutuals, cooperatives, or as partnerships between public, private, or not-for-profit sector organizations (Brennan & Ackers, 2004; Easterly-Klaas, 2005; Maitland, 2006). Moreover, some social ventures are privately held or incorporated as private sector corporations. For example, Chilmark Chocolates (in Martha's Vineyard, MA) is a privately-owned company that trains and employs individuals with severe cognitive and physical disabilities. The company's mission is to promote the inclusion of individuals with disabilities within the broader community through equitable employment and paying living wages (Easterly & McCallion, 2007). Another example of a for-profit social venture is Cafedirect (United Kingdom), a publicly-traded Fairtrade social venture that was established to help reduce poverty among coffee growers in the Southern hemisphere. The company pays fair wages and helps improve the infrastructure of impoverished communities by paying above the world market price for coffee and marketing it to Western countries (Cafedirect, n.d.).

Other social ventures may be established as a subsidiary of a public sector entity. For instance, a psychiatric hospital located in a high unemployment region of Canada recently converted its hospital-based employment programs into social ventures including an industrial contract factory, a car wash, a sewing shop, a greenhouse, and three cafés (Krupa, Lagarde, & Carmichael, 2003; Krupa, McCourty, Bonner, Von Briesen, & Scott, 1999). Hospital administrators realized that its employees with psychiatric disabilities no longer needed the support of the hospital program to perform their jobs, but since no employment could be located for them in the community the government chose to use the employment program funds to start the social ventures (Krupa et al., 1999; Krupa et al., 2003).

However, the vast majority of social ventures that have been reported on are legally structured as not-for-profits, as a subdivision of a larger not-for-profit organization, or as a subsidiary not-for-profit or for-profit corporation held under the control of a parent not-for-profit organization (Dees, 1998; Paton, 2003). The following are some examples of the different legal structures used by social ventures.

MOPA Housekeeping (in Shanghai, China) is a stand-alone social venture that is not affiliated with a larger not-for-profit organization. This not-for-profit social venture aims to reduce high rural unemployment by relocating unemployed migrant workers to the city where they work in its housekeeping venture (Chen, Pan, & Wu, 2006). Differing from the stand-alone model is the subsidiary model used by Pioneer Human Services (in Seattle, WA). It is a not-for-profit that operates several legally separated not-for-profit social ventures which offer job training and employment to chronically unemployed ex-offenders and substance abusers (Paton, 2003). Both of these types of models have the advantage of not posing a financial risk to a parent not-for-profit organization because they are not legally part of one.

In contrast are social ventures that are a subdivision of a larger not-for-profit organization. CREATE (in Liverpool, United Kingdom) is one such venture (Brennan & Ackers, 2004). It provides employment to the chronically unemployed by refurbishing and reselling used white goods (e.g., washing machines, refrigerators, freezers, ovens, etc.). CREATE is legally part of Bulky Bobs, a much larger not-for-profit, but has a separate funding contract from the government and operates with a slightly different mission than the rest of the Bulky Bobs social ventures.

As is common in many not-for-profit organizations that operate social ventures, all three of the organizations described here provide social services to the impoverished and unemployed (including job training, housing, and counseling) in addition to operating the social venture. Having the dual purpose of fulfilling a social purpose mission and of operating a viable business creates a strain on the social venture that most for-profit businesses do not have to contend with.

Constraints on Competitive Strategy

While not-for-profit charity organizations address a wide range of social and environmental issues, social ventures are distinctly different from the organizations that create them (Emerson & Twersky, 1996; Thompson & Doherty, 2006). Social ventures are established to engage in competitive business activity, whereas not-for-profit charity organizations typically do not seek to become businesses and often remain heavily dependent on grants, gifts, donations, and government funding (Thompson & Doherty, 2006). When not-for-profit charity organizations engage in social venturing, they are faced with the challenge of fulfilling both their not-for-profit mission while at the same time striving to achieve profitability in the social venture. This dual mission focus may interfere with the not-for-profit organization's ability to operate a viable social venture (Dees, 1998). To maintain tax-exempt status, not-for-profit organizations must adhere to strict legal codes. To be considered tax-exempt, income produced by a social venture has to be directly related to the not-for-profit organization's mission or social purpose, otherwise the not-for-profit organization's tax exempt status could be revoked (Brady, 2000; Hopkins, 2005a).

Not-for-profit charity organizations typically operate as institutional organizations due to government control, soft budget constraints, disincentives for cost saving structures, and bureaucratic organizational structures (Bryson, 2004). These organizations do not operate to generate a profit and are legally prohibited from distributing financial surplus to those who own or control it (Brady, 2000; Hopkins, 2005a). In fact, as not-for-profits they are expected to distribute their surplus revenues back to the community that supports them. They are traditionally viewed as tools of the government for achieving social objectives (Low, 2006). This climate is not favorable to entrepreneurship, which is the process of creating a new business (Brinkerhoff, 2000).

Many new businesses started by not-for-profit charity organizations fail because they are not competitive in the early stages after business start-up; indeed, one survey found that remarkably 71% of 41 high-profile U.S. not-for-profit business ventures were unprofitable between 2000 and 2001 (Foroohar, 2005). Further, because not-for-profit organizations typically serve as contractual agents and do not compete for customers, their organization leaders and board members often lack such business management skills as managing risk, market awareness, and understanding their position in the competitive market (Dees,1998; Emerson & Twersky, 1996). Since their resources are often tied to service delivery (fee-for-service), they often lack the financial resources to compete in the open market (Dees, 1998; Emerson & Twersky, 1996). Added to this are competing stakeholder demands from community members, clients, family members, tax-payers, donors, and governmental funders, all of which limit the not-for-profit organization's ability to operate a viable business (Brinkerhoff, 2000; Paton, 2003).

What Competitive Advantages Do Not-for-Profit Social Ventures Have?

The not-for-profit's tax-exempt status offers several advantages. For instance, social ventures can solicit donations to operate, get government funding to pay for support staff to assist individuals with disabilities who work in the business, are often not required to pay income tax on the business' profits from sales, and may not be required to pay property tax on any space the organization owns and operates the business from as long as the business activity is directly related to the organization's mission (Hopkins, 2005b). These advantages may allow some social ventures to sell their products at lower prices than their for-profit competitors can. In fact, more than 20,000 representatives at a White House conference for small businesses reported that competition with not-for-profits was one of the most significant issues they faced (Brady, 2000). But these benefits to operating a tax-exempt social venture rarely become a sustainable competitive advantage because they are typically outweighed by the costs of the disadvantages (Emerson & Twersky, 1996; Shuman & Fuller, 2005).

STRATEGIC MANAGEMENT FOR SOCIAL VENTURES

Several authors on social venturing have suggested that not-for-profit charity organizations will successfully operate a business only if they shift their decision-making process to one that requires strategic management and planning (Brinkerhoff, 2000; Dees, 1998; Easterly-Klaas, 2005; Emerson & Twersky, 1996; Paton, 2003). Briefly, strategic management involves decisions and actions that affect an organization's long-run performance. It includes environmental scanning, strategy formulation, strategy implementation, and evaluation and control (Hofer & Schendel, 1978). Just as in the classic board game of battlefield strategy that bears its name, the Greek word *strategos* is derived from combining *strat(ós)* (army) with *égos* (to lead) to mean "a general." Indeed, the earliest popular usages of the term were in the military (e.g., Sun Tzu's *The Art of War* c. 453 B.C.E. and Clausewitz's *On War* in 1832) and politics (e.g., Machiavelli's *The Prince* in 1517). Following WWII, these applications took hold in businesses as policy and planning to provide direction for large organizations buffeted by turbulent environments. Following the establishment of the *Strategic Management Journal* in 1980, the discipline continued to evolve through competitor analysis, core competencies and the resource-based view, leadership and vision, entrepreneurship and innovation, organizational learning, and globalization.

Since the early 1990s, the not-for-profit sector has similarly adapted the business practices of strategic visioning, strategic planning, and core competency analysis to identify strategies that enhance organizational responsiveness and improve performance (Bryson, 1995; Young & Steinberg, 1995). Conducting an analysis of the organization's strengths, weaknesses, environmental opportunities, and threats (SWOT) and identifying the organization's strategic vision can help define it both internally and in relation to the larger environment (Bryson, 2004). Strategic planning has been used to determine where an organization's resources should be focused and defines a sequence of strategic moves the organization should take to help it fulfill its mission (Bryson, 2004).

The challenge for creating a sustainable social venture is to establish a business strategy that supports the not-for-profit organization's mission, makes efficient use of its scarce resources, is financially sound, is adaptable to changing pressures, and is attainable (Brinkerhoff, 2000; Dees, 1998). Several authors have suggested that having a management strategy for the social venture is important to help it overcome the institutional and legal constraints placed on not-for-profit organizations and help organization members change their focus from charitable service delivery to one of strategic competitive business (Brinkerhoff, 2000; Dees, 1998; Easterly-Klaas, 2005; Emerson & Twersky, 1996; Paton, 2003). In the following sections we will examine how social ventures are being used to reduce poverty, why they have been effective where for-profit businesses have not, and how strategic management practices have played a role in their viable operations.

SOCIAL VENTURES: A GROWING BUSINESS MODEL

Not-for-profit organizations in the developed world are faced with unparalleled challenges in environments characterized by growing needs for all types of human services and a shrinking resource base (Chen et al., 2006; Choi, Cheng, Kim, & Eldomiaty, 2005). In developing countries characterized by widespread poverty, the situation is often much worse since those governments are often unable to meet even the basic needs of their people (Seelos & Mair, 2005; Thompson & Doherty, 2006). Traditionally, not-for-profit organizations have been concerned with assisting the impoverished, those who experience long-term unemployment, and those who exist on government subsidies to acquire the job skills and job training they need to secure employment.

Certain disadvantaged groups throughout the world, such as individuals with disabilities, convicts, the homeless, and individuals with substance abuse histories, have disproportionately experienced long-term unemployment and have been helped into the labor market through social ventures started by not-for-profit organizations (Emerson & Twersky, 1996; Harris, 2004; Krupa et al., 2003; Paton, 2003; U.S. Census Bureau, 2004/2005). The loss of manufacturing and unskilled labor jobs in developed countries such as the United States and the United Kingdom has contributed to the development of regions in those countries characterized by chronic unemployment, with social ventures used to reduce unemployment in those regions (Brennen & Ackers, 2004; Easterly-Klaas, 2005). Other countries such as China are experiencing a shift from an agricultural to a manufacturing economy, as well as growth in the not-for-profit sector spurred by a decrease in government management of human services. These factors combined have resulted in social ventures being created to help relocate unemployed agricultural workers into urban areas of the country (Chen et al., 2006). In other countries such as Bangladesh and Kenya, social ventures are established in rural regions to provide job training and employment for unemployed agricultural workers (Dees, 1998; Thompson & Doherty, 2006).

As the population grows, so do the numbers of impoverished that need services. Further, many new global problems have emerged—such as HIV/AIDS, terrorism, and repeated natural disasters—that require immediate attention. With the rising costs of health care and other products and services, governments find it difficult to adequately fund all the services needed to reduce poverty (U.N. Development Program, 2003). Pressure has been placed on corporations to take more responsibility for addressing social and environmental concerns throughout the world (Seelos & Mair, 2005). However, since helping the impoverished, homeless, and needy is very likely to be "unprofitable," for-profit corporations have shown little interest in addressing these concerns (Peredo & Chrisman, 2006; Seelos & Mair, 2005). This lack of interest has burdened not-for-profit organizations with finding solutions to poverty and unemployment that governments and for-profit corporations have been unable to address. To make up for the lack of governmental funding, not-for-profit organizations usually turn to donors (Bryson, 2004). However, the pool of grant and donor funds has not kept pace with the increasing demand for them (Brinkerhoff, 2000; Viravaidya & Hayssen, 2001). The increasing demands for services combined with the decreasing availability of governmental and philanthropic resources has led many not-for-profit organizations serving disadvantaged groups to start social ventures to generate additional revenue to support their services or to create employment for the people they serve (Krupa et al., 2003; Shaw, 2004; Shuman & Fuller, 2005).

In spite of the special challenges they face, social ventures have often succeeded in business activities not typically attractive to for-profit corporations. Consider the thrift shops operated by the Salvation Army and Goodwill Industries, both of which are international not-for-profit organizations that have been operating for over a century. The Salvation Army provides food, clothing, housing, and support services to the homeless and impoverished. Fifteen percent of its $3.04 billion in annual revenue comes from sales within its used goods thrift shops (Salvation Army, 2006). Goodwill Industries' mission is to reduce chronic unemployment and poverty through job training and employment. The lion's share of its $2.65 billion budget comes from the $1.65 billion in thrift shop sales (Goodwill Industries Int., 2006). However, the viability of both of these organizations' thrift shops comes largely from donors and volunteers who generously give cash, used goods, and physical labor to these social ventures because they believe in the parents' mission of serving the poor and chronically unemployed.

Since for-profit corporations have a mission of profitability rather than serving the poor and they cannot receive tax-free donations and voluntary labor, it is unlikely they could competitively operate similar thrift shops and fund programs for the poor. For-profits interested in helping the poor typically take advantage of legal incentives for corporate giving by making tax-deductible donations to a not-for-profit organization that has a mission of serving the poor rather than trying to operate such businesses (Hopkins, 2005a).

Social ventures often engage in businesses that would not be viable without the support of public funds and grants. One such venture is Energywise Recycling (in Liverpool, United Kingdom), that started operating in 2000 as a not-for-profit recycling business for paper, cardboard, toner cartridges, glass, and drink cans. Its mission is to create local jobs and training opportunities for the region's chronically unemployed (Brennan & Ackers, 2004). The market for recycled goods has become drastically more competitive over recent years, making it less likely that starting this type of business would be profitable and therefore making the start-up of such a business unattractive to many for-profit corporations (Porter, 1998; U.S. Census Bureau, 2002; U.S. Department of Commerce, 2004).

Energywise was able to operate as a sustainable venture with the assistance of government and grant funds. The Liverpool City Council was especially interested in supporting Energywise because the city was recycling only 2% of its waste. Through funding to Energywise and other recycling projects, the city hoped to increase the recycling of its own waste as well as decrease the number of chronically unemployed receiving government assistance by moving them into the labor market. Liverpool recycling social ventures, including Energywise, have added value to the community not only by reducing local waste but also by providing jobs in this high unemployment area (employing 85% of those trained). The community retains local wealth as the newly employed purchase and spend more locally thus improving the standard of living. The larger community benefits from decreased government assistance payments to the unemployed, increased taxpayer contributions from the newly employed, and improved community self-sufficiency from being able to recycle more of its waste rather that outsourcing the task. The venture has also increased social capital in the community by creating a pool of trained workers who have enjoyed increased self-esteem, self-worth, and confidence due to their new employment (Brennan & Ackers, 2004).

Honey Care is another not-for-profit social venture that is concerned with reducing poverty through job creation in rural regions of Kenya (Honey Care Africa, 2006). Through cost sharing or loan agreements, Honey Care provides hives and bee keeping equipment to impoverished communities and individuals. Training and technical assistance is provided at no cost. Honey Care then purchases the honey from the producers at above market prices. This social venture has helped reduce poverty in several poor communities by developing sustainable employment that directly benefits over 38,000 individuals annually (Honey Care Africa, 2006). It has also helped build community self-sufficiency through producing honey and bee products locally, rather than importing them. The success of this venture has been partly due to choosing a location that for-profit companies would typically find unattractive. Since honey production is much lower in developing countries than in developed countries, for-profits have not found it financially attractive to establish a business in the rural regions of Kenya (Thompson & Doherty, 2006). By taking advantage of this market opportunity, Honey Care has succeeded in reducing poverty in regions where for-profit companies have not.

As these examples highlight, social ventures have decreased poverty and unemployment through job training and job creation. They have improved the local standard of living and increased community self-sufficiency through the production of value-added goods and services. Social ventures have helped retain local wealth as the newly-employed both buy and spend more, circulating money throughout the local community. They have increased social capital by building a pool of trained workers, fostering community trust, strengthening community networks, and fostering norms of self-sufficiency through employment. Communities have also benefited from increased taxpayer contributions from the newly-employed with the workers experiencing increased self-esteem, self-worth, and confidence from their new-found employment. There are other benefits to the community specific to the venture's function such as reducing local waste through recycling. By starting businesses that rely heavily on donations or choosing businesses that appear unprofitable to for-profit companies but add value to the community, social ventures have succeeded in reducing poverty and chronic unemployment where for-profit businesses have failed.

BUSINESS STRATEGIES TO IMPROVE SOCIAL VENTURE PERFORMANCE

Several experts on the topic have suggested that aspects of strategic management are needed to operate a sustainable social venture (Dees, 1998; Easterly-Klaas, 2005; Emerson & Twersky, 1996; Paton, 2003; Viravaidya & Hayssen, 2001). We now turn to summarizing lessons learned from examining sustainable social ventures and present ten elements of business strategy that should be included if their operators wish to increase their likelihood of being successful.

1. Mission, Possible.   All organizations must have a reason for being, their raison d'être. The late management guru Peter F. Drucker wrote that "the first job of the leader is to think through and define the mission of the institution" (Drucker, 1990). This statement should be concise and precise, specifying what the organization does that includes the stakeholders it serves or relies on, the business(es) it is in, the client needs that are currently being served, and its key philosophical values and core purpose. While for-profit businesses can have missions to maximize their profits, not-for-profits must have an overriding mission that addresses their service orientation and good works (e.g., economic development, education, preservation, etc.) to retain their tax-exempt status. In the case of social ventures, their mission should be based on the community's needs (e.g., insufficient job training, competitive employment, providing a product, transportation to existing jobs, supporting unfunded or under-funded services, etc.). Moreover, the mission must consider the venture's unique cultural setting (Peredo & Chrisman, 2006) and be based on the demands of all potential stakeholders and funders (Dees, 1998).

If not-for-profits do not have a strong mission focus when they engage in social venturing, they are in danger of becoming so profit focused they may lose sight of their original purpose (Dees, 1998; Viravaidya & Hayssen, 2001). One example is the YMCA that for many years offered its health and fitness facilities at very low cost to the community in support of its mission "to put Christian principles into practice through programs that build healthy sprit, mind, and body for all" (YMCA, 2007). In recent years, the YMCA has generated substantial revenues by operating its health facilities and fitness clubs for middle-class families, causing critics to charge that the organization has lost sight of its original not-for-profit mission in the pursuit of profits (Dees, 1998; Shuman & Fuller, 2005) and uses its not-for-profit status to compete unfairly against for-profit health clubs (Brady, 2000). Therefore, when not-for-profits engage in social venturing they must do so with a strong view of the organization's mission or it could lose community respect and its not-for-profit status can be called into question (Brady, 2000; Lewis, French, & Steane, 1997; Spear, 2006).

2. Metrics Matter. Unfortunately, service orientation and good works often have vague or ambiguous outcome measures (Letts, Ryan, & Grossman, 1997; Paton, 2003). The extent to which the broad mission is attained must ultimately be measured by results, often described in terms of quantity, quality, timeliness, or cost. While for-profits share a common overall measure of accountability, the same is not true for all organizations. Hence, it is critical that social ventures measure their overall added value to the community rather than only one performance dimension (Darby & Jenkins, 2006; Paton, 2003). One way to do this is by benchmarking their performance against similar programs and measuring overall systems costs and benefits that include both financial and social benefits (e.g., number of jobs created, increased self-esteem of workers, etc.). Regardless of the approach, the performance metric should focus on the client (such as improving knowledge or economic status) and the resources expended. The performance standards must be known and understood by those responsible for results (Easterly-Klaas, 2005; Letts et al., 1997; Paton, 2003).

The previously-mentioned Pioneer Human Services (PHS) has operated several sustainable social ventures for many years (PHS, 2007). Its mission is: "Improving lives through jobs, social services and housing." Nearly one half of its $55 million budget comes from revenues generated in its social ventures, which employ over 1,000 chronically unemployed ex-offenders and substance abusers.

To maintain the viability of their ventures, PHS has a wide range of performance measures including tracking financial performance using generally accepted accounting practices with a goal of maintaining a minimum 13% margin, using quality assurance measurements to achieve customer satisfaction (including meeting ISO 9002 standards), and inspecting and auditing the ventures for quality improvement (Paton, 2003). Because this is a human service organization, mission-related and client outcomes on social venture-related goals are key to determining the viability of each venture (Paton, 2003). Information reported monthly includes operational data (activity, throughput levels, completions), quality data (error rates, rule violations, incidents, internal client/external customer satisfaction surveys), and professional assessment data (risk reduction, improved client functioning, progress toward client goal attainment) (Paton, 2003). PHS has used performance measurement as a tool for sustaining the viability of its social ventures by putting procedures in place for data gathering and reporting. It also uses graphical displays (i.e., "dashboards") of performance over time that are clear and easily understood by top managers and the board of directors to determine progress toward goal attainment. Outcome data are in turn used to set goals and targets, which may include closing poor performing ventures (Paton, 2003). Using multiple performance measures and standards that are accessible and valuable to top decision makers, PHS has been able to operate sustainable social ventures that have reduced poverty for many unemployed individuals.

3. Develop a Business Plan.   In order to attain the performance metric, organizations must conceive an original and well-considered idea. It is important to detail the products or services offered and how they compare to the local competition's offerings, including a summary of market size, expected customers, and key financials including revenues, cash flow, and surplus. This should also include action plans and milestones, particularly the roles and responsibilities of the management team members. Since not-for-profits do not have the same market pressures as for-profit businesses, it is important for them to have complete and up-to-date business plans that are overseen by the board of directors and/or a chief executive officer skilled in business. A common mistake is to hire a business consulting firm in lieu of having skilled business management within the organization to develop the business plan. Finally, it is important that the organization plans to grow the social venture slowly and deliberately so that the business activity does not distract them from fulfilling their social purpose mission.

Easterly-Klaas (2005) reported on a spice company social venture that did not have business management skills among the board members or executive management within the not-for-profit organization that started the venture. Its board of directors decided to hire a business consulting and market research firm to devise a business plan to penetrate the wholesale seafood store market. When it was discovered that the business was not growing at the projected rate and it was rapidly losing money, the organization members did not possess the management skills to discern how to revise the business plan and were unable to devise strategies to improve the social venture's performance. The organization's board members and executive management became very reactionary in their approach to running the venture, taking such steps as implementing a new, poorly formulated plan for the business. When that plan did not produce rapid results, they would quickly try another approach. It was decided that the spice company would leave the wholesale seafood store market (for which a business plan had been written) and instead attempt to penetrate the retail grocery store chain market. No business plan was created to penetrate this new market, so the organization management overlooked critical aspects of the businesses' needs and available resources and had no clear idea of how much capital was required to penetrate it. For instance, they reported they "forgot to include hiring a sales force" as part of their business plan and had initially assumed that if they offered a quality product "it would sell itself." Not only did this venture fail to provide employment for individuals with disabilities, but it also left the not-for-profit parent organization with $500,000 in debt that had to be paid for with funds intended for other human service programs the organization delivered. Without a comprehensive business plan, this social venture veered off on a course of action that ultimately drained resources away from the parent not-for-profit's mission and depleted the quality of service offered to the individuals with disabilities the organization served.

4. Dare to be Different.   If you build it, they will not come unless the plan specifies how the business will be unique. According to conventional strategic theory, there are two polar opposite generic strategies: Being the lowest delivered cost provider or being the highest differentiator. Organizations must make choices that distinguish them from the competing offerings (Porter, 1998). Price competition is a race for the bottom to be avoided and, as already pointed out, can be problematic for not-for-profits that receive cost advantages from government or other sources. Hence, it is important for these organizations to avoid price-sensitive markets if they are to maintain the public's good will and avoid being accused of using their not-for-profit status to compete unfairly with for-profit businesses. It may also not be feasible for social ventures to compete on price when their poverty reduction mission includes paying higher wages than their for-profit competitors, hiring less skilled workers, providing extensive job training, and purchasing products from impoverished business owners at above market prices. These added costs make it nearly impossible for social ventures to compete on price. Moreover, customers prefer a value proposition that offers the best combination of product and service attributes for the price. Organizations can be unique by balancing their quality (e.g., Mercedes) and reliability (e.g., Caterpillar), cost of delivery (e.g., Dell), level of convenience (e.g., Amazon.com) and service (e.g., Nordstrom), engineering innovation and design (e.g., Apple), image (e.g., Nike), and overall customer satisfaction (e.g., Toyota).

Cafedirect, mentioned previously, has become the United Kingdom's largest Fairtrade hot drinks company with 8.1% market share in the roast and ground coffee market (Cafedirect, n.d.). To achieve a brand image of exceptional quality, 86% of operating profits fund initiatives such as business development, marketing, and management training to support growers in building the expertise necessary to produce the highest quality products. Cafedirect works with 33 producer organizations in 11 impoverished countries. By competing on quality, Cafedirect has been able to pay growers above market prices for their product while supporting the growth of their businesses that results in over a quarter million growers receiving a decent income as a benefit of this social venture.

5. Know Thy Market. Every business should know the market it wishes to occupy by paying attention to why, who, what, where, how, and when: Why are you targeting that customer, who will you be competing against, what are the alternative product and service offerings, where will you get the competencies you need, how is the product or service delivered, and when will you be profitable? Answers must be thought out and actions must be deliberate to develop viable strategies to penetrate the chosen market (Porter, 1998). A common mistake within social ventures is to try to operate the business with only a handful of customer contracts, because when these contracts expire the social venture fails (Dees, 1998; Easterly & McCallion, 2007). Social ventures may fare better at increasing their customer base or repeat sales by offering specialized or niche products and services, or locating in areas that competitors choose to ignore (Easterly-Klaas, 2005; Pelham, 2000). These approaches also avoid highly competitive markets that require economies of scale that not-for-profit organizations typically cannot generate given their limited resources to penetrate these demanding markets (Perlmutter & Adams, 1990; Young & Steinberg, 1995). Alternatively, a creative strategy can capture emerging markets (e.g., aging population), create new markets (e.g., tap unmet needs), develop new products (e.g., collaborate with other organizations), become indispensable (e.g., a monopoly position, contract, patent, high switching costs), or fortify (e.g., promise long-term commitments, obtain financial support).

A janitorial company in the Northeastern United States hires individuals with disabilities in a region characterized by high unemployment. Since the economy is declining in the area where the social venture is located, many of its customers are relocating to other regions of the country or are filing bankruptcy. Nonetheless, it has been very successful at maintaining a 35% profit margin in an economically depressed region by continually assessing the performance of its customers and revising its business plan based on how its customers are performing (Easterly-Klaas, 2005). By continually assessing the performance of the venture's customers, upper management is able to curb potential losses from customer default by limiting the amount of credit extended. Upper management continually engages in networking and environmental scanning to seek out new customers with strong financial performance and discontinues service to those exhibiting poor performance. Costs are controlled by continually keeping a close watch on the market size. This social venture has been able to offer stable employment to chronically unemployed individuals with disabilities and generate excess revenue to the parent not-for-profit organization enabling it to fund housing, job training, transportation, and clinical services.

6. Hire for Talent, Pay for Performance.   Human resources are often the most neglected and taken for granted of all resources, and ironically also the most unique and indispensable. Nowhere is this truer than in the case of the executive talent ranging from the top management team to the chief executive officer and board of directors. Not-for-profits have often been accused of hiring managers that lack business skills and experience (Dees, 1998; Maitland, 2006) and skimping on the salaries they pay their managers (Easterly-Klaas, 2005; Viravaidya & Hayssen, 2001). Not-for-profits should not short-change the organization by neglecting the people responsible for day-to-day operations of the business. Rather, they should hire skilled management and pay them competitive salaries. One way to increase the managers' financial incentives is to tie their salaries to the venture's performance (this is not legal for the CEO or board in not-for-profits) (Easterly-Klaas, 2005).

Many social ventures have failed financially because they ignored the dangers of hiring unskilled management and deferred business decision-making to them (Easterly-Klaas, 2005; Viravaidya & Hayssen, 2001). One water bottling social venture that was started to create jobs in a high-unemployment region of the Eastern United States created $500,000 in debt for the parent not-for-profit organization that started it (Easterly-Klaas, 2005). The CEO and board members later realized that even though they thought they were paying a lot of money for the manager they hired, they had only paid about half the average salary. Because he was considered "the business expert," they allowed him to make all of the decisions for the venture until the not-for-profit was threatened with bankruptcy. This social venture was forced to close and the not-for-profit organization spent many years diverting funds from its mission-related programs to pay off the venture's debt.

7. It's Who You Know.   Creating and maintaining linkages with stakeholders when resources are scarce creates a competitive advantage (Collis & Montgomery, 1998). Not-for-profits should choose local (or specialty) markets where their organization's networking skills are an advantage (Brennan & Ackers, 2004; Easterly-Klaas, 2005). For instance, board interlocks can provide access to information and contacts, sharing product lines or processes can create mutual interdependence, entrepreneurial initiative and creativity can gain access to customers, experience, and knowledge (Covin & Slevin, 1989; Davidsson & Honig, 2003), and engaging the community in developing a social venture can build consensus and support (Peredo & Christman, 2006).

Energywise, the previously-mentioned recycling social venture, probably would not succeed in regions other than their local market because of the competitiveness of the recycling market, high start-up costs, and low profit margins (U.S. Census Bureau, 2002; U.S. Deptartment of Commerce, 2004). Energywise networks with several departments of the local government and nongovernmental organizations interested in reducing waste and supporting economic development in the local region (Brennan & Ackers, 2004). It has been able to access a variety of grants and donations because the social venture focuses on reducing local waste and providing employment to the chronically unemployed in the area. These networks have made it possible for the recycling venture to operate as a sustainable venture, whereas it probably would have failed without these networks.

8. Establish Financial Oversight.   The not-for-profit organization's CEO and its board members must be skilled in business to exercise their decision making authority competently as well as to provide proper governance, oversight, and control over the business' financial accounts, market strategy, and exit planning. In addition, the amount of financial risk the social venture assumes should be established by specifying such performance baselines as expected profit margin, programmatic support required for breakeven, and the amount and source of donations (Dees, 1998).

Maintaining proper financial oversight does not always require the social venture to operate self-sufficiently without the assistance of grants or donor assistance. For example, the Bangladesh Rural Advancement Committee (BRAC) operates several social ventures to reduce poverty and empower the poor in war-torn countries such as Afghanistan, Sri Lanka, and Bangladesh employing 97,192 people in their ventures (BRAC, 2005). However, not all of their ventures are self-sufficient. BRAC intended to operate all parts of its silk industry in Bangladesh without the cash assistance of donations and grants. It engaged in all parts of the industry's value chain including sapling production, silkworm seed production, mulberry cultivation, silkworm rearing, reeling, weaving, and marketing with the goal of employing thousands of women and landless poor (BRAC, 2005). Due to the poor quality of the cocoons, the silk reeling plants were very inefficient (Dees, 1998). Financial losses had to be incurred at this stage of production to be able to pay the workers a living wage (Dees, 1998). Since closing this production stage would have endangered the entire silk venture and forced thousands of workers back into poverty, BRAC chose instead to continue seeking cash assistance to sustain the venture while it devises a strategy to make the plants profitable (Dees, 1998). By maintaining close financial oversight of the silk venture, BRAC has been able to protect itself from incurring losses that could have diminished the organization's capacity to serve the poor elsewhere (BRAC, 2005).

9. Manage Risk Carefully.   While all start-ups are more likely to fail because of their "liability of newness" (Stinchcombe, 1965), social ventures are especially at risk because their missions place them at a disadvantage in the competitive market. For instance, social ventures often allocate more resources to social purposes to fulfill their mission than their competitors do. They also hire workers their competitors consider unqualified, forcing them to try to compete with a less-skilled workforce (Emerson & Twersky, 1996). Although it can structure the social venture as a separate for-profit company to protect its finances and increase bankability, doing so might jeopardize its not-for-profit status if the venture becomes too profitable (Hopkins, 2005a). To mitigate the operating risks, not-for-profit organizations should enter businesses that are easily learned, require a limited amount of technical skills to operate, or where employees already possess the knowledge and skills to be successful (Easterly-Klaas, 2005). To minimize the financial risks, not-for-profit organizations should choose a business that requires little start-up capital and has low overhead because most of these organizations have limited liquid resources (Perlmutter & Adams, 1990; Young & Steinberg, 1995). They should also have sufficient capital to see the venture through the first few years of operation (Emerson & Twersky, 1996).

The previously mentioned Canadian psychiatric hospital used several strategies to minimize risk when it started its social ventures (Krupa et al., 2003). First, it structured the ventures under a separate not-for-profit umbrella organization so that the hospital would not be legally liable for any financial losses incurred in the ventures. Then, it started only ventures that require operating skills the business managers, hospital administration, and employees with disabilities already possessed. Finally, it minimized overhead costs wherever possible by locating the venture in donated space. Although not all of the ventures are yet sustainable, these risk management tactics have helped the ventures grow slowly toward becoming viable.

10. Obey the Law and Abide by Ethical Principles.   While it seems obvious that managers and companies should not break any laws or violate ethical principles, not all not-for-profit organizations are actually aware of and follow the laws governing their social venture. Since not-for-profit organizations are given tax-exempt status because they operate to perform good for the community, they should go beyond simply obeying the law, engaging in ethical business practices, and avoiding "unfair competition" such as using tax-payer dollars attained through governmental funding to lower prices and under-cut local business competition (Brady, 2000). In fact, several not-for-profits have been accused of violating their tax-exempt status and misusing taxpayer and donation funds when engaging in social venturing (Brady, 2000). CEOs of not-for-profits have been accused of engaging in unethical practices such as acquiring personal and financial benefit from the social venture or allowing the business to collapse, leaving the organization with large debts (Dees, 1998; Shuman & Fuller, 2005). Board members have also been found guilty of violating their fiduciary responsibility as trustees for not-for-profits by neglecting to maintain oversight of financial and CEO activities and thus allowing the organization to incur large financial losses (Bart & Deal, 2006; Low, 2006; Shuman & Fuller, 2005). Consider the Milwaukee YWCA that allowed its computer software venture and plastics factory to collapse in 2003, leaving it with millions of dollars of debt while some board members collected stock options from the ventures. Ethical practice means not taking advantage of bankruptcy laws whenever possible by considering the impact that such filing could have on the not-for-profit organization and its relationship with stakeholders. For instance, taxpayers in the community who already have contributed tax dollars to a social venture's operation should not have to cover its bankruptcy losses. Rather than giving back to the community that supports them, these unethical practices have contributed to draining precious not-for-profit resources away from the organization's philanthropic mission. Situations like these have led to increased pressure being placed on not-for-profits to improve their legal and ethical business practices when engaging in social venturing (Dees, 1998; Shuman & Fuller, 2005).

CONCLUSION

Through the use of innovative business approaches, social ventures have challenged and redefined the traditional roles of not-for-profit organizations at reducing global poverty. The examples given here demonstrate how social ventures add value to impoverished communities throughout the world through job creation for the chronically unemployed, fostering community self-sufficiency through production of their own products rather than importing them, creating markets for products produced by impoverished communities, and providing job training to help the chronically unemployed acquire employable skills.

Although social ventures often target markets or hire employees that for-profit companies would typically find unattractive, thereby putting them at a competitive disadvantage, many succeed at achieving their mission of reducing poverty. They do so through a strong mission focus, performance measurement, business plan development, market awareness, avoiding highly price-sensitive markets, skilled management, networking, financial oversight, risk management, complying with the laws governing the business, and engaging in ethical business practices. Although constrained by legal limitations, lack of resources, and conflicting stakeholder demands, social ventures that have applied innovative business and strategic management practices have reconfigured the wealth generation dynamics within several impoverished communities in areas where charities and for-profit businesses have failed.

REFERENCES

Bart, C,. & Deal, K. (2006). The governance role of the board in corporate strategy: A comparison of board practices on 'for profit' and 'not for profit' organizations. *International Journal of Governance and Ethics, 2*(1/2), 2-22.

Bangladesh Rural Advancement Committee. (2005). *About BRAC.* Retrieved January 31, 2007, from http://www.brac.net/about.htm

Brady, D. (2000, June 26). When nonprofits go after profits. *Business Week,* 173-178.

Brennan, S., & Ackers, S. (2004). Recycling, best value and social venture: Assessing the 'Liverpool model.' *Local Economy, 19*(2), 175-180.

Brinkerhoff, P. C. (2000). *Social entrepreneurship: The art of mission-based venture development.* New York: Wiley.

Bryson, J. M. (1995). *Strategic planning for public and nonprofit organizations.* San Francisco: Josey-Bass.

Bryson, J. M. (2004). *Strategic planning for public and nonprofit organizations: A guide to strengthening and sustaining organizational achievement.* San Francisco: Josey-Bass.

Cafedirect. (n.d.). Retrieved January 3, 2007, from http://www.cafedirect.co.uk

Carroll, A. (1998). The four faces of corporate citizenship. *Business and Society Review, 100*(1), 1-7.

Chen, M., Pan, L., & Wu, H. (2006). Developing China's nonprofit sector. *The McKinsey Quarterly.* Retrieved November 10, 2006, from http://www.mckinseyquarterly.com/article_abstract_visitor.

Choi, C., Cheng, P., Kim, J., & Eldomiaty, T. (2005, Spring). Dual responsibilities of NGOs: Market and institutional responsibilities and ethics. *The Journal of Corporate Citizenship, 17*, 26-29.

Collis, D., & Montgomery, C. (1998). Creating corporate advantage. *Harvard Business Review, 76*(3), 70-83.

Covin, J. G., & Slevin, D. P. (1989). Strategic management of small firms in hostile and benign environments. *Strategic Management Journal, 10*(1), 75-87.

Darby, L., & Jenkins, H. (2006). Applying sustainability indicators to the social venture business model. *International Journal of Social Economics, 33*(5/6), 411-431.

Davidsson, P., & Honig, B. (2003). The role of social and human capital among nascent entrepreneurs. *Journal of Business Venturing, 18*(3), 301-331.

Dees, G. J. (1998). Enterprising nonprofits. *Harvard Business Review, 76*(1), 54-61.

Dees, G. J. (2001). *Enterprising nonprofits: A toolkit for social entrepreneurs.* New York:: Wiley.

Drucker, P. F. (1990). *Managing the nonprofit organization.* New York: HarperCollins.

Easterly-Klaas, L. (2005). *Employing people with disabilities: Perceptions of the critical elements of agency sponsored entrepreneurial business success.* Ann Arbor, MI: Pro Quest UMI Dissertation Services.

Easterly, L., & McCallion, P. (2007). Affirmative business: Examining the relevance of small business research. *The Journal of Rehabilitation, 73*(1), 13-21.

Emerson, J., & Twersky, F. (1996). (Eds.). *New social entrepreneurs: The success, challenge, and lessons of nonprofit enterprise creation.* San Francisco: Roberts Foundation.

Foroohar, R. (2005, September 5). The $1.6 trillion non-profit sector behaves (or misbehaves) more and more like big business. *Newsweek International.* Retrieved August 8, 2006, from http://msnbc.msn.com/id/9108631/site/newsweek/.

Goodwill Industries International. (2006). *About Goodwill Industries.* Retrieved November 27, 2006, from www.goodwill.org

Harris, L. (2004). *2004 National Organization on Disabilities/Harris survey of Americans with disabilities.* Washington DC: National Organization on Disability.

Hofer, C. W., & Schendel, D. (1978). *Strategy formulation: Analytical concepts.* St. Paul, MN West.

Honey Care Africa. (2006). *Honey Care Africa: On site in Kitui, Kenya.* Retrieved January 18, 2007, from http://en.wikipedia.org/wiki/Honey_Care_Africa

Hopkins, B. (2005a). *Starting and managing a nonprofit organization: A legal guide* (4th ed.). Hoboken, NJ: Wiley.

Hopkins, B. (2005b). *650 essential nonprofit law questions answered.* Hoboken NJ: Wiley.

Krupa, T., Lagarde, M., & Carmichael, K. (2003). Transforming sheltered workshops into affirmative businesses: An outcome evaluation. *Psychiatric Rehabilitation Journal, 26*(4), 359-367.

Krupa, T., McCourty, K., Bonner, D., Von Briesen, B., & Scott, R. (1999). Voices, opportunities and choices employment club: Transforming sheltered workshops using an affirmative business approach. *Canadian Journal of Community Mental Health, 18*(2), 87-98.

Letts, C. W., Ryan, W., & Grossman, A. (1997). Virtuous capital: What foundations can learn from venture capitalists. *Harvard Business Review, 75*(2), 36-43.

Lewis, D., French, E., & Steane, P. (1997). A culture of conflict. *Leadership & Organization Development Journal, 18*(6), 275-282.

Low, C. (2006). A framework for the governance of social venture. *International Journal of Social Economics, 33*(5/6), 376-385.

Maitland, A. (2006, October 26). How the good become great: Social venture is all the rage. But companies in the sector may struggle to scale up operations. *Financial Time,* p.12.

Meehan, J., Meehan, K., & Richards, A. (2006). Corporate social responsibility: The 3C-SR model. *International Journal of Social Economics, 33*(5/6), 386-398.

Paton, R. (2003). *Managing and measuring social enterprises.* Thousand Oaks CA: Sage.

Pelham, A. (2000). Market orientation and other potential influences on performance in small and medium sized firms. *Journal of Small Business Management, 28*(1), 46-67.

Peredo, A. A., & Chrisman, J. J. (2006). Toward a theory of community-based enterprise. *Academy of Management Review, 31*(2), 309-328.

Perlmutter, F. D., & Adams, C. T. (1990). The voluntary sector and for-profit ventures: The transformation of American social welfare? *Administration in Social Work, 14*(1), 1-14.

Pioneer Human Services. (2007). *Products with a mission: Social venture.* Retrieved January 29, 2007, from http://www.pioneerhumanserv.com/products.html

Porter, M. E. (1998). *Competitive strategy: Techniques for analyzing industries and competitors.* New York: Free Press.

Salvation Army of the USA. (2006). *Beacon of a brighter light: National annual report.* Retrieved November 27, 2006, from http://www.salvationarmyusa.org

Seelos, C., & Mair, J. (2005). Social entrepreneurship: Creating new business models to serve the poor. *Business Horizons, 48*(3), 241-246.

Shaw, E. (2004). Marketing in the social venture context: Is it entrepreneurial? *Qualitative Market Research: An International Journal, 7*(3), 194-205.

Shuman, M., & Fuller, M. (2005). Profits for justice. *Nation, 280*(3), 13-22.

Spear, R. (2006). Social entrepreneurship: A different model. *International Journal of Social Economics, 33*(5/6), 399-410.

Stinchcombe, A. L. (1965). Social structure and organizations. In J. G. March (Ed.), *Handbook of organizations* (pp. 142-193). Chicago: Rand McNally.

Thompson, J., & Doherty, B. (2006). The diverse world of social enterprise. *International Journal of Social Economics, 33*(5/6), 361-375.

U. N. Development Program, Human Development Report. (2003). *Millennium Development Goals: A compact among nations to end poverty.* New York: Author.

U.S. Census Bureau. (2002). *Economic census 2002.* Washington, DC: U.S. Department of Commerce Economics and Statistics Administration.

U.S. Census Bureau. (2004/2005). *Statistical abstracts of the United States: The national data book* (124th ed.) Washington, DC: U.S. Department of Commerce Economics and Statistics Administration.

U.S. Department of Commerce. (2004). *3 R's initiative roundtable.* Washington, DC: Author.

Viravaidya, M., & Hayssen, J. (2001). *Strategies to strengthen NGO capacity in resource mobilization through business activities.* Retrieved August 8, 2006, from PDA and UNAIDS Joint Publication, UNAIDS Best Practice Collection Web site: http://data.unaids.org/Publications/IRC-pub06/JC579-Strategies_NGO_en.pdf

Waddock, S. (2004). Parallel universes: Companies, academics, and the progress of corporate citizenship. *Business and Society Review, 109*(1), 5-42.

YMCA. (2007). Retrieved May 9, 2007, from http://www.ymca.net/

Young, D. R., & Steinberg, R. (1995). *Economics for nonprofit managers.* New York: The Foundation Center.

CHAPTER 2

REDUCING POVERTY THROUGH SOCIAL ENTREPRENEURSHIP

The Case of Edun

Brett R. Smith and Terri Feldman Barr

ABSTRACT

This chapter discusses the emerging role of social entrepreneurship as a means of reducing poverty, particularly in developing nations. The chapter has 2 aims: (1) to provide an initial understanding of the concept of social entrepreneurship; and (2) to offer an in-depth understanding of social entrepreneurship through the example of Edun. Social entrepreneurship involves the creation of innovative, sustainable solutions to immediate social problems with an emphasis on those who are marginalized or poor. While many examples are not-for-profit organizations, the domain of social entrepreneurship also includes for-profit businesses that deliver both economic and social value. Edun, launched by Bono, Ali Hewson, his wife, and a New York fashion designer, Rogan Gregory, is a for-profit socially conscious clothing business focused on developing sustainable employment in poverty stricken regions like Sub-Saharan Africa. Edun was launched to shift the focus from aid to trade in the developing world.

Innovative Approaches to Reducing Global Poverty
pp. 27–41

INTRODUCTION

In 2005, humanitarian and rock star Bono, his wife, Ali Hewson, and fashion designer, Rogan Gregory, launched a socially conscious clothing company. A primary mission of the company was to help reduce extreme poverty in Sub-Saharan Africa by increasing trade and providing sustainable employment to the region. The basic premise of the company, named Edun, was to shift the emphasis from providing aid to stimulating trade as a solution to reduce extreme poverty in this region of the world. Consistent with research that suggests that the most effective approach to reducing poverty is raising the income of the poor (Karnani, 2006), Bono and his colleagues have utilized the ideas and principles of social entrepreneurship as an innovative vehicle for long-term change to address poverty in the developing world.

The use of social entrepreneurship to affect change in impoverished populations is increasing. Much like the work of Muhammad Yunus, the recipient of the Nobel Peace Prize in 2006 for his work as a banker to the poor of Bangladesh, Edun uses the ideas of social entrepreneurship as the vehicle for change to address poverty in the developing world. These initiatives demonstrate the potential effectiveness of social entrepreneurship as a means to reducing poverty. Over the last few years, social entrepreneurship has been occurring on a scale that has never been seen before (Bornstein, 2004). Paralleling this trend, social entrepreneurship is also rapidly emerging as a subject of research and teaching within academia. Unlike commercial entrepreneurship, social entrepreneurship is focused on creating social rather than economic value. In the case of Edun, the social value is that of poverty reduction, increased self-sufficiency of community members, and hopefully, long-term sustainable economic growth of the community.

This chapter discusses the emerging area of social entrepreneurship, provides an in-depth explanation of Edun as one example of social entrepreneurship, and highlights the innovative strategies Edun is using to maximize its social impact.

SOCIAL ENTREPRENEURSHIP

While the practice of social entrepreneurship has a relatively longer history, the domain of social entrepreneurship within academia is still emerging (Austin, Stevenson & Wei-Skillern, 2006). Given the nascent stage of scholarly work in this area, the definition of social entrepreneurship is still being clarified. In reviewing 11 different definitions of social entrepreneurship, Zahra, Gedajlovic, Neubaum and Schulman (2006) found that all definitions share the common theme that social entrepreneurship is motivated by the aspiration to achieve some socially desirable objective.

Before developing their own definition of social entrepreneurship, Zahra and his colleagues introduced the construct of social wealth. According to these authors, social wealth is defined as the social value generated minus direct economic and opportunity costs incurred. In this way, the construct of social wealth calls attention to the overall net value added to society. After reviewing the different definitions of social entrepreneurship and introducing the construct of social wealth, these theorists defined social entrepreneurship as "the processes related to the discovery of opportunities to create social wealth and the organizational processes developed and employed to achieve that end" (Zahra et al., 2006, p. 11). For our purposes, we will follow this definition.

While social entrepreneurship exists on a continuum that encompasses both not-for-profit and for-profit firms, primary attention in the literature has been directed toward not-for-profit organizations. Not-for-profits have increasingly engaged in earned-income strategies to advance the mission of their organizations (Dees, 1998). For example, the Girl Scouts annually sell cookies as a means of generating additional funds to continue their mission. In this way, the earned-income strategy of the organization reduces the organization's reliance on donations and therefore increases its self-sufficiency.

At least two factors contribute to this disproportionate focus on not-for-profits as examples of social entrepreneurship. First, it is easier to identify not-for-profit examples of social entrepreneurship. The identification of these organizations is facilitated by the publicly available data. As such, data on not-for-profit organizations are readily obtained in databases such as Guide Star. By comparison, the vast majority of for-profit social ventures are privately-held or privately-funded organizations. The second factor that contributes to this disproportionate focus is that not-for-profit organizations are likely overrepresented in the population of social entrepreneurial ventures. Given the primary focus on creating social value, many start-up social ventures opt for organizing as a not-for-profit organization. While a not-for-profit structure facilitates tax benefits, this decision may also be driven, in part, by the belief that social and economic value creation may conflict with each other. Therefore, one way to minimize the potential for such conflicts is to structure the organization as a not-for-profit.

Despite the common focus, social entrepreneurship is not confined to not-for-profit organizations. Rather, the organizational form of social entrepreneurship can occur anywhere on a continuum ranging from not-for-profit to for-profit entities. One of the most prominent examples of social entrepreneurship, the microfinance organization of Grameen Bank, is a for-profit business venture. While Grameen Bank was developed to provide credit to the poor in rural Bangladesh without any collateral and to fight poverty as a catalyst in the overall development of socio-economics, it is run as a for-profit social venture (Yunus, 1998). One of the perceived tensions in for-profit social ventures is between the social and economic considerations of the organization. Assuming a for-profit venture's primary mission is the creation of social value, a for-profit social venture does not necessarily experience any more tension between these dimensions than a not-for-profit organization. For example, the decision for a not-for-profit organization to enter into an earned-income strategy will likely contain similar tensions. "Commercialization can often change the character of a not-for-profit's relationship with its beneficiaries" (Dees, 1998, p. 62). However, in for-profit and not-for-profit social ventures, the social dimensions take precedence over the economic dimensions of the organization. The economic considerations serve as both a guide for which opportunities to pursue and as a means of facilitating sustainability of the organization. Yunus (1998) explained that at Grameen Bank tried to show that social consciousness-driven enterprises involving the poor as owners, suppliers, vendors, and franchisees can offer services just as efficiently as they had been previously provided but additionally attaining important social objectives.

Through the Lens of Entrepreneurship

While the domain of social entrepreneurship is still emerging in academic circles, the field can draw on knowledge gained in other academic fields particularly those that may be closely related. "We should build our theory of social entrepreneurship on [the] strong tradition of entrepreneurship theory and research. Social entrepreneurs are one species of the genus entrepreneur" (Dees, 2001, p. 2). The utility of this approach is that we can more rapidly advance the field of social entrepreneurship by leveraging existing knowledge of entrepreneurship and then identifying both the similarities and differences between commercial and social entrepreneurship. To highlight the value in this approach, we will illustrate the commonalities in commercial and social entrepreneurship.

Commonalities in Commercial and Social Entrepreneurship

The academic domain of entrepreneurship has been defined as "the scholarly examination of how, by whom and with what effects opportunities to create future goods and services are discovered, evaluated and exploited" (Shane & Venkataraman, 2000). Drawing from this definition, some of the key questions in the field involve the identification and exploitation of entrepreneurial opportunities and the set of individuals who identify and exploit these opportunities.

In many ways, commercial and social entrepreneurship address similar conceptual questions about the processes of discovery and exploitation of opportunities and the set of individuals who engage in the discovery and exploitation. In applying a conceptual model of entrepreneurship, Austin, Stevenson and Wei-Skillern (2006) noted the many similarities between commercial and social entrepreneurship particularly in the areas of the people, the context and the deal. For example, within the "people" dimension, both commercial and social entrepreneurs must be able to attract the necessary human capital to be able to execute an opportunity. To attract these human resources, both types of entrepreneurs need to rely on reputation and social networks to build their organizations (Austin et al., 2006).

In a similar way, both commercial and social entrepreneurship are focused on large-scale radical innovations. Based on the classic work of Schumpeter (1942), the entrepreneur is one who engages in creative destruction and radical innovation. For the commercial entrepreneur, such innovation often serves to completely alter the prior method of serving a market. Likewise, the social entrepreneur is focused on creating large-scale systemic change that significantly alters the current manner in which a problem is addressed. It is this focus on social innovation that is fundamental to social entrepreneurship. For example, Muhammad Yunus challenged the imbedded assumption that collateral was required to obtain a loan. By challenging this assumption, Yunus significantly altered the landscape of banking and lending practices that led to the widespread practice of micro-loans in developing nations. As such, the emerging field of social entrepreneurship can build on the theoretical and empirical tradition of entrepreneurship to further the academic inquiry into the large-scale innovations of social entrepreneurship.

Differences in Commercial and Social Entrepreneurship

While entrepreneurship may serve as the foundation on which social entrepreneurship is built, it is also important to identify some of the differences between commercial and social entrepreneurship. The most important differences are interrelated and concern the type of value being pursued and the type of opportunity being exploited.

One of the most important distinctions between the commercial and social entrepreneur is the type of value being pursued. In commercial entrepreneurship, the primary focus is on the achievement of private economic gain. The commercial entrepreneur is willing to engage in entrepreneurial activity when the financial rewards of engaging in such action exceed the personal risks of doing so. In commercial entrepreneurship, "the primary focus is on economic returns while in social entrepreneurship, the focus is on social returns" (Austin et al., 2006, p. 6).

By comparison, the social entrepreneur is focused on the achievement of social value and ultimately seeks to better the human condition (Dees, Emerson, & Economy, 2001). While the commercial entrepreneur is focused on economic value, the social entrepreneur is motivated by social value. In many cases, both economic and social value is created by commercial and social entrepreneurs. However, the important distinction is the type of value that is the top priority. While the commercial entrepreneur may create social value, the primary motivation is the creation of economic value.

For example, many commercial entrepreneurs contribute social value through the creation of employment opportunities. However, job creation is generally a byproduct rather than a purpose of commercial ventures. Similarly, the social entrepreneur may create economic value in the process of generating social value. For the social entrepreneur, this economic value is simply a means to increase the social value created. For example, the creation of Paul Newman's line of salad dressings results in the creation of significant economic value. However, the use of the proceeds from the sale of the dressings is to support a number of not-for-profit entities including the creation and development of Hole in the Wall camps. In this way, economic value is viewed by the social entrepreneur as a means to an end rather than an end itself.

A second difference between commercial and social entrepreneurs lies in the type of opportunities they pursue. Driven by an interest to achieve different forms of value, commercial and social entrepreneurs are likely to discover and exploit different types of opportunities. In comparing commercial and social entrepreneurs, Austin and his colleagues (2006) suggested one of the primary differences is the nature of the opportunity discovered and exploited by the entrepreneur (Austin et al., 2006). The nature of the opportunity exploited by commercial and social entrepreneurs is related to an underlying issue of motivation that causes the entrepreneur to act (Smith & Stevens, 2007).

For commercial entrepreneurs, one of the most important issues is the expected economic value of the entrepreneurial opportunity (Shane, 2003). As such, the potential economic reward provides the motivation for the commercial entrepreneur to act. For the social entrepreneur, the motivation to act is the creation of social value. When the social entrepreneur identifies an opportunity to generate significant social value, the desirability of the opportunity contributes to the exploitation of the social innovation (Smith & Stevens, 2007). As a result, the commercial entrepreneur is not likely to consider an opportunity that may be extremely attractive to the social entrepreneur.

For example, Martin Fisher and Nick Moon of KickStart identified a socially entrepreneurial opportunity to build water pumps in Sub-Saharan Africa to provide better irrigation for subsistence farmers in the region (Fisher, 2006). The goal of this venture is to reduce poverty in sub-Saharan Africa by providing a mechanism that allows for greater productivity for the farmers. In this case, the social innovation was the identification of a mechanism to reduce the poverty of the subsistence farmer through increased productivity of the existing asset of farming land. Not surprisingly, no commercial entrepreneurs have yet pursued this same innovative opportunity because the economic expected value is extremely low.

EDUN: A FOR-PROFIT SOCIAL ENTREPRENEURSHIP VENTURE

Edun was founded in 2005 as a socially conscious clothing company dedicated to bringing the issue of sustainable employment in the developing world to the world of catwalks and high fashion (Kemp-Griffin, 2007). Following several visits to Africa, rock star and U2 frontman, Bono, and his wife, Ali Hewson, decided to create a social venture focused on providing sustainable employment in poverty stricken regions with emphasis on Africa. In contrast to many of Bono's macrolevel humanitarian efforts, Edun was a microlevel, innovative approach to reducing poverty.

To develop Edun, Bono and Ali joined Rogan Gregory, a fashion designer who was developing his own brand using only organic cotton, to design and produce a line of socially conscious designer clothes.[1] Edun's principals sought to identify and build opportunities for trade in the developing world, rather than simply to provide aid to the people of African nations. Empirical research suggests that poverty will not be solved by capital intensive (such as heavy manufacturing) or skill intensive sectors (such as information technology), but through labor intensive, low skill sectors such as clothing production (Kochhar, Kumar, Rajan, Subramanian, & Tokatlidis, 2006).

Edun's mission is to help increase trade and create sustainable employment for developing areas of the world with an emphasis on Africa. To do so, the company focused on building and improving the skill sets of the workers who would be involved in the production of the clothing. The goals of the company were two-fold. First, Edun wanted to provide increased trade to poverty-stricken regions so the workers could become self-sufficient. In their words, the goal was to provide the fishing rod rather than the fish. Second, the company also wanted to generate a financial profit.

The ability to generate a financial profit was important because it related to both the sustainability of the organization and the likelihood of replication. Social value creation was paramount rather than making money. Rather, the profit was important for the creation of social value. If Edun was unable to generate a financial profit, then the social value they could deliver would be limited to the amount of capital the principals were willing to lose. In contrast, if Edun could generate a financial profit, then the company could not only continue to expand the amount of business it could offer to the developing nations but could also use the surplus profits to invest back into the regions where the work was being performed. However, as a social entrepreneurial venture, Edun was not focused on profit maximization. Rather than focus on producing goods at the lowest possible price, Edun focused on producing goods where the work was most needed, in poor areas such as Sub-Saharan Africa. Edun also wanted to develop a sustainable business model that other companies could replicate. While Edun was motivated by the creation of social value through the sustainable employment opportunities, other for-profit companies would need to see a path to profitability before they would follow suit. As such, the importance of a profitable business model was directly related to the amount of social value that would be created for these poor countries.

To achieve both of their goals, the company's initial business plan focused on the production of high-end, designer clothing, made of all organic fibers. Workers in these underdeveloped regions such as Sub-Saharan Africa were trained with skills that allowed them to produce the garments, and in the process, raise themselves and their families out of poverty. Edun then markets the clothes to the high-end fashion markets around the world. Beginning in 2005, Edun began producing their first collection of socially conscious clothing. While the clothing was made available to the United States and Europe, the majority of the sales occurred in the United States. Today, the clothing line is sold in higher-end retail shops such as Saks Fifth Avenue and Anthropologie (Miller, 2007).

The Creation of Different Forms of Social Value

The creation of social value—the increase or betterment of society or some social condition—may be more involved than first meets the eye. Social entrepreneurial ventures "often create social value through both their end product and their processes" (Dees, 1994). As such, the social innovation is often embedded in the process of social entrepreneurial ventures. In the case of Edun, social value and the innovative ideas that bring it about are created at several different steps in the process.

Consistent with the founding purpose, Edun delivers its first form of social value through the creation of sustainable economic employment in sub-Saharan Africa. Each garment produced under the Edun label is manufactured in factories in poverty-stricken regions. In this way the company contributes "trade" rather than "aid." In essence, this innovative approach takes the notion of assistance from one of charity to one of economic development. The preference for trade rather than aid arises from its sustainability. From the perspective of Edun, the economic value created in these regions through the employment of the factory workers is considered social value. In addition, the factories are all operated in accordance with fair trade principles. The importance of trade to these regions has become increasingly critical. In 1980, Africa had a 6% share of the world's trade. By 2002, Africa's share of the world market had declined to just 2% of the world market despite its population making up more than twelve percent of the world's population. As such, the need for economic development and a reversal of the declining trade percentages can be achieved at least partly by social entrepreneurs in the garment and other industries.

Beyond economic development, a second form of social value generated by Edun is the increased skills of the factory workers. By focusing on high-end clothing, the workers in the factories of Sub-Saharan Africa were encouraged to upgrade their skills beyond those required to produce commodity materials. One of the important motives of Edun was to facilitate the increased acquisition of high value skills through training of the factory workers. Much of the previous work in the region relied on basic skills to produce commodity clothing at the lowest possible price. By providing both opportunities and training, Edun enabled the workers to acquire higher value skills that command a higher premium in the marketplace.

A third form of social value is created by increasing awareness of the plight of workers in sub-Saharan Africa and in the garment industry. Coupling the high-end fashion runway with the celebrity status of the founders, Edun raised the profile of the issue of impoverished workers in these regions with members of the fashion industry and with consumers. In this way, "Edun acts as a voice to encourage the fashion community to do business with Africa as a means of bringing the continent out of extreme poverty" (Edun, 2007). In raising consumers' awareness of the practices within the garment industry, Edun hopes to stimulate ongoing, long-term change for some of the unacceptable practices and conditions in that industry. In a recent presentation, Ali Hewson suggested, "We don't just vote and affect change at the ballot box, we can vote and affect change with the dollar in our pocket and how we use it" (Cornwall, 2007).

Edun's Strategies for Scaling Social Impact

After developing innovative solutions to social problems, social entrepreneurs are generally interested in maximizing or "scaling up" their solution. Scaling up is the process of expanding social innovations to increase their impact on the social problem or need (Dees, Anderson, & Wei-Skillern, 2004). Previous research has identified three major approaches for scaling up the impact of social entrepreneurial ventures (e.g., Alvord, Brown, & Letts, 2004; Dees, Anderson & Wei-Skillern, 2004; Uvin, Jain, & Brown, 2000). In the case of Edun, scaling up is to be achieved through all three of these approaches: (1) the replication of the sustainable model of business in Africa; and (2) the evolution of subbrands; and (3) the integration of their supply chain.

The first strategy used by Edun to scale their social innovation is the development of a model that can be replicated. Edun has spent significant time and money trailblazing a path to create a model of sustainable production in Sub-Saharan Africa. From a commercial entrepreneurship perspective, such investment spending would be viewed as a means to establish first-mover advantage in a market. That is, the first-mover advantage is associated with the creation a longer-term competitive advantage for the firm. However, when the primary goal is the maximization of social value a very different perspective is used. In the case of Edun, the company is pioneering microlevel efforts in poverty-stricken regions such as Sub-Saharan Africa to illustrate that an economic model is possible. As such, their model serves as a model for other companies to emulate. This scaling up approach is consistent with previous research that describes how the initiation of activities that change the behavior of other social actors increases their impact indirectly (Alvord et al., 2004).

Driven by a desire to expand social rather than economic value, social entrepreneurs engage in cooperative rather than competitive activities. When Coca-Cola developed its secret formula, they patented the formula and sold it only to franchisees who paid significant franchise and royalty fees. By comparison, Grameen Bank was happy to give away their successful formula of micro-finance to anyone who was interested in expanding the distribution of micro-finance. In a similar way, Edun is content to develop a successful model for sourcing in Africa and to offer the model to any company that is willing to follow suit. Again, this willingness stems from the desire to increase the social value of the sustainable employment for poverty-stricken regions. In this way, the microlevel social innovation can scale more quickly as other companies replicate the model.

A second strategy used by Edun to expand social value is the creation of subbrands. Initially, Edun was founded as a high-end fashion company to bring socially conscious clothing to the high-end runways of the fashion industry. While this focus remains integral to the overall strategy of Edun, its innovative social venture model has also evolved to maximize its social value through the creation of subbrands. Realizing that the market for high-end designs is relatively small, company executives began to consider clothing markets where they could generate high volume sales. After several considerations, the company decided to produce premium t-shirts under the Edun LIVE subbrand (see Figure 2.1). By producing and selling premium T-shirts, Edun LIVE was able to sell significantly more clothes, thereby increasing the amount of trade conducted with factories in poverty-stricken regions. In addition, the high volume of sales also enabled Edun LIVE to provide a number of other services (like medical treatment for HIV/AIDS and a water-well for a community) to their factory workers.

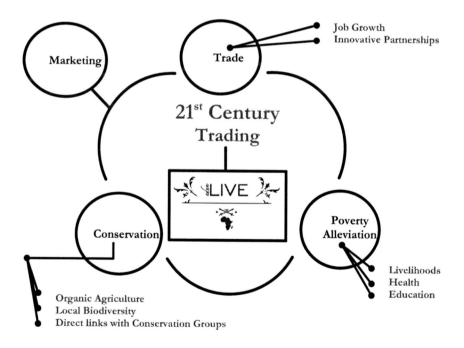

Figure 2.1.   Edun LIVE.

Unlike the production of high-end garments, the production of T-shirts represented a major opportunity for creating sustainable employment in Sub-Saharan Africa. With a significant chance for high volume production, the workload would be large and consistent. Also, the production of T-shirts involved a relatively low-skilled workforce. While the long-term goal was to increase the skills of their workers, the short-term goal was to provide immediate employment opportunities.

In the development of the subbrand Edun LIVE, company executives noted the significant size of the college student market for T-shirts. At the same time, Miami University was in the process of launching an academic program and center focused on the study of social entrepreneurship. One of the goals of the Center for Social Entrepreneurship was to provide opportunities for students to gain real experience with organizations engaged in the practice of social entrepreneurship. Through a series of e-mail, telephone, and personal exchanges, the center director and the CEO of Edun Apparel Ltd. explored opportunities of mutual benefit. The outcome of these exchanges was the development of an agreement to create Edun LIVE on Campus. Recalling the exchanges, the CEO recalled, "When the Center for Social Entrepreneurship approached me, one thing led to another and an innovative idea (of Edun LIVE on Campus) emerged" (Bradshaw, 2007). To achieve the joint goals of both Edun and Miami, Edun LIVE on Campus allowed Edun LIVE to further its social impact by penetrating the college market and by providing students an opportunity for "hands-on" learning of social entrepreneurship (for a complete description of the development of Edun LIVE on Campus, see Smith & Barr, 2007). While still in the pilot stage, the Edun LIVE on Campus model also provides an opportunity to scale social impact through a rollout to other college campuses across the world.

A final strategy used by Edun to scale its social impact is the integration of its supply chain. After moving into the t-shirt business through the subbrand of Edun LIVE, the company began to develop a "grower-to-sewer" approach to sustainable economic development. This approach to reducing poverty examines every process in the supply chain beginning with the cut and sew operations and moving backwards. Edun is currently working to integrate important social considerations into every aspect of the production of the T-shirt.

In outlining this approach, Edun suggests there are several important considerations that affect its decision-making process. These considerations include such questions as: "Where do people most need our business? Where are the workers paid and treated most fairly? Where are we helping the development of rural livelihoods and not destroying the land where these people live?" (Kemp-Griffin, 2007). For example, Edun is working with cotton farmers in Africa to assist them in the transition from using pesticides to growing organic cotton. In this way, Edun is adding social value to the supply chain through the reduction of the pesticides harmful to the environment, through the education of the farmers about how to do organic farming and through the sustainable employment made possible by purchasing the farmers' cotton. From the growing of organic cotton through the milling/ginning operations to the cutting and sewing of T-shirts, Edun is adding social value at each stage of the supply chain. Each process provides additional opportunities for employment, leading to the reduction of poverty and the building of long-term sustainable economic growth.

CONCLUSON

This chapter provides a starting point for an in-depth look at the potential for social entrepreneurship to reduce poverty. As developed, social entrepreneurship offers innovative solutions to persistent social problems such as extreme poverty. Leveraging the extant knowledge of entrepreneurship, the emerging area of social entrepreneurship offers great hope for the future. Through the example of Edun, this chapter detailed several examples of how social entrepreneurs create social value and how social entrepreneurs scale up their social innovations. In order to reduce poverty significantly, the microlevel solutions created by Edun must be emulated by many other companies.

Edun represents an innovative approach to reducing poverty through the use of social entrepreneurship. At one level, the social innovation can be seen in the entrepreneurial approach to develop a new line of socially-conscious clothing focused on delivering sustainable employment to sub-Saharan Africa. Utilizing factories in poverty-stricken regions, Edun is focused on pioneering a sustainable model that other companies can replicate. At a second level, the social innovation can be seen in the processes used in the creation of the venture. In this way, innovative approaches are used to increase the skills of the impoverished workers, to increase the awareness of the plight of Sub-Saharan Africa, and to expand the social value created. This is accomplished through the creation of subbrands to capitalize on social entrepreneurial opportunities and through the integration of a more environmentally-friendly supply chain that seeks to benefit African suppliers from "grower to sewer."

NOTE

1. The information about Edun comes from a working relationship with the company over the last year. As such, the information comes from personal correspondence in a variety of forms including e-mail, face-to-face meetings, and phone conversations.

REFERENCES

Alvord, S., Brown, D., & Letts, C. (2004). Social entrepreneurship and societal transformation. *Journal of Applied Behavioral Science, 40,* 260-300.

Austin, J., Stevenson, H., & Wei-Skillern, J. (2006). Social and commercial entrepreneurship: Same, different or both? *Entrepreneurship, Theory and Practice, 31*(1), 1-22.

Bornstein, D. (2004) *How to change the world: Social entrepreneurs and the power of new ideas.* Oxford, England: Oxford University Press.

Bradshaw, D. (2007, March 4). The T-shirt that helps alleviate poverty. *Financial Times.* Retrieved June 28, 2007, from http://us.ft.com/ftgateway/superpage .ft?news_id=fto030420071721446817

Cornwall, L. (2007, January 22). Bono goes to college for business pilot. *Boston Globe.* Retrieved June 28, 2007, from http://www.boston.com/news/education/ higher/articles/2007/01/22/bono_goes_to_college_for_business_pilot/

Dees, G. (1994, November 30). Social enterprise: Private initiatives for the common good. *Harvard Business School, 9-395,* 116.

Dees, G. (1998, January-February). Enterprising non-profits. *Harvard Business Review,* 55-67.

Dees, G. (2001). *The meaning of social entrepreneurship.* Retreived March 7, 2007, from http://www.fuqua.duke.edu/centers/case/documents/dees_sedef.pdf

Dees, G., Anderson, B., & Wei-Skillern, J. (2004). Scaling social impact: Strategies for spreading social innovations. *Stanford Social Innovation Review, 1*(4), 24-32.

Dees, J. G., Emerson, J., & Economy, P. (2001) *Enterprising nonprofits: A toolkit for social entrepreneurs.* New York: Wiley.

Edun. (2007). Retrieved June 28, 2007, from www.edun.ie

Fisher, M. (2006). Income is development. *Innovations, 1,* 9-30.

Karnani, A. (2006). Fortune at the bottom of the pyramid: A mirage how the private sector can help alleviate poverty (University of Michigan Ross School of Business Working Paper Series, Working Paper #1035).

Kemp-Griffin, C. (2007). *Edun LIVE: Fair trade for the 21st century, creating jobs in sub-Saharan Africa.* Presentation on Social Entrepreneurship at Miami University.

Kochhar, K., Kumar, U., Rajan, R., Subramanian, A., & Tokatlidis, I. (2006) India's Pattern of Development: What Happened, What Follows? *Journal of Monetary Economics, 53*(5): 981-1019.

Miller, K. (2007, January 10). Students market clothing with conscience. *Business Week.com.* Retrieved June 28, 2007, 2007, from http://www.businessweek.com/ print/bschools/content/jan2007/bs20070109_917953.htm

Schumpeter, J. (1942). *Capitalism, socialism and democracy.* New York: Harper.

Shane, S. (2003). *A general theory of entrepreneurship: The individual-opportunity nexus.* Northampton, MA: Edward Elgar.

Shane, S., & Venkataraman, S. (2000). The promise of entrepreneurship as a field of research. *Academy of Management Review, 25,* 217-226.

Smith, B., & Barr, T. (2007). *Contributing to the U.N. Millennium Goals through social entrepreneurship: The launch of Edun LIVE on campus* (Miami University working paper).

Smith, B., & Stevens, C. (2007). *Social entrepreneurial action: The role of knowledge and motivation and the effects on different types of social entrepreneurs* (Miami University working paper).

Uvin, P., Jain, P. & Brown, L. (2000). Think large and act small: Toward a new paradigm for NGO scaling up. *World Development, 28,* 1409-1419.

Yunus, M. (1998). Poverty alleviation: Is economics any help? Lessons from the Grameen Back experience. *Journal of International Affairs, 51*(1), 47-65.

Zahra, S., Gedajlovic, E., Neubaum, D., & Schulman, J. (2006, February). *Social entrepreneurship: Domain, contributions and ethical dilemmas.* Presented at the University of Minnesota Conference on Ethics and Entrepreneurship.

CHAPTER 3

SUSTAINABLE WORKFORCE MODELS

Lessons From India on Training and Development of Unskilled Labor

Cynthia S. Cycyota and Wendy Volkland

ABSTRACT

This chapter explores the research on developing economies and describes a unique model used in India for worker training. The model seeks to reduce poverty by encouraging and training those living in poverty to earn a living wage. The model involves developing strategic and sustainable links between governments, nongovernmental organizations, and not-for-profit organizations to work in concert to develop skills and work ethics in the lower socioeconomic levels of society. A case study of a group of organizations working together to reduce poverty in India illustrates how the model is being used.

Innovative Approaches to Reducing Global Poverty
pp. 43–66
Copyright © 2007 by Information Age Publishing
All rights of reproduction in any form reserved.

INTRODUCTION

Economic policy, social policy, and regulatory strategies seeking to achieve sustainable development are all tied to and reliant on the development of ways to assist the lowest echelons of the population to lift themselves out of severe poverty and to become participating citizens in a viable economic system (Fowler, 2000; Seelos & Mair, 2006). However, the enormous scope of poverty makes reliable solutions difficult to imagine and more difficult to implement. Where does society begin to solve problems that have existed for thousands of years and that are magnified by sweeping globalization (Ahluwalia, 2006; Bala Subrahmanya, 2005)? We suggest that the issue may be effectively, if slowly, addressed by an approach that begins with individual businesses and builds up to a level that involves governments, nongovernmental organizations and multinational companies. The end result is an innovative and sustainable model that harnesses the resources and abilities of multiple levels of organizations. By developing individuals in a manner that enhances their own abilities, this approach, or model, allows these individuals to innovate and create new opportunities of their own.

The idea of building sustainable frameworks for social development from the bottom is not unique to our research. A strategic approach for building on available resources and capabilities has long been a cornerstone concept that relies on identification of available resources and focuses on improving those assets and skills to be competitive (Barney, 1991; Penrose, 1959; Wernerfelt, 1984). More recently, Prahalad (2005a) identified the myriad opportunities for business, development, and sustainability available at the lowest socioeconomic levels, in his terms: the "Bottom of the Pyramid" (BOP). On the surface, the opportunities identified by Prahalad relate to selling to the poor and adapting products and plans appropriate for individuals with smaller budgets and with fewer technical attribute requirements. These BOP opportunities can constitute a viable market for large corporations to address (Katz, 2006). At a deeper level, however the thesis of BOP development strategies attracts attention to the development of profit motivations and essential business skills in underserved poor populations (Prahalad, 2005b) and reflects both a basic need of society in many developing countries and a potential role for global businesses in serving that need.

The idea of assisting the poor to develop their own business models and skills is also well developed (Harper, 1991, Kumar & Liu, 2005). There are numerous studies of microlending (Barefoot, 2005; Hudson & Wehrell, 2005), enterprise development (Harper, 1991), nongovernmental organizations (Fowler, 2000; Handy, Kassam, & Ranade, 2002) and other means of serving the needs of the poor. These studies illustrate the positive effects that attention to this segment of the population may have both on the citizens themselves and on the community at large. Indeed, the idea of helping people to help themselves is central to the concept of social entrepreneurship (Dees, 1998) which emphasizes the value in combining traditional entrepreneurship with a mission to help society (Seelos & Mair, 2005). BOP modeling can present excellent examples not only of market opportunities but also of social entrepreneurship.

The best ways to manage or achieve the goal of sustainable business and to help the impoverished are subject to rather intense debate that includes nongovernmental organizations (NGOs) as providers of assistance, governments as political entities seeking to further the interests of the country, and businesses that seek profitable operations within a region. NGOs have historically taken the lead in helping the poor. Most NGOs were established through charitable entities to help those with few resources to help themselves (Fowler, 2000; Heap, 2000). However, it has been argued that years of working with and around government and political agencies have led to a decrease in the ability of NGOs to aid the poor and an increase in bureaucratic policies and inertia (Fowler, 2000). These organizations were typically (although not exclusively) established to serve the poor through aid aimed at feeding, clothing and housing the poor, not at developing businesses that would be self-sustaining. This aid granting approach has lead to a decrease in their effectiveness. In addition, even if NGOs wished to develop a self-sustaining business to reduce poverty, they typically do not have the knowledge resources to provide assistance in the form of business development, staff training or market analysis (Heap, 2000).

Government efforts to aid the poor may be easily swayed by political interests, bureaucratic policies and a host of conflicting goals (Fowler, 2000). The poorest members of society who have little voice or systematic influence are easily overlooked amid the shifting political interests and government reforms aimed at economic development and liberalization of the economy (Ahluwalia, 2006). The political complexities of coordinating the regulatory and economic aspects of foreign direct investment and globalization often leave few resources available for aid to the poor (Veron, Corbridge, Williams, & Srivastava, 2003).

Businesses within a country and external organizations seeking to operate in a country have obligations to owners to make a profit. They are often attracted to outsource operations to developing countries by the prevailing lower wage market (Dhungana, 2003; Friedman, 2006). A broader social mission for multinational companies is not typically a top priority (Hudson & Wehrell, 2005; Kumar & Liu, 2005).

Another group exists, however, with a specific mission to help the poor in a manner that can make them self-sustaining. Social entrepreneurs

seek to establish business systems whereby the poor, unskilled, and inex-
perienced can gain the knowledge and assistance needed to permanently
eliminate the need for aid except in situation of humanitarian disasters
(Seelos & Mair, 2005). Through these efforts, the original entrepreneurs
can participate in the practice of value creation and hire others, perpetu-
ating the cycle of poverty reduction (Dakhli & De Clercq, 2004; Dees,
2005).

This chapter does not attempt to explain how social entrepreneurs can
overcome all the obstacles to poverty reduction. Seeking a more modest
aim, it focuses on a case example of a single company founded by a group
of well-intended business people. The business faces many obstacles in
operations, yet in many ways represents a model for others to follow. To
provide a context for this business' experience, historical information on
the development of human capital in India is reviewed followed by a discussion of the traditional roles of NGOs, social entrepreneurs, multinational corporations and others' attempts to address poverty in emerging
and innovative ways. Information from the business the authors worked
with is then presented along with the challenges the company faces on a
daily basis. The chapter concludes with a discussion of suggestions for
helping this and similar organizations operate more efficiently and
achieve organizational objectives. The discussion describes a model of
interconnections between such organizations that could serve to help each
of them accomplish individual organizational goals as well as serving society at large.

India and Human Capital Development

The remarkable advances of India as a developing nation in trade
(Som, 2006), education (Friedman, 2006), and outsourcing (Bandi & Srinvasan, 2005) reflect the success of government policies and efforts to
encourage foreign direct investment, trade, and participation in the global economy since opening the borders in the early 1990s (Ahluwalia,
2006). For many citizens of India, the liberalization has brought higher
paying employment opportunities in growing industries for both domestic and multinational companies in the country's growing industries. Multinational companies find a significant number of highly skilled
engineers, software programmers, and medical professionals who are willing to work for lower wages than workers in more developed nations such
as the United States or Europe (Ratnam & Venkata, 1998). In addition,
the services industry has found that a significant number of Indian workers speak languages and have the skills required for employment in outsourced call-centers and other service operations (Friedman, 2006). Out-

sourcing allows companies to control their costs while providing comparatively high-paying jobs in the host country (Krugman, 1995).

However, in India, like many developing nations, not all members of society are equipped to take advantage of these new opportunities. The lower echelons of society remain homeless, unskilled, and underclassed, without the benefits of a reliable social umbrella to assist them. Although government programs for poverty assistance, workfare, and welfare exist (Besley & Coate, 1992; Veron et al., 2003) the historical forces of the caste system work to maintain a permanent or inevitable underclass of people who are unable to meet the costs of becoming part of the competitive labor market (Scoville, 1996). The lowest caste, the Shudras or labor class, does not have the educational opportunities of the higher classes, the Brahmins (intellectuals), Kshatriys, or Vaisyas. The Dalits, untouchables, have no opportunity to gain the needed skills for personal and professional development. Although the Indian government has worked to outlaw discrimination based on the caste system, it is very difficult to overcome the social and practical ramifications of the tradition (Ratnam & Venkata, 1996). Women in the lowest caste and untouchables are further hampered by traditional views that subordinate their position to men, further reducing opportunities for education, training and advancement (Handy, Kassam, & Ranade, 2002).

The lack of education and training in the underclasses of society creates problems for the reduction of poverty. Human capital development (Dakhli & De Clercq, 2004) and human potential development (Kalra, 1997) both suggest that individuals must receive basic training in employment skills and basic education for the individual to be an effective and contributing member of society. Dakhli and De Clercq (2004) found that increases in the value of human capital are related to an increase in innovation in developing countries. In short, the beginning of human capital development is the development of policies, procedures, or alternatives that insure potential workers have basic skills to be gainfully employed (Lewis, 2002). While a number of government programs exist in India, it is also useful to consider other ways to assist the poor. Programs to assist the poor have been mainstays of NGO commitment for many years.

Nongovernmental Organizations

NGOs play an important role in relationships between countries and in humanitarian operations within developing countries. Some NGOs operate as direct aid organizations, providing basic assistance for food, shelter and medical care to those in need due to natural or man-made disasters or disruptions (Fowler, 2000). Increasingly, NGOs are formed to function as policy advocates to influence government or business policies on issues such as health care, environmental issues, and human rights (Schepers, 2006). Each NGO's structure and practices vary according to its purpose and the origin of its supporters. One useful approach to understanding NGOs involves distinguishing between northern and southern NGOs. Northern NGOs, from the Americas or Northern Europe, typically concern themselves with human rights and environmental issues. Southern NGOs, from less developed countries, focus primarily on social and economic aspects of development (Schepers, 2006). Regardless of the origin or role of the NGO, organizations of these types have the opportunity to assist in the development of social entrepreneurs in these emerging markets by assisting potential employees in the acquisition of basic business skills. However, few NGOs have established systems to teach specific workplace skills (Roberts, Jones, & Frohling, 2005).

NGOs could play many roles in this type of development (Heap, 2000). They could assist employees in the development of basic employment skills such as language, hygiene, decorum and reporting relationships. These skills are important because homeless people encounter difficulties finding a job without the ability to establish a clean and pleasant presentation or to learn about the basics of reporting to work, interacting with co-workers and bosses and other aspects of holding a position. In addition, the NGOs could assist potential employers in finding employable individuals that have not previously had the opportunity to be employed. Many shelters, food banks and other assistance agencies work with the homeless underclass on a daily basis. NGO employees have knowledge of individuals that may benefit from employment opportunities and can aid in their identification. Finally, NGOs that do offer shelter can assist the newly employed by providing temporary housing and support for workers while they gain employability skills—the from streets to factory transition.

Social Entrepreneurship in Emerging Markets

Social entrepreneurship combines the "resourcefulness of traditional entrepreneurship with a mission to change society" (Seelos & Mair, 2005, p. 241). Although numerous authors have defined social entrepreneurship, perhaps the most interesting perspective comes from Gregory Dees who suggests that social entrepreneurship is intended to concentrate more on innovation and impact than on income (Dees, 2005). This perspective fits well with businesses in developing markets whose overall goal is to teach and train workers without effective skills while operating a for-profit business. This type of enterprise creates value, the traditional goal of entrepreneurs, but does so in a manner that creates sustainable social value. The model of social entrepreneurship and social development for emerging markets presented in this chapter attempts to capture efforts aimed at the lowest echelons of society to gain skills and abilities in the workplace by progressing though a series of graduated skill-level jobs. The intent is not to take care of people in this class, but to prepare them to earn their own way and to become forces for innovation, impact and value creation within their own communities.

A number of other organizations have pursued similar approaches. For example, the Skoll Foundation assists a number of social entrepreneurs in establishing sustainable businesses that aid the overall community such as a water and sanitation project in India. It also supports a number of micro lenders helping women in Pakistan to obtain financing to start their own businesses and other social entrepreneurs throughout the world (Seelos & Mair, 2005). Other social entrepreneurs work to develop hybrid organizations that combine social responsibility, ecological sustainability and business development.

Multinational Corporations and Local, Small-Scale Industry

Multinational corporations (MNCs) also have a multifaceted interest in the training and development of unskilled workers in developing countries such as India (Ratnam & Venkata, 1996; Som, 2006). From one perspective, the interest of multinationals is self-serving. As competition for employees in these countries increases, the availability of highly skilled workers competing for lower level jobs will evaporate, forcing companies to look to other levels of society to fill entry level positions and basic service roles. The days of having engineers and scientists working in call centers are rapidly drawing to an end (Bandi & Srinvasan, 2005). It is in the best interest of these companies to participate in programs to help workers acquire basic skills and to support government policies that provide education and related services (Powell, 2006).

Other benefits for the MNC and its shareholders arise when the identification and management of social issues creates reputational value. A clear demonstration of voluntary corporate social responsibility sends a strong and positive message to consumers and the marketplace that the corporation values positive and responsible actions to aid the community (Bonini, Medonca, & Oppenheim, 2006).

Finally, the small-scale businesses (SSB) in India may have much to gain by affiliation with programs of social entrepreneurs. Many companies in this sector continue to face the challenges that resulted from the liberalization of government policies in the 1990s that allowed an increase in foreign direct investment and increased in the pace of competition and innovation (Bala Subrahmanya, 2005). These SSBs continue to face barriers to their progress such as a lack of infrastructure in electrical power, clean water, reliable telecommunication, and transportation, as well as the increase in competition from multinational and foreign imported products. If the SSBs , NGOs, social entrepreneurs, and multinational corporations were to address issues related to infrastructure, employee training and government corruption jointly, it could serve to strengthen their competitiveness and create overall improvement in conditions. In addition, the potential to hire workers trained by the social entrepreneurship businesses could serve as a resource to smaller organizations.

The potential for social entrepreneurs to act as catalysts for change in developing countries is enormous. Although the complete process is beyond the scope of this chapter, the study described in the following sections may serve to generate interest in the creation of links between organizations and the development of networks to further innovative training processes and business development. The activities of the three organizations described, a not-for-profit manufacturer, a for-profit manufacturer, and a charitable group, provide information and spawn questions critical to thinking about sustainable economic growth and social transformations in developing countries, through innovations that reduce poverty.

A CASE-STUDY IN INNOVATING AWAY POVERTY—PUNE, INDIA

Background

Early in 2003, an engineer from the Netherlands embarked on a multi-level strategy of business development in India with an Indian engineer from Pune in the state of Maharashta. Recognizing the scale of poverty in India and the impoverished Indian people's need for training and empowerment, the management team set up a three-part venture: a self-sustaining training program in a candle factory, a for-profit manufacturing company, and a not-for-profit orphanage for HIV positive children. Like other social entrepreneurs in emerging economies, the directors intentionally blur the traditional lines between for-profit and not-for-profit ventures with the goal of social and economic growth for impoverished people. Mirroring the venture's setting in India, its successes have been as fragrant as the challenges have been pungent. However, the challenges become less daunting when the plethora of resources and partners are recognized and connected. This case explores this threefold model as a possible part of the solution to innovating away poverty in the developing world. Where challenges and shortfalls exist, the discussion presents suggestions for improvement and partnership.

The consistent theme across each of the three ventures lies in the directors' focus on transitioning the underprivileged population into the profitable marketplace through idea generation, recruitment of workers, training, day-to-day operations, and transition up the ladder of skills and economic prosperity. In their research of the local economy, the two directors sought to identify potential employees whose skills could be improved or retrained to be competitive (Barney, 1991; Penrose, 1959; Wernerfelt, 1984). Looking for a group of people oppressed by the caste system and in need of training to displace the prevalent discrimination hampering them from entering the competitive marketplace, the directors chose to focus on women in the Dalit ("untouchable") class engaging in the commercial sex trade. These women experience triple oppression in the forms of poverty, their status as females, and further, their status as being female Dalits (Grey, 2005). Two hundred to 250 million Dalits live in India and 75-80% of these Dalits subsist below the poverty line, with 50% of these Dalits being women (Grey, 2005). Grey argues that the Dalit women's "lack of self-esteem or low self-esteem is the single most inhibiting factor for women's transformation and achievement of dignity" and that the most acute area of suffering experienced by the Dalit women exists in "the lack of control over their own bodies and sexuality." The directors decided to attack these two factors by focusing on providing retraining to prostitutes to enable them to enter the job market. They also recognized the possible secondary effects of educating and training women echoed in the United Nations Development Program's 2006 Annual Report, reporting that "women's empowerment helps raise economic productivity and reduce infant mortality. It contributes to improved health and nutrition. It increases the chances of education for the next generation."

The directors wanted the program to be self-sustaining and have few barriers to entry (such as equipment costs, specialized training, etc.) so that it could weather volunteer shortages and be independent of international aid. They specifically searched for a shortage of simple products in the local market that could be made quickly and easily with a minimum amount of training or technical skills. They did not expect the women to have many skills with which to start due to cultural barriers and the remnants of the caste system. They desired to help them overcome the discrimination noted by Ratnam and Venkata (1996) by providing them with employable skills. They determined the program must be able to take individuals from a different work background and transition them into an 8- to 10-hour work day, focusing on learning work ethics, technical skills, taking a product from start to finish, and learning how to manage teams and the production process at a microlevel.

Candle Factory

The training program developed is a self-sustaining candle-making factory. The high end candles are sold to local shop owners and rented out for large weddings and other engagements. Currently, the operations are run by a full-time paid employee who is an engineering technician from the Netherlands. He supervises and trains the women (3-5 women in training 6 days per week). To recruit the women, the directors hired a local Indian woman, familiar with the prostitutes and the slums. Free housing is provided at the orphanage and about half of the women who have come through the candle-making factory have utilized this option. Interestingly, these women are the only women who have made it through the training and have proceeded to the manufacturing factory. The others have returned to the street after intermittent success at the candle-making factory.

The women first learn basic working discipline that includes reporting to work from 9:00 A.M. to 4:00 P.M. daily. They are taught how to mold the candles, die them, fragrance them, and package them. Once they have mastered the basic work ethics and technical skills, they are then taught basic bookkeeping skills, followed by small team leadership skills—being given small steps of authority in supervising the other women. After 3 months of proven aptitude with the new work ethic, and technical, administrative, and supervisory skills, the women are allowed to move to the for-profit manufacturing company where they begin learning how to assemble the manufactured pieces, more bookkeeping, computer skills, and increased supervisory and quality-control skills.

For-Profit Company

The for-profit manufacturing company was started by the Dutchman and the Indian engineer about 6 months after the candle-making factory to provide a transition into the competitive marketplace for these women. Using his engineering education and connections, the Dutchman created the company to take advantage of the outsourcing trends in the United States and Europe. He focuses on recruiting a local management team to run the day-to-day operations, training them to think strategically about new business ideas and opportunities, how to develop these opportunities, and how to grow the company to service more underprivileged workers while simultaneously providing cheap, quality products to international customers. The Dutchman intends to transition complete ownership and management to the Indian engineer and his selected team within the next 10 years. Seed capital came primarily from the Dutchman's friends and family in the Netherlands and from the sale of his personal property.

The business' focus is to manufacture a variety of engineering goods (ranging from brass components to designer lamps to hand-carved wooden furniture) for small and medium scale Western enterprises. From 2004-2005, export sales grew to 5,000,000 INR (U.S.$113,000) and projections for 2006 were 7,650,000 INR (U.S.$173,000). Opening a zinc plating factory and doubling export sales in the next year were under consideration. Connections with the University of The Hague in the Netherlands and with an engineering design company in the Netherlands have been critical to the growth of the company. The company has also developed what they call strategic partnerships in Australia and the United States—personal connections who look for business outsourcing opportunities in their local country and then connect the companies with the Indian venture, receiving a small percentage of the profits when they are realized.

Currently, the Dutch director handles all strategic vision issues and new partnerships/customers. The Indian director handles the day to day operations in the factory, pricing decisions, and interaction with suppliers. The staffing comes from two sources: an orphanage that raises and trains orphans for administrative work and provides funding for technical schools and/or colleges and the candle factory training program designed to retrain prostitutes into factory work. Currently, the company employs four women and one man full-time in the factory. It offers company housing at the orphanage where the employees can live free of charge and it also offers company transportation. The factory employees typically work 10- to 12-hour days, 6 days per week. Bonuses are offered in connection with superior performance and low-interest company loans are available for any of the employees with demonstrated need. As the skills of the employees improve, the directors generate new positions for them to utilize the new skills and new employees are brought in through the candle-making training program. They try to match the growth rate of new business ventures to the output of the training program and vice versa. These business operations are also intertwined with a not-for-profit orphanage for HIV positive children, as 30% of the company's profits go to running the orphanage, and the women working at the factory and the candle-making factory can live at the orphanage free of charge.

Orphanage

The idea for the orphanage surfaced from a demonstrated need in the community, as a father left a 4-year old malnourished, HIV-positive child at the doorstep of the Dutch director's home. Unable to find a suitable care facility for the orphaned child, the director and his wife decided to intertwine an idea for an orphanage with the training program and their company. The living space in the orphanage provides underprivileged women an opportunity to transition into their first place of employment. Currently, there are three women caregivers who receive room, board, and a small salary to take care of the children. The directors also recruit interns from local and international NGOs.

The orphanage has grown from the one to five children over the last 3 years. A social worker at the government hospital finds the children that need care and brings them to the directors. The children have been integrated into the local school system and receive free health care and anti-AIDS medication from the government hospital. Although the successes abound at the orphanage, the challenges are just as plentiful. The approach the directors have taken is to help as many orphans as they can in the present—however imperfectly—and work toward making it better in the future.

Successes and Challenges

Table 3.11 provides a listing of some of the successes and challenges faced by these organizations.

Successes in the training program have fueled the entire venture—providing much needed training to the women and providing a source of labor for the manufacturing company. The successes come in four forms: the break down of the caste system mentality, removal of the women from the pressures of their former environment, accountability with the other women, and the learning platform that proves critical to the women's success at the factory. From the first moment of interaction, when the women are recruited, the recruiter, the engineering technician and the directors start intentionally breaking down the oppressive caste system mentality. The women's first interaction with the middle class Indian director happens as he makes candles next to them in the candle-making shop. A foreigner, the Dutch technician, takes a keen interest in their training and development, teaching them not only to look him in the eyes with self-confidence, but also to look over the progress of other women in the shop, with the promise of a promotion to manufacturing facilities in the near future..

The company provided housing at the orphanage has also proved instrumental in the success of the women, as it removes the women from the pressures of street/slum life and allows them to start anew together with the other women working at the candle-making factory, the orphanage, and the manufacturing facilities. In cases where the women have not moved in off of the streets, their male counterparts on the streets have

Table 3.1.   Successes and Challenges of the Three Organizations

		Training		*Company*		*Orphanage*
Successes	1.	Initiate breakdown of caste mentality	1.	Quick growth path in India	1.	Only orphanage in Pune that accepts HIV+ children (5 children removed from streets)
	2.	Women lift themselves off of streets into living wage w/ aid of accountability systems	2.	Continued breakdown of caste mentality	2.	Provides jobs to women raised in nearby orphanage
	3.	Critical job training (work ethics & skills) for further employment	3.	Women continue in upward trend toward small group leadership		
Challenges	1.	Throughput too low for company's operational needs	1.	Costs not fully understood because intertwined with donations and training/not-for-profit ventures	1.	Finances complicated among candle factory, business, & orphanage
	2.	Lack of connections with other organizations	2.	Government corruption	2.	Lack of skilled workers
	3.	Future possibility inability to compete in saturated candle market	3.	Natural hazards	3.	Life issues with women raised in orphanage
			4.	Power grid	4.	HIV+ risk to workers and schools
			5.	Views on Quality	5.	Lack of connections with other organizations
			6.	Endemic bribery in local university system		

tended to exert unresistable pressure for them to continue in the street life and to sabotage the discipline necessary to move into the competitive working world. The women see each other progress, holding one another accountable, and start to feel like a part of the working society—their first chance to grasp the ladder up from the BOP.

Once the women make this successful step into the 9-4 job, other aspects of the discipline and skill set have come much easier than originally anticipated by the directors. In just three months, the women progress from learning a technical skill set to learning bookkeeping and small team management. Thus far, five of the nine women recruited have graduated to working at the manufacturing facility and four new women are in the training process.

Apart from these successes, the largest challenge encountered has been recruiting enough women to provide sufficient manpower for the manufacturing facility, especially around peak assembly times. As noted in Table 3.1, this training system has not been sufficient to provide enough workers for the factory to operate at full capacity. The directors have not established connections with local organizations to aid in recruiting women and are hesitant to do so due to hand to mouth dependencies they fear the aid organizations have created in the Pune community. The recruiter they hired trisects her time recruiting, working at the orphanage, and cooking for the director and his family. The amount of time available for recruiting and the receptiveness of the recruits have proven to be challenges. The directors have also attempted to use local NGOs to connect to possible recruits from the streets and slums, but the NGOs were not very successful in providing this assistance. They have not been willing to provide the job screening and recommend candidates due to their own problems with a shortage of employees and the different nature of their work, which usually involves providing aid in the way of food and clothing handouts. The directors are not connected with a wide variety of NGOs, so their experience with one particular NGO has skewed their perception of the value that other NGOs might add.

Successes arise on three fronts in the manufacturing company: revenue growth, caste system shrinkage, and the women's leadership growth. From 2004-2005, the company's export sales grew to 5,000,000 INR (U.S.$113,000) and projections for 2006 were 7,650,000 INR (U.S.$173,000), with the possibility of opening a zinc plating factory and doubling export sales in 2007. The company experiences, first hand, the accelerated growth model that Prahalad (2005a) claims is possible in developing countries. In addition to revenue growth, the success of bringing women in off of the streets and watching them progress into leading small teams in factory work underpins all aspects of the business. The directors lease space at a small factory and have made an impact by working among the women. These activities have empowered the women and made the factory owner question his own more hierarchical nature, once again breaking down the caste system mentality. When interacting with suppliers and government officials, the directors explain their business and their goals of empowering women which leads the suppliers and officials to question this business' mode of operations and value. Once they see the successes of the business, they start to question their own assumptions about the Dalits and the place of women in Indian society. They also see that when someone values these untouchables, they can begin to value themselves and play productive roles in society and the marketplace.

Although the directors consider these successes significant, with regard to the manufacturing facility, there are challenges. Specifically, the corruption in the Indian government hampers productivity, the prevalence of natural hazards and the fluctuations in the power grid interrupt the schedule frequently, the differing view of acceptable rates of defective workmanship and products slows progress, and the endemic bribery at smaller universities makes determination of qualifications for prospective employees difficult. Providing resistance at every turn, the corruption in the government excise office prevents shipments from getting to port in Mumbai on time. Paperwork must be filed before each shipment and, each time, the paperwork is delayed while hints are given that there are ways to speed things up, if the company is willing to pay, otherwise, come back again another day. The company takes a stand against the corruption in not paying bribes and, thus, must make 10-14 trips to the office to check on the shipping documents and encourage the government to sign the paperwork. The directors found even more bribery pressure present when the local Indian director made the trips versus the foreign director. Because of these experiences they do not feel that it would be effective to hire an administrative person to make the trips and feel it necessary for the foreign director to continue to make his presence known until transparency increases and bribery pressure decreases. As a result, shipments have been delayed from 2 days to as long as 2 weeks.

The natural hazards such as flooding and mudslides and the power grid fluctuations also hamper the company's efficiency and interrupt delivery schedules. Every monsoon season, the city releases the dam on the river at the wrong time (just before 2-3 days of forecasted solid rain). Not surprisingly, flooding of roads and slums occurs, disrupting all travel throughout the city and between Pune and Mumbai. Mud and rock slides threaten the mountain pass between Pune and Mumbai weekly throughout the monsoon season. Mumbai also floods frequently during monsoon season causing shipments to be delayed from the port. In April of 2006, the city of Pune finally secured "uninterrupted" power in all locations. While a drastic improvement from four to six power outages per day and some locations without power completely, the electricity in its current "uninterrupted" state still blacks out all day on Thursdays (scheduled) and four to six times per week for unknown lengths of time (unscheduled).

In addition to the challenges of natural hazards and government corruption, the company has found it difficult to communicate quality and delivery time standards to suppliers of raw materials and manufactured goods. It is not uncommon to receive raw materials or products 2 weeks to 1 month late and then have to reject 80% of the materials/products for defects. Several dimensions exist in this problem. First, suppliers will agree to any delivery date without question and with an agreeable head bob, saying "no problem," stemming from a cultural bias toward telling people what you think they want to hear. When the actual delivery time expires, the suppliers ask for more money to get it to the company with less delay. Second, difficulties arise when the directors try to change well established mindsets. For example, when they tried to reduce schedule and defect delays by ordering extra materials and ordering all necessary raw materials in bulk at one time, the factory owner did not understand their reasoning and refused to spend more money initially—seeing only the necessity to buy the materials needed for the next month, not the next 6 months. In his view, if the supplies are needed after the first month, they must be ordered later to save money initially. When the scheduling delays are addressed, it is as if time has no standard dimension and the factory owner replies with a comment that that is the way it works in India; why does the customer need the product at a certain time?

One method the directors have successfully implemented is the practice of shorter contract deadlines, spanning 2 weeks to 1 month versus 1 to 2 years and establishing milestones in the schedule for the factory owner, versus focusing on the overall delivery of product and allowing the factory owner to set his own milestones. To enforce the sanctity of the contract, something that Prahalad (2005a) notes as a problem within the developing world, the directors tie the possibility of future work to the successful completion and delivery of each milestone.

Another obstacle affecting day-to-day operations is the difficulty in recruiting skilled workers, once again stemming from a bribery issue, but this time with the university system. When looking for skilled administrators, accountants, or financial managers, the company frequently encounters fake schooling credentials obtained by a mere $5 bribe to university officials.

The ultimate success of the factory in overcoming these obstacles and turning a sizeable profit determines the scale of the third venture, the orphanage. The orphanage somewhat speaks for itself as a success, in that it is one of the only places in Pune that accepts HIV positive children due to the social stigma attached to them and it also provides jobs to women raised in a nearby orphanage. Challenges include confusion amongst the finances of the three ventures, problems hiring skilled workers or trainers, issues with the women raised in an orphanage, and risks inherent with HIV-infected people.

Due to the lack of skilled financial managers, as noted above, and the intricacies involved with the workers and women-in-training living at the orphanage, the finances are somewhat confused among the candle factory, manufacturing company, and orphanage. The result is that many charities and individuals are reluctant to make donations, fearing their money will be used for the for profit venture.

In addition, the caretakers were themselves raised in an orphanage with no treatment or counseling for mental, physical, and emotional hardships experienced previously in life or at the orphanage. Thus, behavior problems abound and the directors have had to fire three women in the last 8 months. The women also have no understanding of basic hygiene, nutrition, or safety with HIV-positive children. The risks inherent in trying to raise HIV-positive children without educated care-givers include the balance between educating the children or keeping them at home. The orphanage has chosen to integrate them into local schools without notifying the school that they are HIV positive. The children are often handled and sent to school with open, bleeding sores all over their bodies. The children's illnesses escalate quickly due to their suppressed immune systems (causing them to miss many school days and also causing the caretakers to err on the side of taking them to the hospital at the first sign of any problem). Another issue with HIV infected orphans is the apparent lack of birth certificates, once again offering an opportunity for bribery pressure with the government—pay them $5 to draw up a false birth certificate. This problem echoes the identity problem that Prahalad raises, where people at the fringe of society do not have a legal identity and "because they do not have a legal existence, they cannot be beneficiaries of modern society" escalating their situation into that which Hernando de Soto recognized as confinement to a cycle of poverty (Soto, 2000).

Unfortunately, the social stigma associated with HIV-positive children prevents local educated adults from working with them on either a paid or voluntary status. An additional barrier presents itself when workers are notified that they would be housed in the same building with the children and exprostitutes (the current "orphanage" is in a three-bedroom apartment). The United Nations Development Programs (UNDP) cites this stigma as "one of the main hurdles in the fight against HIV/AIDS" (UNDP, 2006). Although these problems might be surmounted with the right connections to NGOs, training programs, or universities, the directors are not actively seeking organizations that could help provide educated caretakers or medical attention. They retain a generalized bias against NGO's because of the one local NGO with whom they tried to work. Instead, they rely on short term foreign volunteers from churches or Dutch/American-based NGOs. This is an extremely expensive and unreliable option as international travel plans change often and the expense prevents volunteers from coming often, while the distance prevents them staying for long periods of time.

DISCUSSION

As this model touches each sector of society, it provides the necessary connection between the growing business world in India and the lower echelons of society. To magnify the successes and mitigate some of the risks and challenges involved in such ventures, several issues that permeate the entire case should be addressed. These include undermanning, time, and isolation from other organizations such as MNCs, NGOs, government organizations, and businesses. Addressing these issues successfully will make it easier to hire qualified people and therefore enable the ventures to empower and train more people at the bottom of the pyramid. The following suggestions and model (as depicted in Figure 3.1) tie together C.K. Prahalad's (2005a) suggestions and the UNDP suggestions in the 2006 annual report in light of the first-hand experience of the threefold venture discussed in this case study.

First, this case presents an organization experiencing severe undermanning and a shortage of the requisite management and political skills. These skill shortages prevent the company from affecting large-scale change and from participating in the accelerated growth rate that Prahalad (2005a) notes is taking place in industries in India and China. This manning and skills shortage also results in a lack of time committed to making needed connections with other NGOs, multinational corporations, government organizations and other businesses, leaving each problem to be dealt with on an individual basis with no lessons learned garnered from others, no existing supplier connections, no influence with the government, and no established distribution channels for products. Economies of scale are next to impossible to achieve with the current manning shortage and mode of operations with the suppliers and manufacturing facilities. On the positive side, the directors have embraced Prahalad's

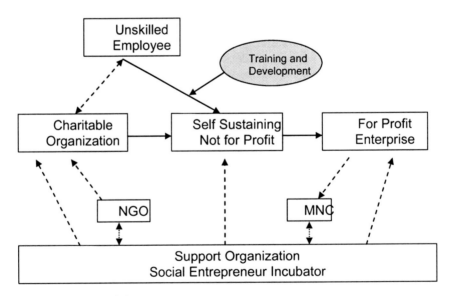

Figure 3.1.   A model.

(2005a) view of seeing the people at the BOP as possible entrepreneurs rather than victims and they have taken a necessary step in providing initial training and labor opportunities to these people that will then empower them to start ventures of their own or move on to different training or work. On the other side, they have not utilized the many organizations embarking simultaneously on this journey in the different sectors with valuable skills and relationships that could be harnessed together. They are simply unaware that these organizations exist or they do not know how to use them in their area of expertise. As the model in Figure 1 suggests, the organizations established by the directors could utilize a number of other sources to assist them in their operations. The model provides a mechanism for implementation and amplification of the ideas expressed by Prahalad (2005a), the UNDP (2006) and other social entrepreneur organizations as it addresses the needs of the people at the bottom. The potential for each branch is explored in the next section.

Multinational Corporations

A relationship between social entrepreneurs and MNCs may provide benefits for both parties. Many MNCs actively seek ways to overcome international reputations as exploiters of the poor and to participate in social change (Steidlmeier, 1993). For example, social entrepreneurs such as the directors in this case may be able to work with MNCs to provide them with a source of labor once the women have progressed through the candle-making and manufacturing facilities. In addition, this connection might also enable the company to utilize the MNCs' power in withstanding bribery with the government (Vittal, 2001) and their connections to trusted suppliers and a plethora of management resources and skills. Typically, the larger firm in an alliance or network relationship may appropriate more of the value created in terms of profitability (Alvarez & Barney, 2001), thus creating value for their organization while assisting not-for-profits in achieving their mission. In this situation, the MNC can benefit from the access to labor as well as from the goodwill generation from assisting a not-for-profit.

Nongovernmental Organizations

The connections with NGOs can prove vital in understanding the culture, providing language training and influencing government policy, (Fowler, 2000; Handy, Kassam, & Ranade, 2002; Roberts et al., 2005). Unfortunately, the directors in the case have, instead, tried to use the NGOs only as a source of skilled labor and business partnership without a great deal of success. Their experience with one NGO has unnecessarily skewed the directors' opinions, causing them to question the value of all NGOs as partners in developing the society and economy through business ventures. As the role of NGOs evolves, more are partnering with business and local organizations to achieve their stated goals (Heap, 2000). Utilizing the expertise of these organizations to understand more about the people and culture appears to be an appropriate way for social entrepreneurs to acquire information.

Social Entrepreneurship Incubators

Ultimately, a critical organization needs to be included in this model to serve as a support system for social entrepreneurs in developing countries. Entrepreneurship incubators would operate in a manner similar to a business incubator, serving as a resource to connect the different players, and providing internship or work programs for students—benefiting both the students and the organizations. The business incubator idea has been modeled by PRI (2007) in China and venture capital firms such as Seedfund and Erasmic in India (Venturebeat.com, 2007) providing companies with the necessary management expertise and funds to get started. The Skoll Foundation (2007) operates with a similar mission to "connect social entrepreneurs with key people and resources through a number of academic, business and community channels which serve to advance the work of individual entrepreneurs, as well as the field of social entrepreneurship as a whole." The UNDP has also modeled this idea in Turkey, Moldova, and with its Growing Sustainable Business initiative. This initiative seeks to help small and medium sized enterprises improve skills and train entrepreneurs who "often lack skills" as well as encouraging larger business to partner with smaller entrepreneurs to seek solutions that reduce poverty (UNDP, 2006).

The use of business and/or technology incubators to help start-up companies has flourished in recent years both in developed countries (Aernoudt, 2004; Jong, 2006) and in less developed nations (Kim, Lee & Ames, 2005; Sutherland, 2005). The benefits of designing an incubator type support organization could include connecting social entrepreneurs with professional service providers such as accountants, human resource specialists, attorneys and other experienced business people and educators who are willing to provide advice and assistance (Totterman & Sten, 2005) The benefits to the members of such organizations include actively engaging in new businesses as they grow, as well as intrinsic rewards related to aiding in the development of society. The business incubator idea has been modeled by PRI in China and organizations such as Google.org are trying to partner with venture capital firms to do similar work in India—providing companies with the necessary management expertise and seed capital to get started. This model could be expanded by simultaneously embarking on the training efforts and the not-for-profit ventures as did the directors in this case study.

In conclusion, the sights and sounds in India and other developing countries stimulate and overwhelm the senses, just as the opportunities and challenges stimulate, yet pose the risk of overwhelming organizations seeking to affect social and economic development. To avoid being overwhelmed, ventures seeking to affect social and economic development need to build an effective mutual support base to share ideas, glean expertise, and move forward together to affect large scale change. The model presented may allow the people at the BOP to capitalize on the opportunities in globalization to catapult themselves into the competitive marketplace. The model of combining a training program with a business and using the business to fund not-for-profits may be an innovative approach to tying together all areas of social and economic development in the developing world. Doing so may actually enable social transformation, similar to the idea behind Grameen Bank (Hartigan, 2006; Pitt, Shadhidur, & Cartwright, 2006.). On the individual level, these impacts are much smaller than Grameen's impact. However, by connecting the multitude of businesses venturing into this work with business incubators or venture capital firms and focusing on creating new relationships and strengthening/capitalizing on old relationships, this model could be a part of the solution to developing the entire pyramid in developing nations, rather than leaving the bottom behind. The model could also intertwine the necessary agents to help increase transparency and reduce corruption in all sectors—business, government, and not-for-profit. Many courageous social entrepreneurs are single-handedly embarking on these ventures in isolation without the requisite knowledge that others have embarked on similar or symbiotic ventures. This symbiotic view, with business incubators as catalysts and connectors, could prove transformational for the business owners as well as the society. These ventures are difficult ones indeed, and no one entity possesses the right solution. Most likely, each entity exists as a synecdoche—a part of a solution rather than singularly as "the" solution.

ACKNOWLEDGMENT

The views expressed in this chapter are those of the authors and do not necessarily reflect the official policy or position of the United States Air Force Academy, the Air Force, the Department of Defense or the U.S. Government.

REFERENCES

Aernoudt, R. (2004). Incubators: Tool for Entrepreneurship? *Small Business Economics, 23*(2), 127-135.

Ahluwalia, M. S. (2006). India's experience with globalization. *Australian Economic Review, 39*(1), 1-13.

Alvarez, S. A., & Barney, J. B. (2001). How entrepreneurial firms can benefit from alliances with large partners. *Academy of Management Executive, 15*(1), 139-148.

Bala Subrahmanya, M. H. (2005). Small-scale industries in India in the globalization era: Performance and prospects. *International Journal of Management and Enterprise Development, 2*(1), 122-139.

Bandi, R. K., & Srinvasan, V. (2005). Jobs on the move: De-localisation and relocation of ework. *IIMB Management Review, 17*(2), 71-90.

Barefoot, J. (2005). Lending as miracle medicine. *ABA Banking Journal, 97*(2), 12-84.

Barney, J. B. (1991). Firm resources and sustained competitive advantage. *Journal of Management. 17*(1), 99-120.

Besley, T., & Coate, S. (1992). Workfare vs welfare: Incentive arguments in poverty alleviation programs. *American Economic Review, 82*(1), 249-261.

Bonini, S. M., Mendonca, L. T., & Oppenheim, J. M. (2006). When social issues become strategic. *McKinsey Quarterly, 2,* 20-32.

Dakhli, M., & De Clercq, D. (2004). Human capital, social capital and innovation: A multi-country study. *Entrepreneurship & Regional Development, 16,* 107-128.

Dees, J. (1998, January/February). Enterprising nonprofits. *Harvard Business Review,* 55-67.

Dees, G. (2005). *Social entrepreneurship is about innovation and impact, not income.* Retrieved March 16, 2007, from http://www.fuqua.duke.edu/centers/case/articles/1004/corner.htm

Dhungana, B. P. (2003). Strengthening the competitiveness of small and medium enterprises in the globalization process: Prospects and challenges. *Investment Promotion and Enterprise Development Bulletin for Asia and the Pacific, 3*(1), 1-32.

Fowler, A. (2000). NGDOs as a moment in history: Beyond aid to social entrepreneurship or civic innovation? *Third World Quarterly, 21*(4), 637-654.

Friedman, T. (2006). *The world is flat: A brief history of the twenty-first century.* New York: Farrar, Straus and Giroux.

Grey, M. (2005). Dalit women and the struggle for justice in a world of global capitalism. *Feminist Theology: The Journal of Britain & Ireland School of Feminist Theology, 14*(1), 127-149.

Handy, F., Kassam, M., & Ranade, S. (2002). Factors influencing women entrepreneurs of NGOs in India. *Nonprofit Management & Leadership, 13*(2), 139-154.

Harper, M. (1991). The role of enterprise in poor countries. *Entrepreneurship: Theory & Practice, 15*(4), 7-11.

Hartigan, P. (2006). It's about people not profits. *Business Strategy Review, 17(4),* 42-45.

Heap, S. (2000). NGO-business partnerships: Research-in-progress. *Public Management, 2*(4), 555-563.

Hudson, R., & Wehrell, R. (2005). Socially responsible investors and the microentrepreneur: A Canadian case. *Journal of Business Ethics, 60*(3), 281-292.

Jong, S. (2006). How organizational structures in science shape spin-off firms: The biochemistry departments of Berkeley, Stanford, and UCSF and the birth of the biotech industry. *Industrial & Corporate Change, 15*(2), 251-283.

Kalra, S. K. (1997). Human potential management: Time to move beyond the concept of human resource management? *Journal of European Industrial Training, 21*(4), 176-180.

Katz, R.S. (2006). *Base of the pyramid: Sustainable business from the bottom up.* Retrieved October 20, 2006 http://www.greenbiz.com/news/columns_third.cfm

Kim, H., Lee, Y. -J., & Ames, M. D. (2005). Promoting business incubation for improved competitiveness of small and medium industries in Korea. *International Journal of Technology Management, 32*(3/4), 350-370.

Krugman, P. (1995). Growing world trade: Causes and consequences. *Brookings Papers on Economic Activity, 1,* 327-377.

Kumar, S., & Liu, D. (2005). Impact of globalization on entrepreneurial enterprises in the world markets. *International Journal of Management and Enterprise Development, 2*(1), 46-64.

Lewis, D. (2002). Organization and management in the third sector: Toward a cross-cultural research agenda. *Nonprofit Management & Leadership, 13*(1), 67-83.

Penrose, E. (1959). *The theory of the growth of the firm.* Oxford, England: Oxford University Press.

Pitt, M. M., Shadhidur, R. K., & Cartwright, J. (2006). Empowering women with micro finance: Evidence from Bangladesh. *Economic Development and Cultural Change, 54*(4), 791-831.

Powell, S. (2006). Spotlight on Stuart L. Hart. *Management Decision, 44*(10), 1475-1484.

Prahalad, C. K. (2005a). *The fortune at the bottom of the pyramid: Eradicating poverty through profits.* Upper Saddle River, NJ: Wharton School Publishing, Pearson Education.

Prahalad, C. K. (2005b). Learning to lead. *Vikalpa, 30*(2), 1-9.

PRI. (2007). Retrieved April 1, 2007, from http://priusa.com/loc_hohhot2.asp

Ratnam, C. S. & Venkata, C. V. (1996). Sources of diversity and the challenge before human resource management in India. *International Journal of Manpower, 17*(4), 76-112.

Ratnam, C. S., & Venkata, C. V. (1998). Multinational companies in India. *International Journal of Human Resource Management, 9*(4), 567-589.

Roberts, S. M., Jones, J. P., & Frohling, O. (2005). NGOs and the globalization of managerialism: A research framework. *World Development, 33*(11), 1845-1864.

Schepers, D. H. (2006). The impact of NGO network conflict on the corporate social responsibility strategies of multinational corporations. *Business & Society, 45*(93), 282-299.

Scoville, J. G. (1996). Labor market underpinnings of a caste economy. *American Journal of Economics and Sociology, 55*(4), 385-394.

Seelos, C., & Mair, J. (2005). Social entrepreneurship: Creating new business models to serve the poor. *Business Horizons, 48*(3),241-246.

Seelos, C., & Mair, J. (2006). Sustainable development, sustainable profit. *European Business Forum, 20,* 49-53.

Skoll Foundation. (2007). Retrieved June 28, 2007, from http://www.skollfoundation.org/aboutskoll/index.asp

Som, A. (2006). Bracing for MNC competition through innovative HRM practices: The way ahead for Indian firms. *Thunderbird International Business Review, 48*(2), 207-237.

Soto, H. D. (2000). *The mystery of capital: Why capitalism triumphs in the West and fails everywhere else.* New York: Basic Books.

Steidlmeier, P. (1993). The business community and the poor: Rethinking business strategies and social policy. *American Journal of Economics and Sociology, 52*(2), 209-221.

Sutherland, D. (2005). China's science parks: Production bases or a tool for institutional reform? *Asia Pacific Business Review, 11*(1), 83-104.

Totterman, H., & Sten, J. (2005). Start-ups: Business incubation and social capital. *International Small Business Journal, 23*(5), 487-511.

United Nations Development Program. (2006). Annual Report. Retrieved April 10, 2007, from http://www.undp.org/publications/annualreport2006/index.shtml

Venturebeat.com. (2007). Retrieved June 28, 2007, from http://venturebeat.com/2007/02/16/

Veron, R., Corbridge, S., Williams, G., & Srivastava, M. (2003). The everyday state and political society in Eastern India: Structuring access to the employment assurance scheme. *Journal of Development Studies, 39*(5), 1-28.

Vittal, N. (2001). Corruption and the State: India, technology, and transparency. *Harvard International Review, 23*(3), 20-25.

Wernerfelt, B. (1984). A resource-based view of the firm. *Strategic Management Journal, 5,* 171-180.

CHAPTER 4

ECO-STACKING

A Strategy for Success in
Social and Business Agendas

Neerja Raman

ABSTRACT

This chapter describes a strategy for simultaneously achieving competitive advantage in the cut-throat global manufacturing environment and reducing poverty among individuals who are normally unemployable. Southwest Creations Collaborative (SCC) is an entrepreneurial enterprise in New Mexico that keeps production costs low while delivering high quality, custom work. SCC employs low-skill women with family responsibilities—factors that usually render such U.S. workers unemployable and socially marginalized. In SCC's model of poverty reduction, economic value is stacked on a low-cost yet strong social support network. SCC provides basic sustenance, such as childcare, to give low-income women social stability while demanding quality and productivity on the job. Examples of key operational practices that lead to success in SCC's social and business agendas are outlined.

Innovative Approaches to Reducing Global Poverty
pp. 67–90

NEW MARKET FOR A NEW ECONOMY

What do couture glass mosaics for buildings have in common with elegant velour capes for children? Not the same product. No common target market. No common supply chain. No common technology. No common geography. So what is it?

What they have in common is the business of selling creativity and Southwest Creations Collaborative (SCC) (Web site: http://www.southwest-creations.com/).

SCC is in the business of providing customization. The collaborative's operations allow custom specifications to be handled locally in New Mexico while leveraging the efficiencies and value pricing of off-shored manufacturing for high volume. With SCC as a supplier, customization at mass production prices is no longer impossible.

Strategy to Develop the Market for Custom Goods

Erin Adams Design (Web site: http://www.erinadamsdesign.com/), whose office is in Albuquerque, NM, provides hand-mixed artisan glass mosaics for residential and commercial buildings while Magic Cabin (Web site: http://www.magiccabin.com/), a catalog business based in Wisconsin, provides unique crafts that are heirloom quality, fun to play with, and that, most of all, ignite the imaginations of children—which explains the royal velour cloaks and capes. Both Erin Adams and Magic Cabin are small companies that have made a successful business out of selling creativity. Both must customize to create unique designs and, by working with SCC, they can take advantage of volume pricing for standard materials.

The market for individualized, custom goods has always existed, but the premium for such goods has been threatened by price erosion from mass production. Since logistics for large-scale manufacturing are not amenable to customization, converting creative designs into customized products can lead to issues of cost, quality, and time. So, unless customization can be made affordable with appropriate quality, this market shrinks or evaporates.

Southwest Creations Collaborative has made customization affordable for small businesses like Erin Adams Design and Magic Cabin. SCC makes it possible for businesses to incorporate customization and also to deliver value when compared to mass-produced goods. Fortunately for SCC, businesses that sell creativity are specialized but not unique. Southwest Creations Collaborative is a potential supplier to anyone who has a business requirement for custom work at costs that can be competitive in the age of mass production and global pricing of consumer goods.

Interestingly enough, SCC did not start operations with a mission of creating a business out of customization of goods. It started with a mission of providing dignity in the lives of low-income families in New Mexico. Its business model evolved as SCC's leadership gained experience with providing employment to low-skill, low-income women. In developing ways to provide that employment, SCC contributed to the creation of healthier communities. It also developed a viable business that is expected to be self-sustaining by 2009.

Southwest Creations Collaborative's social mission became a strategy that delivered success on social as well as business agendas.

SOCIAL AND BUSINESS AGENDAS

Social Mission

> Southwest Creations supports us in our dreams for a better life for ourselves and our children. It's not just a job, it's a family. (Fermina Lopez, contract sewing worker at Southwest Creations Collaborative)

Fermina Lopez has been with SCC since 1994 and thinks of it as her family unit. Among SCC employees Fermina is not unique in terms of the longevity of her employment.

SCC employs women who would otherwise not find employment and are socially marginalized. Their social status would normally limit their ability to provide for their dependents and lead to the cycle of poverty and societal isolation. The women working in SCC represent a cross section of the local population; recent immigrants as well as those born in New Mexico. Like Fermina, when they start with SCC, traditional metrics of education, English-language skills, and family obligations would have made them unemployable or unable to run their own business. A new hire at SCC may speak very little if any English, may have high school or less for education and typically has childcare or other family obligations.

"We developed our business using an ear-to-the-ground approach," says Susan Matteucci, founder and CEO of SCC. Since the business was started with the social mission of advancing dignity in the lives of families, SCC offered solutions to issues that concern women from day one: health care, day care, job training and an income that can provide stability in their daily lives as well as the ability to perform on the job. Dealing with these issues translates into peace of mind for employees because their personal life is taken care of, not just their life at work. For SCC as a business, this peace pf mind translates directly into higher productivity, employee retention and high morale, which in turn lead to higher quality products and predictability at work.

SCC was started in a section of a church property in Albuquerque in 1994 by Susan, an entrepreneur and local resident. She started the business by providing job-skills training like working on industrial sewing machines. In addition, she helped the cooperative's employees get proper immigration documentation, if needed, and developed programs like education on domestic violence and the need for physical exams for their children (Kamerick, 2006). When she started, Susan's goal was to create a business that could provide employment to 25 women from low-income communities.

Over the years SCC has increased its social impact to 35 families. A sharpened business focus enabled it to expand. In 2005, SCC leased a 13,000-square foot building that once served as a women's detention facility north of downtown Albuquerque and put in $250,000 worth of improvements. This investment in the facilities improved the whole area and was a benefit to the community not just to SCC (Esterson, 2005). In recognition of SCC's contribution to the community, the facility was opened with much fanfare at a fiesta hosted by New Mexico's Lieutenant Governor, Diane Denish.

What stands out most about SCC is the loyalty of employees like Fermina. SCC's programs to support its social mission have delivered an employee retention rate of 97%—a proud metric by any business standard. Its leadership model includes giving full credit to the women employees for creating the business, making it grow and keeping overheads low.

Business Mission

Southwest Creations Collaborative is a 501c3 not-for-profit organization that, as indicated in its brochure, integrates a successful contract sewing and handwork business with a social mission to enhance dignity in the lives of families. Although a not-for-profit, its client list is no different than that of a for-profit contract manufacturer. It is a service business offering customization at a value that generates business for its clients while creating quality jobs for its employees.

Thus it has a "double bottom line" agenda (Boschee, 1997). First, create a business that generates revenue. Second, provide stable jobs to grow the quality of life for its employees and hence the local community. Susan

Matteucci says they funnel revenues back into training and to grow business so they can provide jobs to more women.

SCC's operational mission serves nationwide clients in soft goods and glass mosaic tile industries who have outsourced production needs. It has shown consistent annual increases in revenue and an expanded customer base ranging from apparel and home interiors to government subcontracting.

By lowering costs, SCC can create and grow the market for custom goods. Soft goods, glass and ceramic manufacturers choosing to reduce production costs often face a conflict with their need for speed and customization. SCC uses the technique known as "spackling" to mange its operations. Custom orders receive top priority for quick delivery and the remaining capacity is used to produce standard products in small lots. (Matteucci, 2005). SCC's ability to respond quickly to relatively small, unique orders allows its customers to take advantage of lower cost offshore production for their large volume standard products while utilizing SCC's capacity for mass customization for lower volume goods.

By 2004, 10 years after its startup, SCC had $500,000 in annual revenue and was cash-flow positive on an operational basis. It provided full-time employment to 35-37 women with families to support. By 2009, estimates are that revenues will reach $2 million and the cooperative will be completely self-sufficient, with no philanthropic or grant investment needed. Total investment in getting SCC to sustainability is expected to be approximately $3.7 million. The first $3 million will achieve self-sufficiency. The next $660,000 will fund expansion and growth necessary to achieve sustainable economics.

The "local/global/boutique" nature of SCC that its customers now see evolved as it was finding ways to achieve its social mission. That local/global/boutique persona is now a major element of its business model and business success:

- *Boutique*: To its clients, small-medium businesses, SCC is an artsy, boutique style goods provider, able to fulfill small orders by employing skilled craftswomen—goods that normally come with a high markup.
- *High Quality*: Local—SCC can differentiate on quality of service and goods because it has a local presence for its clients.
- *Low Cost*: Global—SCC has also embraced low-cost manufacturing outside the United States. Instead of thinking of outsourcing as competition, SCC partners globally. By combining orders from many clients to achieve adequate volumes, SCC can outsource the acquisition of some of its own materials and products.

A NEW KIND OF ENTERPRISE

SCC is local and also global; local in delivering social value, global in delivering financial value.

Some call it the "death of distance," some call it a "flat world" (Friedman 2006; Prahalad, 2005), and some call it "globalization," but whatever the label, the fact remains that business, political and social ecosystems have changed. Today we have lower prices for consumer goods because of this phenomenon. But we also have complexity and economic interdependency among companies situated in distant geographies. Large and small companies are faced with this reality and a global economy challenges business models enough to create a demand for new insights and for new ways of delivering value and providing employment.

These changes also make it harder to deliver social benefits at the local community level.

Social ventures are new kinds of enterprises that show great promise in figuring out how to take advantage of the global economy and also to deliver local benefits. Starting with a humanitarian agenda they create businesses that generate revenues and are self-sustaining. Southwest Creations Collaborative, with its double-bottom line agenda of poverty reduction in New Mexico and sustainable business operations, illustrates the benefits of understanding and managing differences between a single and double bottom line business. The fact that it operates in the global environment where manufacturing outsourcing is a fact of viable economics makes SCC a particularly interesting organization for exploring these benefits.

The Price of Success

The private sector, or "for-profit" business endeavors, measure success with metrics of growth and profits. After some initial infusions of cash, the business will, hopefully, become self-sustaining and eventually give a return on the original investment. Continued infusions of cash should not be needed to sustain the business although they may be used to grow it faster than would be possible from only its own operations.

Social and humanitarian causes such as poverty reduction, education, and public health have often been the domain of governments and philanthropists, that is the public sector. Such institutions are not expected to generate revenue or provide a return on investment. Because they do not generate their own revenue streams, regular infusions of new cash are necessary to keep the endeavor operational. Fundraising as an activity must continue as long as the operation exists.

The reward for creating a successful business is freedom to focus on business matters. On the other hand, the reward for a creating a successful social venture is the need to raise more capital while also managing the venture's operations. This need for continuing infusions of cash means that fundraising as well as management issues become ever more demanding jobs. Hence, social ventures face the risk of becoming victims of their own successes.

Business or Philanthropy?

A social enterprise with a humanitarian agenda can escape becoming a victim of its own success if it has income generation incorporated into its business model. Southwest Creations Collaborative is an example of this new breed of enterprises that seek to apply entrepreneurial skills to social agendas to create self sustaining businesses. Naturally this approach raises the question in investors' minds about SCC's mission. Is it for profit or not for profit? Is it a business or is it philanthropy? Should it be considered part of the private sector or part of the public sector? To answer such questions with existing terminology can be confusing. For instance, in the case of SCC the answers would be something like:

"Yes we are for profit but we are a not-for-profit 501c3 organization."

"Yes we are a business but our mission is philanthropic."

"Yes we are in the private sector but our success metrics are social impact."

Such answers do not lend themselves well to 2-minute-elevator pitches and one-sentence-mission-statements often required by busy investors. Therefore social entrepreneurs like Susan Matteucci often seek capital from a new kind of investor.

A New Kind of Investor

Southwest Creations Collaborative enlisted a new kind of investor to get started; one that understood the special challenges of an organization that pursues a humanitarian agenda but wants to be self-sustaining in order to grow and expand its influence on the community.

Businesses created to increase social wealth are still a new concept. While books, magazines (e.g., *Stanford Social Innovation Review*), Web sites (too many to list), even coursework (e.g., Duke University), are starting to appear, there is no institutionalized approval of the business models needed nor agreement on the leadership and management attributes required for social enterprises. Investors willing to provide capital for social entrepreneurship are even rarer. However they are starting to appear. A social mission can be a compelling motivator for many investors and as a social enterprises like SCC become more numerous, their ability to attract capital also grows.

"SCC figured out a model that works for the manufacturing industry in the U.S., and that's no small feat," says Alice Loy, executive director of Social Venture Partners, SVP (Web site: http://www.svpseattle.org/), a group of philanthropists with business management backgrounds that made a 5-year investment in Susan's dream.

- *Scale:*   Social Venture Partners sees the SCC system as one that can be transferred to many different communities. "We saw that her model on how to solve poverty was more progressive and met the goals of improving the economic landscape in New Mexico in a more sustainable and comprehensive way," says Alice (Esterson, 2005).

- *Expertise:*   Investors like SVP not only provide capital they also provide expertise—business and technical. For example SVP did its part by providing technical assistance for SCC expansion. Specifically, former Intel engineers helped Southwest Creations design its new manufacturing space to be as efficient as possible. Other SVP members helped the organization find the building and worked on marketing materials for SCC. Susan Matteucci believes that SVP expertise proved to be invaluable. "I knew how to bring women together to form peer groups but I had not run a business before."

- *Involvement:*   Investor involvement in the early stages of a social enterprise also reduces the burden of documenting fuzzy social metrics of success for the enterprise by giving the investor confidence in its business operations and influence on its management and leadership. By providing capital, operational assistance, and other expertise, investors may increase the chances that the mutually desired win-win outcome will actually emerge.

It is an honor and privilege for our foundation to work with Southwest Creations Collaborative. The model they are developing is one that gives us hope for the future. (EMA Foundation)

SCC manages a fine line of communication between investors, employees and customers and has created new metrics and language to show

Table 4.1.   Investor Concerns

Why is it more difficult to acquire capital for a social venture?

- Motivators are different
- Problems are more challenging as they cut across geographies, socioeconomic groups
- Has often been considered the job of governments (social sector)
- No language to convert "social currency" to money
- Social currency can easily disappear
- It's just new!

progress and accountability to attract new investors like EMA Foundation and keep original investors like SVP satisfied.

Putting private money to work as business for a humanitarian agenda is a relatively recent phenomenon. Investor concerns, which range from novelty to the nitty-gritty of social currency, are listed in Table 4.1. Processes, metrics and language to communicate what works and what does not, developed by SCC, acknowledge that such concerns are valid and must be dealt with. Social entrepreneurs can be better prepared for conversations with investors if they give specifics whenever possible to address the types of issues listed in that table.

ECO-STACKING STRATEGY:
HOW SOCIAL MISSION EQUALS BUSINESS COMPETITIVENESS

So far SCC has had nearly zero employee turnover. Some of the business advantages SCC gains from its low turnover, reliable workforce are:

- domestic on-shore production capacity to produce custom orders quickly;
- production capacity that includes handwork ability;
- high quality and guaranteed delivery;
- flexibility and just-in-time delivery for custom orders; and
- daily drop-shipping.

In the case of SCC, its innovation lies in having a quality workforce at competitive costs. It keeps costs down by providing employment at close to minimum wage to people that might not otherwise be able to find jobs, making the daily workplace an enjoyable place to be and, very importantly, by providing social support to keep employees loyal and motivated. It provides social support through a peer structure, which has great value to the employee, at a relatively low cost to the business.

Table 4.2.   Social Mission Strategy

How to Turn a Social Mission Into a Competitive Business Strategy	What SCC Does
• Create a new *market* or grow an existing one in a new geography • Support an *employee* base that is socially disadvantaged (poverty, education, health, attitude …) • *Innovate*, that is, new technology or new business model that challenges conventional wisdom	• Quality custom as well as mass-produced goods with quick turnaround • Employs low-income women in New Mexico • SCC provides social support to employees as cost of doing business

Successful strategies turn a weakness into a strength. Table 4.2 lists three for-profit operational issues: market, employee, and innovation, where a social mission would be a weakness. Column 1 postulates a generic strategy and column 2 exemplifies how it is being implemented by SCC to gain competitive advantage.

Understanding Social Wealth and Economic Empowerment

David Shipler in his 2004 book, *The Working Poor: Invisible in America*, has documented some heartbreaking stories of people whose fortunes remain unfound. As he says "the term working poor should be an oxymoron." Many of these are women, often in low-income jobs and having high needs with regard to raising their offspring. In spite of a growing American economy, these people (coming from all ethnic and racial backgrounds) remain invisible. Each story is individual and the factors that lead to change are also unique. But what is common to all is that they seem to move from crisis to crisis. Their social support structure is so fragile that an inevitable event, like a health problem, a car accident, or a truant child, affects job performance making them fall off the ladder of self-supportability and when they dust off and get back on, they often start from the bottom rung again.

There is much to be learned about reducing poverty by studying what works and what does not in the field of social work and philanthropy. One lesson is that poverty is real in concept but is not captured by a single metric—it is a combination of a number of social factors that result in a quality of life issue. Poor in America is not the same as poor in Albania, yet the social issues around quality of life may be the same. While the exact definition of poverty can be a topic of debate (Reddy, 2005), the symptoms of poverty, such as lack of access to healthcare, childcare and education, living day to day (Worldbank, n.d., "Understanding Poverty") are common to the poor in all societies. Hence, thinking of empowerment of the poor as a process of creating access to basic needs, can also be thought of as creating wealth—social wealth.

Saying that a social enterprise creates social wealth might appear to be just a different way of saying that it reduces poverty, but this difference is important. It is important because being poor is relative but needs such as access to healthcare, ability to read and write, education, stability to plan for the future are universally understood. In addition, each of these fundamental needs can be addressed and measured to manage and monitor the success of an enterprise. Reduction of poverty as a global metric creates division and debate but creation of social wealth brings people together.

Living standards have risen dramatically all over the world but great regional and social disparity exists within all societies and arguably the gap between the rich and the poor has actually been growing (Worldbank.org, "Measuring Poverty"). By providing employment to the ones who need it most, i.e. those at the lower end of the social stack, it is possible to reduce this poverty gap in every society. Reducing poverty in this way is the fundamental premise of a social enterprise and the strategy can be defined as *Eco-Stacking: provide social support to create an empowered employee who can perform on the job.*

Eco-Stacking Means Creating Social Wealth as a Business

Southwest Creation Collaborative's value proposition is providing customization at mass production costs and its business depends on growing the market for creativity and custom goods that is affordable to many more than a select few. To be economically sustainable it must ride a delicate balance of growing its client list and growing its workforce (employees gain skills while on the job) with no compromise in the factors that make its value proposition viable.

This is where 90-100% employee retention becomes an operational imperative for an enterprise like SCC. The collaborative has adopted the following key operational policies to achieve its high level of employee retention and productivity:

- New hires are unskilled employees who come in at the lowest wage level *(reduced hiring costs)*;
- Experienced employees can get raises *(employee motivation to develop skills)*;
- Promotions happen from within *(recoup investment in training, build loyalty)*;
- Experienced employees train new ones *(lower or no training costs)*;

- Stable workforce for operational predictability *(quality, productivity, volume)*;
- Provide a social support system made up of peers and co-workers *(no additional cost)*;
- Peer management through regular group meetings *(low management overhead, lower costs)*; and
- Seek collaborations for delivering community services to employees *(improved community relations with education, law-enforcement and healthcare providers)*.

Susan Matteucci calls her business model *Leading with Economics: providing for employee welfare, that is, creating social wealth as a business need and managing its associated costs just as you would other business costs.*

SCC has had an excellent return on the investment it has made in employees. As SCC expands its business, promotions to jobs requiring higher skill levels can be done from within senior employee ranks. This process creates the ability to provide employment at entry levels to new recruits who enter with a low skill level and from economically unstable situations. Senior employees help train new recruits saving SCC money. Providing jobs, economic empowerment, to unskilled women means fulfilling a social mission as well.

This process of creating social wealth as a business goal has paid off for SCC. If the goal had been just cost cutting, SCC would not be able to sustain itself. Either the organization would have financial disadvantages over other companies and other countries or it would have product quality issues. Susan's pursuit of the double bottom line has demonstrated the competitive advantage of creating social wealth even in a company competing in the cut-throat business of contract sewing—a business that conventional wisdom would say is sure to be outsourced to countries able to deliver at lower cost.

Table 4.3 borrows the stack metaphor, as in a "network stack" to illustrate the relationship between business and social values. Networks are built as stacks; the most useful application, upper stack, is enabled by the lower software and still lower hardware stacks. Column 1 represents the value stack of a social enterprise and column 2 shows how high on-the-job performance of low-income employees enables visible prosperity and business sustainability.

Why Eco-Stacking Works

For-profit businesses manage their operations for profit and growth. They benefit the community by providing employment. Employee and

Table 4.3.   Eco-Stacking Value

Value Stack	*Business Is Able to:*
Economic Stack = factors that allow a business to succeed—generate revenue	Pay for Performance for employee
	Capital for Infrastructure, Goods
	Employee:
Social Stack = factors that allow an employee to succeed, to perform on the job	Motivated to make future plans
	Income stability and predictability
	Education for employee
	Education for children
	Childcare
	Healthcare

hence community benefits are a consequence of business success. When establishing a business that serves a low-income community, the for-profit company will approach its task the way it would in any community, not from the perspective of the needs of the employees, as is done in social work, but from the perspective of the needs of the business, as is customary in for-profit companies

Starting from the perspective of the needs of employees, a social enterprise like SCC might be more likely to see the importance of building a support system as a basis for effective work and as a social benefit in its own right. As SCC discovered, social benefits can be provided to the employee for free or minimal cost by setting up a peer-support system and by partnering with community service providers like schools and hospitals. Employees are freed from worries associated with being poor, such as the welfare of their child, illness and debt. Removing such worries gives them hope for the future, a drive to continue working and ensures their ability to succeed in performing on the job. Successful job performance by employees leads to a successful business.

Thus, a "not-for-profit" business like SCC benefits the community by providing social success. Economic benefits are a consequence of social success of employees which in turn creates a cycle of self-sustenance.

The difference between the for-profit's way of providing social benefits and a social venture's way is subtle but important because it affects how social enterprises are led and managed. It is a cause-and-effect relationship. A social venture manages the cause, its humanitarian agenda, and the desired economic results follow. A for-profit business manages its business operations and social benefits follow.

At the same time, the difference between the ways a social enterprise and a charity provide social benefits also has a subtle aspect. A charity provides social benefits by acquiring contributions of money and volunteer efforts and uses them to pursue its humanitarian mission. A social venture, in pursing its humanitarian mission, starts from the perspective of the needs of the employee in a very real sense, but with another subtle difference. It cannot operate as a pure charity because of the need to run a profitable business. Therefore, its social investments need to be "earned" by its employees' high performance at work. "Every business needs high performing workers. In demanding the highest performance from employees, while attending to their family needs as a business issue, you engage them as actors and performers in their economic empowerment. At SCC we do not engage with our employees from (only) a position of their needs; rather we engage them with our business needs (as well). *This is the difference between social work and social entrepreneurship*" says Susan. "We empower them to succeed by providing for their basic humanitarian needs as a part of our business practice."

Managing a Socially Motivated Business

Managing a socially motivated business starts with innovative business planning. A cardinal rule is to manage finances of a social venture just as if it were a for-profit business.

1. Find/create a revenue stream—whether it is through product or service delivery. SCC founders first created an online marketing brochure. Then, with a good idea of where craft-work would generate revenue, they focused on giving appropriate employee training.
2. Manage costs of providing social wealth. Engage employees by providing them basic necessities and a stable lifestyle. Remove the barriers to productivity. Include these costs in the business plan. For SCC, the keys to providing employees with their basic needs and a stable life style lie in a series of innovative ways to do so— ways to create social wealth.

KEY PROGRAMS TO CREATE SOCIAL WEALTH

SCC's employee welfare programs are built into the business plan. A combination of innovative practices and the nature of the employee base yield an affordable strategy. The innovation lies in two areas: first how the programs are structured and second the progress metrics that have been applied to keep them on track.

Table 4.4.   Social Programs at SCC

Programs to create social empowerment and business benefits:

- Onsite childcare—Community care makes it low cost (25 cents/day/per child)
- Adult education—English language skills
- Peer mentoring—learn skills on the job
- Affordable healthcare—through community health providers
- Family leadership—a community of workers who support one another

SCC provides full-time employment as well as comprehensive packages of education, child care, health care and other family support services to its employees. This gives employees, the peace of mind they need to meet commitments to their children. Everyday issues like sickness in the family, school commitments and other routine problems do not become career fatalities. Then, having given them something that is of value to them, SCC holds them accountable to the highest standards of performance in their jobs.

In America, while there is greater economic wealth, relative poverty gap metrics between the haves and the have-nots are the same as for other nations. Social isolation leads to the syndrome of the working poor and to those that become invisible even if lack of money is not the key factor in their isolation. In many ways social wealth creation in the United States is just as challenging as in poorer nations.

Key SCC programs responsible for creating social empowerment and business benefits are summarized in Table 4.4. Employee needs like childcare, mentorship and healthcare are common across all businesses—SCC's innovations associated with each item lies in how the programs have been designed to incur low economic cost while delivering high social value.

Metrics and Accountability

Definitions lead to metrics. Metrics lead to measurement. Measurement leads to effective management. Hence the importance of definitions. Social wealth may be created by building community, providing employability, family support, education and a future for children. Social innovation comes in creating affordable programs that create stable support systems—support systems capable of withstanding the normal mishaps of workers' lives. And doing so in ways that generate sustainable business income.

In the case of SCC, specific metrics have been generated to manage and measure success of social programs. Susan's philosophy is to track what employees put back into society, which she believes is an indicator of the success of her social mission. It shows that employees' value being part of the SCC family and this value can be turned into accountability metrics.

A significant benefit of this philosophy is that it leads SCC to see and use appropriate metrics created by the state and various organizations. Kids Count, a venture of The Annie E. Casey Foundation (Web site: http://www.aecf.org/kidscount/sld/databook.jsp) tracks the health and welfare of children in the US and publishes several metrics on a national as well as state-by-state basis. One that is a predictor of future economic advancement is the percentage of kids who graduate from high school. It matters to most women that their children stay in school. *SCC believes that if a woman is paying attention to her child's education, it is reasonable to assume that she is investing in her future which in turn means she is interested in performing on the job.*

SCC applies metrics for the state of New Mexico, which appears in the bottom 10% when measured on some of these poverty index metrics, to quantify and communicate its social impact.

One example of how SCC uses a simple metric can be seen in its involvement in the *Buena Fe* program.

Buena Fe (Familias+Escuelas)

"We are not just any business. We back our vision with the Strong Families program which acknowledges and responds to the barriers faced by women from low-income communities" says Susan.

Buena Fe (families+escuelas) is one of three programs in SCC's Strong Families Initiative to expand support and encourage job retention. It is a partnership with schools and other parent advocacy groups to facilitate the involvement and collaboration of 100% of employees in their children's schools. It is a way to support and track their employees' kids' educational health.

This is how it works: SCC employees must spend 1.5 hours/month (paid) visiting the child's teacher where they discuss insights into things that could affect learning. The teacher and parent are drawn into a contract where they are both vested in keeping the child in school and performing at capability. At the beginning of the school year a formal contract is drawn up outlining expectations and issues to be overcome. This contract is updated and monitored at each visit and submitted at the end of the year to SCC management.

The idea is to set an expectation and SCC management watches progress. Instead of having one-to-one meetings at SCC, monthly group meetings are held. At these meetings information is shared openly with a spirit of supporting one another. This process achieves the right balance of peer pressure to perform without falling into the needy or victim mentality.

These monthly group meetings are a key part of SCC management philosophy. Susan says "we want to avoid getting into the details of solving individual concerns; that becomes too much like the case management scenario in social work. By bringing early visibility to the issue in a group environment we empower and encourage employees to devise their own solutions."

Some other programs that are a part of the Strong Families Initiative are:

- Adult Education which includes English as a second language and GED classes, so employees can become citizens and can earn higher education degrees.
- Health Education and access, *Sabias Y Saludables*, based on priority concerns of the Latino community.

SCC services can be offered very cost effectively because social needs have been accounted for from the very beginning in the "lead with economics" business model. SCC pays employees $9.30/hour (New Mexico minimum wage is $7.50/hr) and benefits. It can provide daycare at $0.25 per day/per child by having its own daycare facility, located in the same building. Women who work there also help out with childcare. Similarly SCC is able to provide healthcare at very reasonable costs by dealing with local health providers as a group to get low cost health insurance. These are the sorts of "hard metrics" SCC uses to prove its operational efficiency but the real value adds up to be much greater; SCC is building a community of productive, motivated people who in turn build a future for their children. The eco-stacking model and SCC programs are condensed in Table 4.5. Columns 1 and 2 are generic while column 3 is specific for SCC. Table 4.5 may be used as a template for other businesses similar to SCC's by replacing the column 3 title and its elements.

A NEW KIND OF LEADERSHIP

Creating a business around a social mission requires its leadership to be well versed in "business speak" (to attract capital and become self-sustaining) as well as "social speak" (to manage operations). Susan has formal education (MA in City Planning from MIT where she specialized in community development) as well as work experience at the executive, operational and financial level in socially responsible organizations.

Table 4.5. How SCC Does It

Value	Business Is Able to:	What SCC Does
Economic stack: revenue model is sale of goods	Pay for performance for employee	Pays employees just above New Mexico minimum wage
	Seek capital for infrastructure, goods	Secured investment $3Million
	Employee:	
Social stack = peer-support model creates social value at low $ cost	Motivated to make future plans	Employee engagement in community and hope for future- kids staying in school
	Income stability and predictability	Creates motivated workers
	Education for employee	Basic skills taught, growth path; peer mentoring, teaching
	Education for children	Relationship with schools/teachers
	Childcare	Affordable, on-site, peer supported
	Healthcare	Relationship with local providers

Prior experience in social and non-profit work led to the innovations that the founders of Southwest Creations Collaborative applied to the business of creating social wealth. As Susan says, "Social entrepreneurship is a messy business. It is about people first and foremost. The objective is economic empowerment but the route to engaging employees in this process is social empowerment. For example, the Grameen people I worked with never talked about money. If you ask them how they manage their business they say all they do is motivate, motivate, motivate. Indeed, their sixteen tenets only talk about community: we will educate our children; we will only drink well water; we will not give or receive dowry, and so on. When people live in poverty, economics is not the first motivator; it is their social worth and the well-being of their children that matters."

Social Entrepreneurship

In its first twelve years of operation SCC has had only one employee leave the company. What creates such strong employee loyalty?

At Southwest Creations Collaborative, Susan's vision was of "women coming together under one roof as a community, where they would feel connected, not isolated." This is the value proposition she gave her employees. To her investors, the value is new business creation. In other words, social entrepreneurs recognize that business rigor is essential in achieving sustainability, but the benefits are far greater than pure economic indicators can capture and the language of the leadership reflects the social as well as financial gain.

Success in managing a business, whose employees are from a low income community, comes when leadership acknowledges the multiple social barriers faced by its workforce and proactively develops programs to address the issues. A shift is required from a language of money and finance. A social leader develops a language that includes dignity, relationships, community; words that capture a value its employees find empowering. Business sustainability demands economic returns but economics by itself is an insufficient motivator for the people who are served by the business.

Susan adapted the micro-finance model of lending to an organization where the community as a whole becomes a support to a peer-management organizational structure. Applying that model to her business Southwest Creations was structured to be a community of workers. In this model, welfare of the worker is the supreme concern of the organization and so the welfare of the organization becomes the supreme concern of the worker.

While economics is what sustains the business, social currency is what gets it off the ground. One can say that the double bottom line isn't about having two goals, there isn't twice as much to do; it's about creating synergy between financial and social goals to ensure sustainability. Creating loyalty through a peer support management style keeps costs low while building organizational flexibility. Susan not only figured out how to make the pitch to her investors, she figured out how to turn her societal mission into a business advantage.

Social Investorship

Social Venture Partners, who provided seed investment and continues to partner with SCC is just as picky about its investments as any other venture capitalist. "We look for small organizations, budget- and staff-wise, with potential to scale or replicate. They must have strong leadership, execution plan and a good fit for what we offer" says Alice Loy (Esterson, 2005). In addition to providing capital, SVP offers its business expertise and stays involved with the operations of the ventures it funds to compensate for the extra obstacles faced by social entrepreneurs in running their ventures.

Investors like SVP realize that a business with a societal mission requires more time than a regular business to become self sustaining (exceptions are when some new technology can be game changing), so they will often start with small investments but commit to a longer period of time. In this respect, investing in a social business is like investing in basic research where breakthroughs are unpredictable but one can recoup value through longer term investment.

The need for long term commitment, in and of-itself, can be an obstacle towards securing capital. But, it is not insurmountable. It can be overcome if metrics are provided to measure how the seed phase is proceeding. Not every investor listens to a social entrepreneur's pitch, but every investor who does wants to know how they will know whether the plan is on or off track. That requirement is not only reasonable, it is good business discipline that can actually help a social entrepreneur become successful. It is also helpful to involve the investor in managing the venture as in the case of SVP.

Table 4.6 is designed to be a template that integrates mission, metrics and wealth generation to create a summary of best practices as exemplified by SCC. As a template for the general case of a socially motivated business, the column 1 title can be replaced with the name of a new business. All other row and column titles remain the same. Table elements should be filled-in by a new social venture as appropriate. The closer the new business is in social mission, geography, economics and community issues to SCC, the more applicable will be the model developed by SCC.

Eco-Stacking Strategy: What Makes it Hard?

Case studies like SCC might make one wonder why every business isn't rushing to use this concept of doing good to the society it operates in as a business strategy. As attractive as the approach is, there are solid reasons why the approach has not been followed by many more businesses.

First, creating businesses to empower underserved communities is new and social entrepreneurs are using different approaches, appropriate for local conditions.

For example, the economic details of running a poverty reduction venture in New Mexico can be very different from those of one in Bangladesh. Understanding local culture and politics plays an equally important role in choosing and developing an appropriate model for the new venture.

Table 4.6.   SCC Social and Economic Metrics

	Southwest Creations Collaborative Case	Social Wealth Generated	Economic Wealth Generated
Social- mission	Enhance dignity through employability	Productive community of workers	Revenue from sale of goods
Sector	Low-skill women in New Mexico	Reduced poverty, undocumented workers made legal	Reduced cost of state programs; downtown rejuvenation
Key insight: competitive advantage	Providing social support to low-income workers creates stability in their family life and hence: • low employee turnover • training gets leveraged • employees able to deliver high quality work	Motivated employees plan for their future and the future of their dependents so as to be able to take care of themselves	Created market for low cost customization
Sustainability model	1. Peer-support model; 2. Achieve cost-effectiveness and quality through employee loyalty and retention	Stability in family life of employee; better able to manage life issues on their own	Growing market in custom goods
Social metrics	1. Employees' children stay and perform in school 2. Acquisition of English language skills by employees	Number of children educated; Number of dependents able to hold jobs	Employee benefits like child-care, healthcare offered at very low cost by business.
Economic metrics	1. Revenue from business 2. Cost effectiveness of services offered	Reduction in social divide across diverse communities; mutual respect in society	Reduced social and law enforcement service costs

SCC's success stems in large part from the vision of its leadership. Susan says that her experience working with Grameen business operations (http://www.grameen-info.org) gave her the insights that later led to the philosophy she developed for running SCC.

At Women's Self Employment project in Chicago, we wanted to replicate the Grameen model of small loans to help women generate an income by starting a business. My job was to go around and find five women that we could then organize into a borrowing circle as they do in the original model that was so successful in Bangladesh. Social workers would come to me and say that their clients, the women they worked with, were very capable and all they needed really was a job and not social services. What I found was that the jobs we gave them never worked out. Small loans did not always generate sustainable businesses. For one reason or another, the women always failed, generally through no fault of their own. Their circumstances, which often involved issues like childcare, lack of any specific skills, family commitments or health did not allow them to deliver a satisfactory performance on the job and they went back to needing social services.

Susan found that the peer group lending model that worked so well in rural Bangladesh did not work in urban United States. There were at least two factors contributing to the different outcomes. First, the culture of informal entrepreneurship where if you have a chicken you can sell eggs does not exist in urban America. Second, there are legal barriers; licenses, policies, certifications to name just a few. Thus the investment required to get a microbusiness off the ground in Chicago is much greater than in Bangladesh. That difference makes return on investment from a micro-enterprise too low and economically unsustainable. Failing in their ventures, the women go back to needing social services; the poor remain poor, unable to participate in their own economic empowerment.

This experience proved invaluable for Susan. She learned that the women in her peer group wanted to stay together for the social support they provided each other, but their failed businesses and jobs did not support them in doing so. She leveraged this knowledge of the desire for peer group support and the need for a viable way to make a living in creating SCC, where her vision was of "women coming together under one roof." To manage the economics she created a viable business that would be their sustenance.

Thus, local understanding plays a noteworthy role in determining a successful outcome for eco-stacking as strategy.

Second, measuring social return is new; there is no accepted language or metric for social wealth. It is also difficult to quantify because much of the economic return is in terms of savings in social programs or metrics like reduction in crime rates which are difficult to attribute directly to the social enterprise.

Third, initial success of one venture does not guarantee replicability of that model because the issues of scaling are tied to local economics. For example, further development needs to be done to ensure that the market for custom goods can continue to grow and that what works in New Mexico will work in other parts of the United States. There are just not enough social ventures yet to be able to develop generic models of the ones that will be sustainable ventures.

Fourth, social entrepreneurs may sacrifice some profitability by reinvesting in their mission as SCC has done, thus delaying a financial return on investment. This practice makes it harder for investors to track progress if they are not involved in managing the venture directly.

Table 4.7. Entrepreneurship Models

Business Entrepreneur	Social Entrepreneur
• *Motivation*: Economic (social benefits follow)	• *Motivation*: Social agenda (economic benefits follow)
• *Metric*: Revenue growth, profits ($)	• *Metric*: Social return sustained by revenue from business
• *Measures Return on Investment*: lower costs enable larger customer base; reduction enabled by supply chain optimization	• *Measures Social Return on Investment*: services to build employee loyalty. Lower costs through peer, community support
• *Philosophy*: Support employee to grow market	• *Philosophy*: Grow market to support employee

Opposing forces of social and business entrepreneurship models are contrasted in the two columns of Table 4.7. Even though all successful entrepreneurship leads to social and economic gain, this table highlights the fact that philosophical differences like business motivation and market dynamics necessitate a leadership and operational model that is quite different for the two. Thus there are aspects of social entrepreneurship that do not fit traditional business models making it appear financially riskier than a standard for-profit business.

New Economy? New Strategy

Companies must think globally to succeed but their impact is felt locally wherever they operate. A global economy demands new insights. Multinationals as well as small ventures must expand into geographies and social strata to grow market share as well as to tap into new employee pools. The case of Southwest Creations Collaborative shows how it is possible to think big to act small for making an impact that matters in the twenty first century.

ACKNOWLEDGMENTS

Sincere thanks, first to Susan Matteucci, executive director, Southwest Creations Collaborative for candid interviews, providing informational materials and permission to analyze operations. Thanks to Silicon Venture Partners International and Trevor Loy (Flywheel Ventures) for hosting the event "A Celebration of Social Entrepreneurship" where some of the material in this chapter was presented. Thanks to Reuters Foundation, Stanford University, Cathy Healy, Digital Vision Fellows and staff for supporting the research for this chapter. This chapter would not have been possible without the expert guidance of Karen Coppock, executive director, Reuters Digital Vision Program, Stanford University.

REFERENCES

Annie E. Casey Foundation (n.d.). Kids Count: A national and state-by-state effort to track the status of children in the U.S. Retrieved June 28, 2007, from http://www.aecf.org/kidscount/

Boschee, J. (1997). *Definition of double bottom Line—Institute for Social Entrepreneurship.* Retrieved June 28, 2007, from http://www.socialent.org/definitions.htm

Esterson, E. (2005). *Social Venturing Benefits Albuquerque Manufacturer.* Retrieved June 28, 2007, from http://www.newwest.net/index.php/city/article/3879/C110/L110

Friedman, T. L. (2006). *The world is flat: A brief history of the twenty first century.* New York: Farrar, Strauss and Giroux

Kamerick, M. (2006). *Women of influence.* Retrieved June 28, 2007, from http://albuquerque.bizjournals.com/bizwomen/albuquerque/content/feature/item.html?item_id=2926&feature_id=290

Matteucci, S. (2006). Overview and market opportunity, Southwest Creations Collaborative [Brochure]. Albuquerque, NM: Author.

Prahalad, C. K. (2005). *The fortune at the bottom of the pyramid: Eradicating poverty through profits.* Philadelphia: Wharton School.

Reddy, S. (2005). An interview with Sanjay Reddy, co-author of "How NOT to Count the Poor." Retrieved June 28, 2007, from http://www.50years.org/cms/ejn/story/68

Shipler, D. K. (2004). *The working poor: Invisible in America.* New York: Vintage Books.

WorldBank. (n.d.). Poverty net. Understanding poverty. Retrieved June 28, 2007, from Bhttp://web.worldbank.org/Whttp://web.worldbank.org/WBSITE/EXTERNAL/TOPICS/EXTPOVERTY/EXTPA/0,,contentMDK:20153855~menuPK:435040~pagePK:148956~piPK:216618~theSitePK:430367,00.html

PART II

**"SOCIAL VENTURES"—
LEARNING FROM, EVOLVING THROUGH,
AND SURVIVING BUMPS IN THE ROAD**

CHAPTER 5

BANKING ON WOMEN FOR POVERTY REDUCTION

Portrait of Kenya Women's Finance Trust

Faith Wambura Ngunjiri

ABSTRACT

Poverty in Kenya is so extreme that over 50% of the population survives on less than a dollar a day. Gender has a strong impact on poverty levels with over 70% of the poor being women. Cultural norms, inequitable government policies, lack of access to credit, limited educational opportunities for girls, and other contextual factors limit women's economic opportunities. In the face of these challenges, Kenya Women's Finance Trust (KWFT) has emerged as a microcredit lending institution committed to increasing women's access to financial resources through provision of credit plus financial management education. This chapter describes how KWFT and its CEO, Dr. Jeniffer Riria, have worked toward the reduction of poverty by banking on women. It discusses the business strategies that Dr. Riria and her team utilize to make KWFT both profitable and able to meet the immense credit needs of women entrepreneurs. The chapter is based on a field study conducted in Kenya in the summer of 2005 on leadership for

Innovative Approaches to Reducing Global Poverty
pp. 93–108
Copyright © 2007 by Information Age Publishing

social justice. Data collection included interviews with Dr. Riria and archival documents from and about the institution.

INTRODUCTION

Debate rages on in academic and development circles regarding the viability of utilizing microcredit programs in alleviating poverty and empowering women in global south locations. Some have argued that increased access to credit, which is the focus of many women-in-development programs in global south locations, often does not transform the social and structural dynamics in which women live and work. As such, empowerment of women may or may not take place through access to credit because the structural dynamics that breed inequalities and impoverishment might remain unchanged (Ofreneo, 2005). Programs that concentrate only on providing credit facilities may fail to empower beneficiaries and improve their quality of life. Real transformation takes place only when programs include social change objectives beyond credit to enable political advocacy at the individual and collective levels (Ofreneo, 2005).

This chapter provides a portrait of an effective microcredit institution in Kenya—the Kenya Women's Financial Trust (KWFT)—that has managed to improve the living standards of thousands of women—averaging about 80,000 per year—and the families they represent. The discussion also demonstrates how KWFT benefits the poorest of the poor in Kenya's rural villages, towns, and urban slums through the activities of the women entrepreneurs' it serves. The information for this chapter was gathered through interviews with Kenyan women leaders, archival data from Kenya Women's Finance Trust, and other articles on microfinance. The material was collected as part of a larger study on Kenyan women and leadership.

FEMINIZATION OF POVERTY

Kenya is one of the poorest countries in the world, and also one of the most heavily indebted. Changes in the political landscape in the 70s and 80s, structural adjustment programs (SAPS) instituted by International Monetary Fund (IMF) and World Bank, and limited natural resources have all contributed to the growth of poverty in the country. In the mid-80s, the IMF and World Bank instituted tough Structural Adjustment Programs meant to increase the likelihood of economic growth and debt repayments—these programs served only to fuel inflation and make the poor even poorer. Strategies such as cost-sharing for education and health care brought government institutions to their knees. The poor who most needed the services of these institutions were the worst hit.

Women make up between 60-70% of the poor in Kenya, and about 52% of the entire population of the country (2007). Several factors have contributed to this feminization of poverty (Ngunjiri, in press). First, commercial banking institutions demand collateral before providing women entrepreneurs with loans. Unfortunately, most women do not own land, the most prized possession amongst the majority of Kenyans, because traditional cultures do not allow women to inherit land from their fathers or husbands (Muteshi, 1998; Ngunjiri, in press).

A second source of increasing impoverishment was a combination of the SAPS that demanded cost-sharing in education, and patriarchal culture that placed less value on girls' education than on boys' (Mbugua-Muriithi, 1996; Ngunjiri, 2006a, 2006b). As such, girls had less access to primary and secondary education, because parents who were forced to choose who to pay school fees for chose to pay their sons fees. Without basic education, girls' economic and employment capacities became severally limited. Even though the advent of free primary education in 2003 made basic education equally available to boys and girls, those who are poor are less likely to advance to secondary and technical schools, because they would have to meet the tuition expenses. Again, parents have tended to choose their sons rather than their daughters for continued education.

Third, the tradition of not allowing women to inherit land and own property means that women do not have collateral for loans. The legal system does not protect women who seek property left behind by their deceased husbands; the courts often take the side of the tribal customs (Otieno, 1998). In that case, widows often lose their primary income earner as well as all their property upon the death of their husbands (Muteshi, 1998). The quote below, from one KWFT client contained in *The Pillar*, KWFT's annual magazine, illustrates the destitution that low income women from certain ethnic groups face when their husbands die;

> My in-laws took everything—mattresses, blankets, utensils. They chased me away like a dog. I was voiceless, I had young children who were sick and no one would assist us. I couldn't buy clothes, we couldn't eat and I had no cooking pots. I was destitute, with no land as well.

In addition to forced destitution, most of the poor are concentrated in rural areas. Unfortunately, commercial banks and other nonbank financial institutions concentrate their efforts in cities and towns areas for several reasons. One is that rural agricultural and entrepreneurial activities tend to have limited profitability, especially in low potential areas where most of the rural poor are located (Kiiru & Pederson, 1997).

Additionally, poor technological and infrastructural development discourages most institutions from providing services in rural areas (Kiiru & Pederson, 1997). Furthermore, lack of drought protection, a lack of policy coordination on rural credit schemes, and absence of clear land titles that are required as collateral have all contributed to discouraging commercial and nonbank institutions from investing in rural Kenya (Kiiru & Pederson, 1997). That is where Kenya Women's Finance Trust, as a microcredit institution committed to servicing the poor, comes in.

EMERGENCE AND NEAR-EXTINCITON OF KWFT

In 1981, a group of professional women including lawyers, bankers, financial experts, entrepreneurs, managers, and trainers got together to discuss the challenges that women faced in Kenya. As leading women, they were well aware of the challenges they faced, challenges that were multiplied for low income women who could hardly meet their subsistence needs. Their vision was to set up a financial institution that would address the economic needs of women that were not being met by large national and international banks. Specifically, they aimed at setting up a women-serving, women-led bank. However, due to rather stringent government regulations and requirements for the establishment of a bank, the women established a "Trust" instead.

Dr. Jeniffer Riria, chief executive officer of KWFT since 1991 remembers the context in which the institution was launched as a sensitive period in regard to women's issues: "anyone who initiated interventions to empower women was regarded as a feminist—feminism being perceived as evil and those who were categorized into this group described as women of poor repute." This perception arose from the fact that first-wave feminists were often seen as radical, men-hating, home-wrecking women with whom good women should not associate. This viewpoint did not deter the women leaders who became founding members of KWFT. They knew that low-income women could be responsible borrowers, even though they offered little in the way of collateral. The founding members contributed between U.S.$10-100, depending on income levels These funds constituted the initial capital for establishing Kenya Women's Finance Trust. The members also sought financial support from the United Nations Development Program (UNDP), United States Agency for International Development (USAID), Department for International Development (DFID) and Ford Foundation. As stated in the charter:

> The general aim of Kenya Women's Finance Trust shall be to facilitate the direct participation of women and their families in the money economy of

the country and in particular those women who have not had access to the services of established financial institutions.

Despite having such a lofty purpose, KWFT's first decade was fraught with problems; the institution ended the decade with fewer than 250 members, 30 clients, a loan portfolio of only U.S.$29, 410, very high loan losses, and donors who were ready to pull the plug. The impending failure of the institution threatened to reinforce the very market barriers that it had been instituted to eliminate. In addition to the problems imposed by the prevailing environment, KWFT had serious internal problems. Poor leadership and general mismanagement seemed to be the biggest problem, stemming from the reliance on voluntary services for its top management. This reliance on volunteers led to a lack of full-time focus and commitment on the part of those expected to manage the not-for-profit, and by 1990 operations ground to a halt. Dr. Jeniffer Riria, formerly a university professor and a women-in-development expert, was brought in with the hope that she could turn the institution around and save it from extinction. She remembers her first days in office:

I stepped into my office and what I saw was shocking, papers strewn everywhere on the floor and dust on the walls. The worst sight was that of the employees. Everybody in the office hung their heads and looked at me like "just another passing MD (Managing Director)!" The dusty records that I could gather revealed that the institution was in great debt. Rent was due and the salaries had not been paid. Just as I was coming to terms with the shock, someone from a donor institution came and demanded that KSh 840,000 (the balance of the funds the institution had been given as a grant) should be transferred to another institution. The donor was upset with the nonperforming KWFT and did not want anything to do with it. I pleaded with him because this was the only money the institution had, but my pleas fell on deaf ears. The money was transferred to another institution shortly after.

According to Dr. Riria, the institution's programs ground to a halt because of three main reasons:

(a) There was no structure for reporting and accountability
(b) All the donors who had previously provided grants had abandoned the institution, except for UNDP and Ford Foundation
(c) KWFT had lost credibility as the premier institution serving women in the African region. Even the Women's World Banking, of which KWFT was on of the oldest affiliates, had distanced itself due to the mismanagement and near bankruptcy.

In spite of these challenges, two of the founding members and the two donor institutions that had not abandoned KWFT did not want to see the demise of the organization and their hope of empowering women dashed. As such, they decided to revamp the institution, beginning with an independent assessment and evaluation conducted in 1990. From these evaluations, it was determined that the only way to save the institution was to reconfigure it, starting at the very top with a new board, a new managing director, and professional mid-level managers.

As it turned out, instituting a new board was easier said than done. Four of the original founding members, who had caused most of the problems to begin with, did not want change, and they needed to be removed from board membership. To do this, the newly hired managing director and the reconstruction team instituted a coup d'etat. They called an annual general meeting, in which a new board was elected. The new board and skeleton management staff moved to:

(a) Reestablish a management structure that included separation of the roles of the board from those of the management;
(b) Develop and implement policies and procedures for credit, accounting, and personnel; and,
(c) Create a corporate governance manual, setting up performance standards and indicators, and reporting formats and procedures.

The staff and new Board also had to relaunch the financial and nonfinancial programs, but to do that, they had to reestablish credibility with both members and funding partners. They needed to prove that the institution would not only survive, but thrive as a viable microfinance institution. Many interventions had to be undertaken concurrently to ensure rapid recovery, including the hiring of professional staff to relaunch the products.

RECOVERY AND RECONSTRUCITON

Under the new management, the years 1992 to 1996 were spent not only recovering from the mismanagement and near-extinction of the previous decade, but also on attempting to grow into a viable institution. First of all, a new credit methodology and modes of operation helped to improve outreach to and access for women clients, and contributed to the self-sustainability of the institution. Part of the credit methodology was derived from the preexisting women's groups known as Rotating Savings and Credit Associations (ROSCAs) which undertake savings and lending activities for their members. KWFT encouraged such groups to take loans under three schemes: (a) the Biashara scheme (Swahili for business) which was initiated in 1991 and lent to first time borrowers organized into groups; (b) the Uaminifu Scheme (Swahili for trustworthiness)—which began in 1993 and lent to ROSCAs of women already engaged in microenterprise and (c) the Barclays Bank of Kenya Guarantee Scheme—initiated in 1994 to make loans and provide technical support to selected KWFT clients with larger credit needs (Kiiru & Pederson, 1997). The group based model of intermediation, where group members would keep each individual accountable for repaying her loan was adopted from Kenya Rural Enterprise Program (K-REP), the pioneer in microfinance in Kenya. The Biashara credit scheme is similar to that used by the Grameen Bank of Bangladesh, modified to fit local conditions and practices in Kenya (Kiiru & Pederson, 1997). These three loan programs helped KWFT to recover and even grow, and its array of financial services in those years included group savings, loans and loan guarantees and nonfinancial services such as client counseling and training.

Second, KWFT also grew by creating a small training department for its staff. This department was intentionally kept small because Dr. Riria realized the benefits that would be gained by linking her employees to other training agencies, including Kenya Management Assistance Program and Small Enterprise Professional Service Organization (Kiiru & Pederson, 1997).

Third, to mobilize funding KWFT had to meet two challenges already mentioned: donor confidence, and attracting competent staff. As Kiiru and Penderson (1997) noted,

> The initial situation was complicated by the need to shed the image of an "assistance" program in order to improve loan recovery. The previous decade had embroiled the Trust in serious management problems, and the new organization faced a challenge of operating above local politics and developing a management structure and culture which could manage an effective credit scheme. (p. 3)

After the new board and new management were instituted, Dr. Riria embarked on finding funding sources for specific operational needs. Some of the organizations that came to her rescue included K-REP, International Fund for Agricultural Development (IFAD), Ford Foundation, Barclays Bank, Kenya Gatsby Charitable Trust, the Netherlands Ministry for Development Cooperation, USAID, UNDP, and Overseas Development Agency (now DFID). With their support, KWFT's portfolio expanded from a total outstanding loan value of about KSh 1.5 million in 1992, to 33 million in 1996. The operating income also increased, enabling the trust to cover 52% of operating expenses in 1995, up from 13% in 1991. The loan recovery rate grew tremendously, from a deficit written off in 1990 of KSh, 2 million, to a recovery rate of 97% during 1993-1996. After this period, KWFT was ready for real growth, even the ability to generate profits and thus be on the path to self-sustainability.

As Kiiru and Penderson (1997) noted, the fact that KWFT survived those early recovery years is commendable considering the macro-economic environment between 1990-1995. For example, inflation rates had remained relatively stable in the 1980s, at about 9-10%, but rose steeply to about 27% in 1992. Politically, the early 90s were a very volatile time in Kenya, impacting every aspect of the economy from education to health care. At the same time, there was no significant improvement in the poverty rate, remaining at around 50% in the early 90s. A decline in real wage rates in this same period disproportionately affected the poor. Per capita incomes fell by 10% in the period 1990-1995

ACCESS AND IMPACT

Building on those years of recovery, KWFT was poised for growth. The year 1996 saw KWFT reach its goal of generating internally suffficient income to cover all of its program administration costs. By 1996, KWFT had earned sufficient credibility with international donor organizations for DFID to give the Trust $2.3 million to implement its 5-year organizational growth plan. The plan sought to expand the active client base, standing at 6,800 in 1998 to 27,000 in 2002, and the outstanding loan portfolio from U.S.$700,000 to U.S.$2,700,000. The plan also sought to decentralize the management and operational activities to the district level in order to improve efficiency in service delivery and increase outreach to local communities. In the decade 1996-2006, KWFT became established as Kenya's largest microcredit institution dedicated to serving women, especially rural women, with a reliable and efficient source of credit. As noted, these women would not have been able to access credit from commercial banks and other formal financial institutions, due to their limited access to collateral. Some of the organization's growth indicators are provided in Tables 5.1 and 5.2.

As planned, KWFT again refined its operations by restructuring along functional lines, establishing three departments: credit, finance and administration, each with its own manager. This move reduced top management expenses and increased overall efficiency in the institution. Regional responsibilities were delegated to the regional managers, and they in turn delegated to smaller unit offices. KWFT designed differentiated micro credit products for asset development, working capital financing and other specific activities. In response to market demands, new products were introduced, including individual loans, school fees loans,

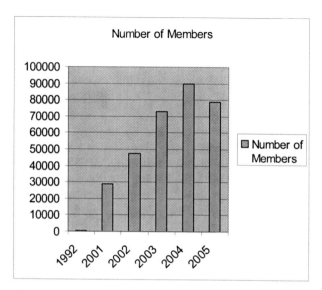

Source: KWFT (2005) annual report and accounts, p. 31 and KWFT Web site, kwft.org

Figure 5.1.   Membership.

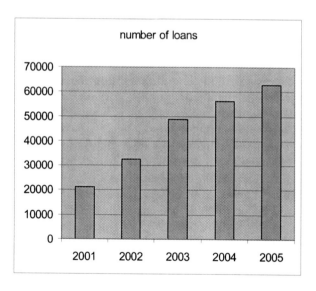

Source: KWFT (2005) annual report and accounts, p. 31 & KWFT Web site, kwft.org

Figure 5.2.   Number of loans.

and medical bills loans,. New credit lines and loan guarantee facilities were negotiated with commercial banks for those KWFT clients who had grown beyond the credit limits imposed by KWFT, enabling such clients to advance to larger loans. As of 2006, most of these customers could access their loans from KWFT, as the minimum loans were increased from KSh 1 million to 3 million.

KWFT also introduced complementary nonfinancial services such as money transfer, business training, and counseling aimed at creating a desirable business culture among the clients and enhanced program activities. To reinforce the training and counseling, KWFT introduced a mentor-learner program where successful businesswomen would train emerging entrepreneurs through observation and apprenticeships. This collection of activities is called "credit-plus" by Dr. Riria. That is, in addition to providing loans, KWFT also provides business training and support services that help the women entrepreneurs succeed and contributes to the high loan repayment rates KWFT enjoys.

SUCCESS INDICATORS IN FIGHTING POVERTY

KWFT has been very successful in meeting its stated purpose of accessing credit and nonfinancial services to women. As of 2006, KWFT introduced new products to the market and rebranded all of its products. Individual loan is now Mwamba loan (Swahili for rock or foundation); mini group loan is now Mwangaza (Swahili for light); school fees loan is now Elimu (Swahili for education) and emergency loan is now Tatua (Swahili for survive or make-it-through). The aim of the rebranding was to put the products in a language that the clients can easily identify with—most of them being semiliterate poor women, Swahili is a more accessible language for them (Swahili is the national language of Kenya). Biashara (group based) loans remained as named (as noted earlier Biashara is the Swahili word for business). Mwamba loan is advanced to individuals, and the loan limit has been raised to KSh. Three million (about U.S.$34,000) paid within 3 years. An additional product, Kinga ya Jamii (Swahili for family protection) was introduced in 2006, a "last expenses assurance product" or life insurance that is affordable to the KWFT clientele. With a benefit of KSh, 30,000, this is a particularly timely product considering the high costs of funerals in Kenya, and the rise of HIV/AIDS related deaths. By providing specialized loans and other financial services for specific needs, KWFT helps women to make better economic decisions, such that loans meant for business go toward business, and other subsistence and emergency needs such as tuition fees and medical expenses are covered by their own special loans. This distinction is important because the borrowers might otherwise spend their business loans to cover family needs and expenses, thus making it easier for them to default.

In terms of growth in numbers of active members, KWFT has increased from less than 250 in 1992, to over 78,000 in 2005, with a peak year of 89,775 in 2004 (Table 5.2). Perhaps the decrease between 2004 and 2005 could be attributed to both natural attrition speeded up by deaths due to HIV/AIDS, and the fact that the economy did not grow as fast as had been anticipated when the new government took over in 2003.

Perhaps another way to communicate the success of the trust is to use short portraits of women entrepreneurs who have benefited from its services. These stories are contained in Pillar, KWFT's annual magazine.

The Road Less Traveled

Most of the clientele targeted by KWFT are poor women—that is, those who support a family of six on less than a dollar a day; who live in urban slums or rural areas; whose loan size is less than KSh 20,000 or about U.S.$230; and whose businesses involve selling foodstuff and other household amenities from their doorsteps or a small shopping center near their homes. However, lower income and struggling entrepreneurs can also access loans from the trust. Take Mrs. Joyce Muyoka, a 32 year old woman entrepreneur who has become a leading businessperson in her local town. She grew up in a farming and business environment, her father was a shrewd businessman and farmer who had many wives and children to support. At the time of starting her business, Joyce had just completed an accounts course at a technical college. She started a hardware shop and later a construction company, because "I identified the niche in this type of business after realizing that there was no hardware retail outlet in this area," she explained. The residents of Lugari town in Western Kenya had problems procuring building materials because the area is very rural and its infrastructure is underdeveloped. Demand from her customers led her to make changes in her business, adding farm implements to her list of merchandise. Not only is she a highly respected and sought after construction contractor, she is also an ardent farmer. She has employs 25 workers, and also hires casual laborers on her construction sites. As she says, "in terms of poverty alleviation, I have done my best. I generate income for many families and I also pay taxes to the government. These are channeled back to the community." In addition, she has acquired property such as residential housing in towns. She has also been able to pay college tuition for her sister who is pursuing a master's degree. Her husband is her partner, and serves as debt collector and director. She has received loans from KWFT ranging from her first of

KSh 50,000 to her most recent of 500,000; in total, she has borrowed KSh 1.2 million. She said that those loans helped her to grow her business, having begun with a paltry KSh 50,000 worth of building materials, her fixed assets are now worth over KSh 2 million.

Creating Employment for Young People

Dorcas Mandere's greatest achievement is paying school fees for her four children who attend various learning institutions around the country, and assisting others in her extended family. The 40-year old runs a hardware and beauty shop in Ogembo, Gucha district (Western Kenya). The mother of five and former teacher provides fulltime employment for five people who would otherwise be among the very poor. "Some of them have built decent houses and are learning to save through my guidance. I would want to see everybody leading a gratifying life where everybody can afford the basic needs and some luxuries in life" she said. Her experience with KWFT started in 1999 when a friend introduced her to the trust, where she borrowed her first KSh 30,000 (about U.S.$340) to increase the stock in her hardware shop. Since then, she has borrowed and repaid loans of varying amounts, the largest being KSh 250,000 (about U.S.$ 2800). Her next goal is to acquire property in the near future, and also to open a beauty salon.

From Wheelbarrow to a Retail Store

Stella Papa quit her poorly paid job as a government typist in order to settle down in one place and provide proper care for her children. Unfortunately, quitting her job meant going without the measly government paycheck. So she got creative. "It all started on a wheelbarrow, moving from shopping center to shopping center on market days to sell my little wares" recounts Stella. With an initial capital of 1,500KSh (U.S.$200) she bought groceries in small quantities and sold them in her "mobile shop." Then one day she heard an announcement from the local leader that there was an organization granting loans to women entrepreneurs. The leader invited women to attend a meeting to learn more about KWFT. To get a loan, Stella and other women in her area formed a self-help group and were trained in business management for 8 weeks. Stella then applied and received her first loan of KSh 10,000 in early 2001. With this she increased her stock and continued hawking from her wheelbarrow. She repaid the loan in 3 months. Her second loan of 30,000 in October 2001 enabled her to rent premises within which to operate her business, and purchase more stock in larger quantities. She repaid the second loan in 3 months as well. Her largest loan was KSh 130,000 with which she further expanded her retail store, adding more products to meet her clients' needs With her profits, she has also bought a dairy cow, set up a poultry project, acquired land and built a permanent house on it for her family, as well as investing in a machine for processing sunflower oil. Additionally, she has provided employment to two people, has been able to pay for decent education for her children, and provided goods that her local community needed—now they don't have to travel long distances to find items like bicycle spare parts, a very important service needed by those who operate "bicycle taxis" called Boda Boda.

Breaking Cultural Barriers

Memzee Seif Bendera is a rarity in her Digo community. As she narrated, "in the Digo community, a woman does not own land or any tangible property. This makes it impossible for her to access loans from banking institutions." The lack of property did not deter Memzee from starting a business. Using money she received from her ROSCA women's self-help group she acquired training in dressmaking and set up a tailoring shop. That was back in 1986, and for the next 8 years business was difficult because she did not have sufficient capital to invest in it. But in 1994, her women's group starting working with KWFT, and she received her first loan of 10,000 (U.S.$120). This loan helped her to diversify her products by adding school uniforms. Her ROSCA group continued to save KSh 50 per week, money that served as security for the group loans. With her second loan of 20,000, she employed a second tailor and bought two sawing machines. This enabled her to earn a tender to supply uniforms to secondary schools in the district. As her business flourished, so did her fellow group members and they increased their savings to KSh 100, with some members saving 150-200 each week. These savings enabled them to borrow larger loans. Memzee's business diversified further, from tailoring and supplying uniforms, to supplying foodstuffs to schools and hospitals and delivering coconuts to the market. Memzee confides that hers was a long journey, from the humble housewife who was worried about her first KSh 10,000 loan, to the businesswoman who could borrow and repay KSh 350,000 with confidence. She is happy about her own ascent from poverty, as well as her ability to help others by providing employment. She has five permanent workers, and hires others on a casual basis as demand arises.

From Peasantry to Propertied Wealth

Jane Muthoni was a peasant farmer and housewife who lived from hand to mouth, in spite of her daily toils. Her first contact with KWFT was in 1999 when the trust offered her a KSh 10,000 security-free loan, which she used to open a food kiosk. From these humble beginnings and several loans later, Muthoni has a hotel and a clothing boutique in the town of Molo, Rift Valley. She has also been able to move from peasant farming to commercial farming, and employs three permanent workers on her farm, as well as 20-35 seasonal workers during planting, weeding and harvesting periods. Such workers represent those who survive on less than a dollar a day. In recognition of her own humble beginnings, Muthoni reaches out to other women to assist them to grow. "My suppliers in the two businesses are women because I would like to help them out of poverty," she says. She has also spearheaded the formation of two self-help groups and three groups of merry-go-rounds (the local name for ROSCAs) which have facilitated teamwork and improved the standards of living of the women.

These five portraits illustrate how women make use of the loans they access from KWFT to raise their own standard of living as well as provide employment to others. Whereas these four do not represent the poorest of the poor, they demonstrate how, by providing loans to women entrepreneurs, KWFT is contributing to reducing poverty because such women are able to provide employment, support their own immediate and extended families, and contribute to the development of their communities.

LESSONS LEARNED: MICROFINANCE AND THE FIGHT AGAINST POVERTY

The women whose portraits are included here are a very small example of the almost 80,000 thousand served directly by KWFT currently. (the number of loans includes those given to groups, which are then disbursed to members). Those 80,000 individuals represent about half a million family members whose standard of living is elevated through the women's business enterprises. Additionally, many other poor people are served as they gain employment opportunities in those business enterprises. If the 80,000 loans create paid work for an average of five additional individuals for each loan and if those workers live in six member households, then another 2,400,000 individuals would be positively impacted by KWFT, yielding about 3 million Kenyans being positively impacted by KWFT. With the current estimate of 56% of the country living on less than a dollar a day (that is about 16 million people), reaching almost 20% of those poor people is quite an achievement. As the women entrepreneurs themselves attest, empowering women directly translates into empowering families and the communities they represent. Women are conscious of their social responsibility not only to uplift themselves, but also to uplift their communities. In an interview Wahu Kaara, a global social justice activist, had this to say about African women:

> The driving force which is the greatest attribute that the African women have is self determination; self drive which is to serve society. Because mothers of Africa, their self determination is not to look nice and go for beauty contests, it's to serve humanity. They provide and they protect, they secure the community ... look at the microcredit thing emerging from the women's groups, which is not anything that anybody came to energize, it is the creativity and innovativeness as we look to meet these budget lines without any budget, and people came up with a very viable way of mobilizing resources, out of goodwill. Collateral is goodwill based on our being members of one community, or you are friends, the goodwill you have, you make it collateral, the human goodwill.

As Wahu observed above, the women's self help group emerged long before institutional microcredit came into being. Institutions such as KWFT utilized an already existing modus operandi to develop credit facilities for women. Once this women's self-help process was proven to be an effective way to reach women and to ensure accountability, KWFT decided to adopt it.

The changes that KWFT has instituted such as diversifying the types of loans, accessing loans to both groups and individual women, and ensuring that women are trained in basic business management skills has enabled the institution to thrive and become sustainable. KWFT is a model of a microfinance institution that has reached sustainability, and that is helping to alleviate poverty for thousands of families. It demonstrates how women are able to solve their problems creatively, once they have access to the necessary financial resources and the training to succeed. It further illustrates women's active engagement in their own emancipation from the poverty that breeds ignorance and disease.

REFERENCES

ITDG, & Istanbul+5. (2007). *Poor people's participation in shelter solutions.* Bourton-on-Dunsmore, Rugby, United Kingdom: ITDG. Retrieved June 28, 2007, from http://practicalactionconsulting.org/docs/advocacy/habitatpos_final.pdf

Kiiru, W. K., & Pederson, G. D. (1997). *Kenya Women Finance Trust: Case study of a micro-finance scheme.* Washington, DC: World Bank, Africa Region.

Mbugua-Muriithi, J. T. (1996). *Strategies for survival: Women, education and self-help groups in Kenya.* Unpublished doctoral dissertation, Ohio University, Athens, Ohio.

Muteshi, J. K. (1998). A refusal to argue with inconvinient evidence: Women, proprietorship and Kenyan law. *Dialectical Anthropology, 23*(1), 55-81.

Ngunjiri, F. W. (2006a, March). *Gender and power: Deconstructing the positioning of African women leaders.* Paper presented at the Women as Global Leaders annual conference, Abu Dhabi, United Arab Emirates.

Ngunjiri, F. W. (2006b). *Tempered radicals and servant leaders: Portraits of spirited leadership amongst African women.* Unpublished doctoral dissertation, Bowling Green State University, Bowling Green, OH.

Ngunjiri, F. W. (in press). Corruption and the feminization of poverty in Sub-Saharan Africa. *Jenda: Journal of Culture and African Women Studies.*

Ofreneo, R. P. (2005). Problematizing microfinance as an empowerment strategy for women living in poverty: Some policy directions. *Gender, Technology & Development, 9*(3), 373-394.

Otieno, W. W. (1998). *Mau Mau's daughter: A life history.* Boulder, CO: Lynne Rienner.

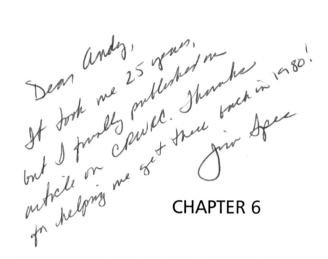

Dear Andy,
It took me 25 years,
but I finally published on
article on CRWRC. Thanks
for helping me get there back in 1980!
Jim Spee

CHAPTER 6

REDUCING POVERTY THROUGH STRATEGY AND INNOVATION IN A BANGLADESH COMMUNITY DEVELOPMENT PROJECT

James Spee

ABSTRACT

Over a 30-year period, Bangladesh Extension Education Services (BEES) diffused worked to reduce poverty in six innovative ways:

(1) Introducing new, high-yielding crops, nutritious vegetables, and the seeds and fertilizers needed to grow them.
(2) Developing a new management by objectives (MBO) process that allowed BEES to support improved farm productivity growth with an understanding of the implications of differing family sizes.
(3) Combining introduction of hand powered irrigation pumps with agricultural credit to assist very small farms.
(4) Undertaking early experiments in microcredit.

Innovative Approaches to Reducing Global Poverty
pp. 109–127

(5) Delivering health and nutrition programs for mothers of young children.
(6) Dispersing BEES' knowledge and expertise across a wide geographic area.

These innovations were driven by strategic decisions made in response to changes outside the organization. The result is a resilient organization that can survive without assistance from international funding sources This chapter explores how BEES started as a faith-based program sponsored by donors from churches in the United States and Canada and operated by expatriates, developed a series of innovative approaches to reducing poverty, adjusted to the loss of external donor support, re-established itself after that loss, and grew to become the tenth largest domestic nongovernmental organization (NGO) program in Bangladesh.

EARLY INNOVATIONS

In the 1970s many NGOs that originally had the mission of providing disaster relief began to shift their missions toward community development. The Christian Reformed World Relief Committee (CRWRC), founded by the Christian Reformed Church of North America in 1964 was part of that shift. It sent two agronomists to Bangladesh in 1974 to work with the Mennonite Central Committee in Noahkali District. The agronomists and committee members surveyed available sites and applied for permission to begin a CRWRC project in Bogra District, about 250 miles northwest of Dhaka.

By 1976, CRWRC had begun to set up its project in Bogra. Rick DeGraaf, a young Canadian agronomist, arrived and began setting up agricultural extension offices in nearby villages. Initially, efforts were aimed at encouraging farmers to grow high-yielding varieties of rice created by the International Rice Research Institute. Members of the offices also planted demonstration gardens to show local farmers how to grow nutritious vegetables such as broccoli, cauliflower, spinach, and squash. They created a research farm to test which varieties grew best in Bogra and to experiment with varying levels of fertilizer and water. This was the first set of innovations the project would diffuse, the introduction of new crops.

One of the first employees DeGraaf hired was Abdus Salaam, a graduate of Mymensingh University. When John Brouwer, a member of CRWRC, moved to Dhaka to set up an office there, he hired Saiful Islam Robin to be his office manager. Ten years later, Abdus and Robin would become the program director and executive director of Bangladesh Extension Education Services (BEES) when CRWRC spun off the program.

In 1978, CRWRC hired a new executive director, John DeHaan to run its domestic and international community development and disaster relief programs from the Christian Reformed Church's home office in Grand Rapids Michigan. DeHaan was a fan of Peter Drucker (1974) and specifically of the Management by Objectives (MBO) philosophy

When John Brower's period in Bangladesh came to an end, CRWRC chose Peter VanderMeulen, of Grand Rapids, Michigan, to replace him. CRWRC gave VanderMeulen the mandate to bring MBO into the Bogra project. By 1980, when James Spee arrived in Bogra, VanderMeulen had instituted a twice yearly strategic planning process that included:

1. Examination of target groups to provide assistance to
2. Review of the project mission
3. Creation and review of project objectives by program
4. Creation and updating of each objective including measurable outcomes, time lines, and responsible parties.

The team developed strategic plans for improving the economic well being of a defined target population. They delineated measurable objectives for client farmers and used simple inputs such as seeds, fertilizer, water, and access to credit to improve their clients' ability to feed their families from their own production. This management by objectives process was the second innovation that the organization came to diffuse across Bangladesh. The principles of MBO were embedded deeply in the organization and survived the transition from international to domestic ownership. Whenever staff from the project visited other development agencies, their first question was always, "How do you measure your success?" When they found that their hosts had none, they would smile knowingly, realizing that they could point to concrete results of their work, rather than wishful thinking that someone, somewhere might be better off as a result of their work.

EVOLVING APPROACHES TO PROVDING ASSISTANCE DURING THE CRWRC ERA

During the CRWRC era, the Bogra project was staffed by a series of expatriates from the United States and Canada. Their contracts ran for 3 years. Typically, they received a few weeks of cross cultural awareness and language acquisition training in the United States then 3 to 6 months of language training with a private tutor once they arrived in country. In 1980, the Bogra office had two Land Rovers and several Honda motorcycles. The expatriates were each assigned a motorcycle and shared the Land Rovers as needed. Since most of them were young men in their 20s the motorcycles provided an adventurous means of navigating the local streets and highways, which were often clogged with riksas, pedestrians, and livestock.

By the late 1970s CRWRC expatriates had opened nine agricultural field offices around Bogra District. Each field office had a "crop promoter" and a "crop promoter assistant." They interviewed local farmers, identified those who fit the target group, and created annual plans for increased output from each of the farmer's plots. At that time, the average farmer had about an acre of land, but it was scattered in five or six different plots, each with different soil and water patterns. One plot might be wet enough for rice while another would be more suited to wheat or vegetables. The crop promoters and their assistants had bachelors degrees (similar to an associate degree in the United States) or BSc degrees (similar to a bachelors degree in the United States). They also received monthly training at the CRWRC office in Bogra.

After approximately 2 years and 8 months of their 3-year commitment to CRWRC, the expatriates left for home. They spent a week or 2 in Grand Rapids, Michigan working on a presentation about their work and then went on public relations tours to churches that supported them individually, the project in particular, or CRWRC in general. These presentations were important because in the early 1980s CRWRC was raising about U.S.$7 million a year for its global operations, nearly 100% from voluntary donations by members of the Christian Reformed Church. Unlike some faith-based organizations, CRWRC workers received a guaranteed salary and did not have to conduct their own independent fund raising before or during their work overseas.

The remainder of the 4 months that was not devoted to presentations was considered "furlough," a concept borrowed from the practice of the mission board. Missionaries were given a 4-month "home stay" every 4 years. The assumption was that you would return to your assigned country after the furlough. In Bangladesh, however, CRWRC expatriates did not typically return immediately, although Rick DeGraaf did come back to replace Peter VanderMeulen in 1982 after 4 years back in Canada.

During the late 1970s and early 1980s, the Bangladeshi staff was relatively stable and continued to grow in its capabilities. Abdus Salam was named counterpart to the head of the agricultural extension program in 1978 and took over completely in 1981. After that promotion, some of the expatriates reported to him rather than to the country director. The seeds for eventual independence from CRWRC had been planted, but no one really knew how long it would take for them to germinate.

In 1977, Marvin DeVries and his wife, Peggi, joined the team. Marvin was trained as an irrigation engineer and Peggi had an interest in women's health and nutrition. The agricultural extension offices were beginning to measure the impact of new seeds and fertilizers on crop yields. The CRWRC research farm north of Bogra town, started by David Vanderpuy and continued by Kees Poppe and Paul Brink, continued providing data to help the staff sort out which varieties of rice, wheat, and vegetables were best suited to Bogra's climate and soil types, which were mostly clay or sand. The staff knew that if farmers could irrigate their land in the winter, they could add a second or third crop that could push them from dependency on outside work to self-sufficiency.

Marvin's first experiment was with small cooperatives which he provided with small diesel powered pumps called "shallow tubewells." In the 1960s the World Bank had installed numerous "deep tubewells" around the district. These wells drew from deep in the water table and had the capacity to irrigate about 100 acres. Because of the small size of average land holdings, farmers had to cooperate to share the deep tubewells. Although they formed cooperatives to share the tubewells, most of the cooperatives failed due to weak financial controls and the tubewells wound up in control of the most powerful landowners in the villages. Cooperatives for shallow tubewells were also tried, but they did not work very well either. The groups had trouble sharing responsibility for the maintenance and usage of the pumps and their diesel engines were expensive to repair.

When Vandermeulen arrived in 1978, he instituted a regular strategic planning process. Initially, the expatriate staff was resistant to codifying the project so rigidly. They felt that they were already having some success providing agricultural extension services to the surrounding communities. The program was modeled after the one operated by the Mennonite Central Committee (MCC) in Noahkali District. The first CRWRC staffers in Bangladesh had worked with MCC there while they applied for government permission to open in Bogra.

Before starting the first planning session, VanderMuelen had the staff survey their current client base. They found that on average, their clients had sufficient acreage to grow food for their families and have a surplus to sell to raise cash. Demographic data on the country in the late 1970s suggested that this was a very small group and actually more affluent than 80 or 90% of the population. In discussions with local farmers, the staff members asked what measures they used to determine if a farmer was successful or in danger of losing his land. They learned two terms in Bengali: *kine khawa* means "buying food;" and *gore khawa* means "food in the house." Farmers would refer to how many days or months they were gore *khawa* or *kine khawa*. If someone was buying food 12 months of the year, then they were no longer considered to be a farmer and were dependent on outside work to feed their families. If they had 6 or 8 months of gore *khawa*, then they only had to work half the year or a third of the year and could eat food from their own production the rest of the time. This innovative measure, although in common use among farmers, was not well known in the development community. The terminology was adopted across the organization as part of their management by objectives scheme.

Once they had a viable measure, they were able to define who their target market would be. They used the term "core contact farmer" or CCF for farmers in the target group. Initially, they looked for farmers who were at least 2 months *kine khawa*, or lacking in self sufficiency. If the farmers could be raised to 12 months gore *khawa*, then they would be breaking even and not in danger of selling their land to buy food. This solidified their use of management by objectives allowing bottom up planning to work as client's goals were translated to field worker goals and bubbled up to become the objectives for the entire program.

In the strategic planning process, once the staff identified the target client group and the measure of success, they could brainstorm barriers to self sufficiency. These included lack of access to water, good seeds, fertilizer, and credit to buy inputs. Other barriers included small land holdings broken into minute plots and the lack of a cooperative to sell water from large pumps at affordable prices. Most deep tubewells had been taken over by large landowners or had broken down permanently. Even small two horsepower pumps were too big for the poorer farmers to use.

The staff concluded that the best alternative was a hand tubewell made from a cast iron pump and several lengths of two-inch pipe with a six-foot filter at the bottom. The pumps cost about $75 and could be installed by local "mistris" who used the pipes themselves and pond water to suck dirt out of a hole and sink the pipe for the well. The water table in Bogra district was generally within 14-50 feet of the surface, so 60 feet of pipe was the most anyone would need.

DeVries suggested that hand pumped irrigation alone might be such a strong driver of improved output that it could be provided without the rest of the extension program. To test this possibility, he began an experiment by hiring six irrigation assistants, training them to work with Bangladesh Krishi Bank (BKB) to get small individual loans, and stocking six field offices with hand pumps and pipe from a factory in Dhaka.

Between 1979 and mid 1981, DeVries's team and existing field offices had delivered over 2000 hand tubewells under a memorandum of understanding with Bangladesh Krishi Bank. CRWRC staff assisted farmers in completing the onerous paperwork required for loans. Farmers had to provide land as collateral which meant that they had to document their share of ownership. Because land transactions were expensive, title tended to stay in the name of the owner's parent or grandparent. CRWRC staff learned to draw family trees showing the number of descendants who shared the land on the title. The distribution rules depended on whether the borrower was Hindu or Muslim. Male and female descendants received different shares depending on their religion. This was the system that Dr. Mohammad Yunus rejected when he set up the Grameen Bank. He realized that no one could ever collect on this collateral. CRWRC chose to work within the system.

Their efforts resulted in a steady increase in the number of farmers served and in the months of self sufficiency achieved, as shown in Figure 6.1 and Figure 6.2

Strategically, the irrigation program was a huge success. It became the third major innovation diffused by the project. The combination of inexpensive irrigation and access to credit opened the door for several thousand families to stay on their farms and avoid selling land to buy food.

By 1981-82, the irrigation staff had begun to receive agricultural extension training and the agricultural staff had learned how to process

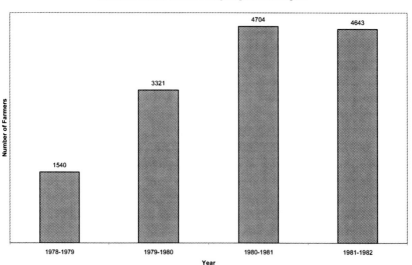

Source: Adapted from CRWRC.

Figure 6.1.   Number of CRWRC farmers in Bogra Agricultural Program 1978 to 1982.

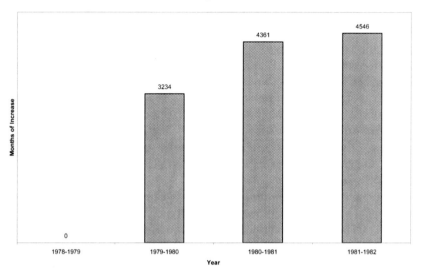

Source: Adapted from CRWRC.

Figure 6.2.   Increased Sufficiency of CRWC Farmers, 1978 to 1982.

loans. Agricultural credit became a corner stone of the extension program along with access to inputs such as fertilizer and seed. CRWRC repackaged large quantities of seed and fertilizer into smaller packets that farmers of limited means could afford. The field offices sold the seed and fertilizer at no markup just as they did with the hand pumps.

James Spee worked on the project from July 1980 to February 1983. Before he departed the United States for Bangladesh, CRWRC gave him a copy of Drucker's (1974) *Management: Tasks, Responsibilities and Practices* to help him gain insight into its management by objectives practices.[1] When Spee took over the irrigation program as part of his first assignment, he began to audit the inventory of tubewells and discovered that the warehouse manager had been stealing components. DeVries had set prices for tubewells of various lengths but had not put a nominal price in for the threaded connectors that held the pipes together, so it was very difficult to match the number of connectors delivered with the revenue collected. In violation of good management practice (which Spee looked up after discovering the theft) the warehouse manager had both keys to the warehouse, so dual control had been compromised. Losses in U.S. dollars were not that great, about $17,000, but it was an important management and accounting lesson: Do not tempt your employees beyond what they can endure.

At its strategic planning meetings every 6 months, CRWRC expatriate staff and their local counterparts continued to analyze the needs of their target population, the "core contact farmer." They were having good success growing both the number of clients served and documenting the growth in farm productivity that would lead to self sufficiency. Nevertheless, the number of landless poor continued to grow. They needed programs that would allow them to generate income without needing property.

Based on the success delivering credit, Spee began investigating credit programs for people who had no collateral, the growing population of landless, nearly landless, or those whose title documents were under dispute. In one village, CRWRC staff discovered that the entire population of several hundred people was tied up in a series of lawsuits disputing boundaries and titles. The case had been dragging on for years in the courts, probably since before the British left in 1947. As a result, no one in the village could apply for credit through a conventional mortgage program.

After several enjoyable visits to Bangladesh Rural Advancement Committee and several other expatriate NGOs, Spee discovered the Grameen Bank. In 1981, it was operating in about three districts: Chittagong, Mymensingh, and Tangail. Spee interviewed Dr. Yunus in Dhaka. He arranged a visit to the Grameen Bank branch in Tangail. From Grameen Bank, Spee learned the principles of microcredit:

1. Nominal groups for savings and peer pressure
2. Individual loans combined with group responsibility
3. Emphasis on business plans for productive income generation.

By early 1982, Spee had written a microcredit proposal based on Yunus's work and presented it to his partners at Bangladesh Krishi Bank. The bank was very cordial in its response and had only one question: How good was our repayment rate on the tubewell program? This was an excellent question. It would prove a very difficult one to answer and an even more difficult issue to resolve. In the early 1980s modern information technology was largely absent in rural Bangladesh. It still is to a large extent in 2007. A bank branch consisted of several rooms in a concrete building with a tin roof. Electricity was used to power a bare bulb and a ceiling fan. Personal computers were rare and expensive. The bank did its record keeping the old fashioned way-with giant ledgers and fountain pens. Each borrower had a page in the ledger that recorded his transactions. The only way to answer the regional bank manager's question was to go through each ledger by hand and calculate the totals.

With the cooperation of each local branch manager, the staff dug into the records. They were appalled to learn that most of the borrowers were behind in their payments. Without a group incentive and peer pressure to repay, and with little cash to spare, the farmers were choosing not to repay their loans. The results meant that BKB would not be financing any additional loan programs, with good reason. It turned out that CRWRC's clients were emulating the more well connected borrowers in their villages, who took out large agricultural loans funded by overseas development funds, used them for consumption and defaulted, knowing that the banks would never collect or foreclose. The loans were often a form of political patronage, going to supporters of the local elected officials. The program DeVries designed was successful at delivering credit and irrigation but not at collecting payments at the other end. CRWRC assumed that the bank would collect and the bank assumed that CRWRC would.

Spee shelved the microcredit proposal and went to work cleaning up the repayment rates on existing loans. Shortly before he left Bangladesh in early 1983, the situation had improved and plans were in place for a microcredit research and development pilot program.

RESPONDING TO EARLY STRATEGIC CHANGES AT CRWRC

Meanwhile, the strategic focus at CRWRC and within its parent organization was beginning to shift. The Christian Reformed Church which supported CRWRC's operations with voluntary donations was also supporting Christian Reformed World Missions, which had a very different focus on strengthening existing churches and building new ones. CRWRC and CRWM ran a joint program in Sierra Leone that attempted to integrate community development and church development. In other parts of the world cooperation between the two organizations had been weak due mainly to their conflicting missions. The target audience for community development, such as Muslim and Hindu farmers in Bangladesh might not be the target audience for church development. In Bangladesh, Christians make up less than one half of one percent of the population, so working through local churches would entail a major revision of the strategy. A new director of international programs for CRWRC, Gary Nederveld, came to Bangladesh in 1982 for a site visit and floated the idea of spinning the program off as a Bangladeshi NGO. Although it had been in the back of everyone's minds, the initial suggestions came as quite a shock. No one understood what he was saying or why. Later, when Rick DeGraaf returned as program director, the expatriates came to a better understanding of what Nederveld intended, which was to open the dialogue on handing off, not shutting the program down. It would take another 4 years before the hand off was accomplished but everyone knew that CRWRC's intention was to shift its strategy to working through churches instead of through a large, religiously diverse, locally-hired staff. In North America, the search began for sources of support outside CRWRC.

New Program Innovation: Experimenting With Microcredit

In the spring of 1983, Abdus trained several of the irrigation promoters to work with microcredit and to form cooperatives. In mid-1983, these individuals formed several cooperative groups in the Mohostan/Bhagopara neighborhood north of Bogra. Abdus left for a 1-year program at Reading University that fall and turned the program over to long time CRWRC employee Shah Alum. When Abdus returned a year later, the program was struggling. Although the groups started with five members and grew to around twenty members and although eventually about 20 groups were fromed, the results were not good. The groups had a mix of members with different social and economic backgrounds. They relied too heavily on the trustworthiness of group members for repayment. Instead, some leaders took unfair advantage of the members. One group leader near the Dhamajani office stole money from the group, took a larger share of the loan, and did not account for his actions to the rest of the group. He had a little more education but he was greedy.

When Abdus returned from Reading University in 1984, he and his colleagues split the project into two target groups: one for farmers and one for landless clients. They made each group more homogeneous with similar education, social, and economic characteristics so that no member would be more likely than another to take unfair advantage of the others. The landless clients met in smaller groups with less input from staff. The farmer groups were better off. The cooperatives had more members and were accustomed to using new agricultural techniques. They were more like the "core contact farmers" CRWRC served before and had more spare time for meetings and training sessions. These groups grew to have between 20 and 30 members.

Former country director Peter VanderMeulen helped the staff secure an outside source of funding as seed money for the landless client loan program and it began to grow. Microcredit would become the fourth innovation that BEES diffused across Bangladesh. At the time of the Bogra pilot program, Grameen Bank was only operating in two districts: Chittagong and Tangail. While Dr. Yunus was glad to share his methodology with anyone who would listen, he did not have the resources or government approval to expand nationwide. The door was open for the Bogra staff to experiment and develop their own program independent of Grameen Bank.

The Bogra site now had several projects. The women's health and nutrition program started by Peggi DeVries and expanded by subsequent local and expatriate staff was improving survival rates for young children by helping them eat better in their first 2 years of life. This program, while small and experimental, provided the fifth innovation that BEES would later diffuse: a program that first provided knowledge of health and nutrition that would keep children healthy during the crucial first 2 years of their lives and then evolved a second part that provided numeracy and literacy education for their mothers.

The agricultural extension program continued to provide education services but was switching to cooperative programs with flexible credit arrangements. The landless program was taking off, providing microcredit opportunities previously unavailable in Bogra District. However, changes back in the United States would soon result in a major restructuring of the Bogra project.

BEGINNING THE TRANSITION TO BEES

CRWRC Bangladesh continued its practice of strategic planning every 6 months. At the 1984 meetings, the topic of transitioning out of CRWRC and into a new, Bangladesh-based NGO was initiated. Over the next year, CRWRC began funneling its budget dollars through a matching grant program provided by the Canadian Government through CETA, Canada's equivalent to US-AID. The first grant of Bangladesh taka 5,600,000 would be used to enable the new NGO to become operational. Top level Bangladeshi program staff and expatriates met frequently to work out financial details and time lines for the transition. CRWRC was experiencing increasing pressure to shift its resources to Christian groups and away from the Bogra project.

At one of the meetings, one of the expatriates, Mrs. Isselstein, suggested that they name the new organization BEES, which translated into "seed" in Bengali and implied a productive honeybee in English. So Bangladesh Extension Education Services was born. In 1986, the remaining expatriates moved to a church-based project location in Mymensingh leaving Bogra for good. Rick DeGraaf served as an ex officio member of the BEES board of directors but could not be officially nominated because he was not a Bangladeshi citizen. The remaining board members were from Bogra and Dhaka. They included Chairman Sahid Ahamed, a chartered accountant and several other professionals. The new board members were not actively engaged in strategic planning for BEES as most planning continued to be done by the program managers.

STRATEGIC CRISIS FOR BEES

According to Abdus, strategic management at BEES worked a little differently than it had under CRWRC. It was more organic and flowed up from clients and field staff to supervisors and managers before being articulated at the top. As the staff developed their mission and objectives, they took ideas from across the organization and combined them into a shared vision. Record keeping from planning sessions was not as formal as before, but the meetings continued every 6 months. The funding from CETA continued steadily for the next 2 years. They reapplied in 1989 and received approval for their 3-year grant when suddenly they learned that the funds had been cut, leaving them with no alternative source of support. The fledgling NGO was facing its first crisis.

With no source of funds in sight, many of the staff members left for more secure jobs. Those who remained took a 50% cut in pay. They also agreed to borrow money from their provident fund (a form of self-insurance) and their vacation fund to cover operating costs in the short run. Abdus equated that time period with fasting during the month of Ramadan. They had to make the sacrifice if they wanted BEES to survive. Their only source of income was the interest they generated from the microcredit program. They continued to provide services to other clients on a limited basis using their profits from microcredit.

By 1991, they were slowly regaining confidence. They noticed that other local NGOs were beginning to get international funding again, so they began applying to various sources. Despite strong urging from Rick DeGraaf, CRWRC was no longer providing any financial support and the Canadian well was still dry. BEES asked CRWRC if it could provide a channel for BEES money into CETA's matching funds program but that could not be arranged. (There may have been legal prohibitions as well.)

The crisis had one positive outcome, and that was the strong bond among the BEES team members who stayed to fight for its survival. They did not blame those who felt they had to leave because they could not survive on a reduced salary. Those who remained did not know where they would get the funds, but they understood that they had to continue to operate as if the money were coming.

As their search continued, they eventually made contact with the Dutch Government and XODA, the British Overseas Development Authority and were able to get funding for the 1992-93 season. For BEES this was like heavy rainfall after a drought. They had learned to accomplish their goals with few resources, now they were grateful for the funding, but wary that it could dry up again. They knew that the funding from the Dutch and British could dry up again at any moment, so they had to become self sufficient in supporting their operations.

To become less dependent on outside funding, they made two important decisions. First, they began searching for sources of microcredit funds that they could relend. They found a small government account but the amount available for Bogra District was not enough to keep everyone employed productively. They also found some money in the Department of Agriculture that was available for micro credit. Once again, the fund was nation wide, with just a little for Bogra District.

The availability of funds nationwide and the strength of their trained staff led them to their second major decision: to expand nationwide into more districts. CRWRC had been restricted to Bogra by its memorandum of understanding with the government of Bangladesh. As a domestic NGO, BEES was under no such restriction. Expansion was a way to ensure survival, to capture more of the resources that were available only if they went outside their home district. They continued to shrink the Bogra operation and transferred their staff to new offices in other districts.

With the new focus on microcredit, they no longer measured farm production or focused as much on self sufficiency from agriculture. They developed two new objectives, which were a balance between generating income to run the infrastructure to provide loans and generating a surplus that could be used to help people.

They continued to recruit groups of 15 to 20 people. BEES made loans to individuals based on individual income generation plans, but the groups took responsibility for ensuring that each individual repaid his or her share of the loan. If an individual did not repay, the other members of the group were prohibited from borrowing additional funds. This created an incentive for everyone in the group to stay current on their loans. BEES combined features it learned from the Grameen Bank model and from its own experience with cooperatives. The groups were larger than Grameen's but the individual and group features were very similar, especially the group responsibility for individual loans.

By 1992, BEES was ready to begin its expansion. Starting with Gazipur District, they went to the top governmental official, the district commissioner and received permission to begin operations. They opened a district field office as a regional center and staffed it with a combination of workers from Bogra and new employees from the local area. In addition to microcredit, they replicated their nutrition and agriculture programs at each center. The combination of income from microcredit and the outside funding was enough to spur their growth through 1998.

STABILITY AND SUSTAINABILITY FOR BEES

As BEES was expanding, other NGOs in Bangladesh were also jumping on the microcredit bandwagon. By 2000, BEES had expanded to 18 districts. In 2004, it was in 40 of the 64 districts nationwide. Their Web site identifies their target group for rural development as those who have less than one half acre of land and depend on selling manual labor for their survival (Target Group of BEES, 2005). For health and nutrition programs, they target women between the ages of 15 and 49. Microcredit is available to anyone between the ages of 18 and 45 who does not have access to formal credit institutions. They have also expanded into funding larger projects by providing a bridge between microcredit and regular bank financing. It is interesting to note that the concept of identifying clear target groups has stayed with BEES for over 25 years. This consistency shows how firmly embedded the management by objectives innovation became within the organization's culture.

In addition to microcredit, BEES continues to provide agricultural support, health and nutrition programs, advocacy and urban development programs, and program support, as shown in Table 5.1.

The lapse in international funding for BEES lead to the sixth diffusion of innovation in their history: BEES' expertise, which had previously been concentrated in only one part of Bangladesh, was spread across the rest of the country. Had BEES continued to receive external support, it would have eventually grown, but not nearly as quickly or as widely. By making microcredit funds available in small amounts across a wide geographic area, the Bangladesh government and its external funders created the opportunity for BEES to move its well-trained staff to new locations and expand its outreach to about 600,000 clients, over 100 times what they had served in the early 1980s. Figure 6.3 shows the location of BEES regional and project offices as well as the original CRWRC office in Bogra.

THE LINKS AMONG ENVIRONMENT, STRATEGY, AND STRUCTURE

The story of Bangladesh Extension Education Services and its growth from a faith-based outreach program in a single district funded from North America to an independent NGO with programs throughout the country illustrates vividly how environment, strategy, and structure are linked. When funding was external, the organization could focus on providing services at no charge other than for the inputs provided. The limitation arising from external ownership was that the government limited

Table 6.1.   2006 Program Activities

Category	Projects	Detail
Rural Development Program	Microfinance Program	Microenterprise Development
		Agricultural Diversification and Intensification Project (ADIP)
	Agriculture and Social Forestry	Smallholder Agricultural Improvement Project (SAIP)
	Poultry and Livestock Program	
	Education Program	
Health, Family Planning, Maternal and Child Health (MCH) and Nutrition Program	Community-based Health Project	Maternal and Child Health Family Planning Component
	Nutrition Initiative Program	
	Urban Poor Development Program (UPDP)	
Special Program	Advocacy Program (Social, legal, and financial)	Gender Awareness and Women's Right
		Social Mobilization Program With Vulnerable Groups
		Legal AID Services
		Financial Services for Poorest
		Promotional Activities
		Social Assistance for Tribal Population
		Water and Sanitation
Support Program	Training	
	Information and Development Communication	
	Research, Monitoring, and Evaluation	

the scope of the organization to a single district to prevent competition with other similar foreign aid groups.

The hub and spoke management structure worked well for disseminating agricultural expertise while the management by objectives control system provided a feedback loop that gave a solid sense of what worked and what did not. BEES continued to operate under the one district structure as long as funding was available from outside Bangladesh. When international funding dried up, and with no internal donor base, BEES turned to microcredit to ensure its survival. Microcredit funds were not concentrated in Bogra District, however. They were available in small quantities across multiple districts. With its cadre of trained field workers, BEES grew like a spider plant, sending its tendrils across the country, replicating

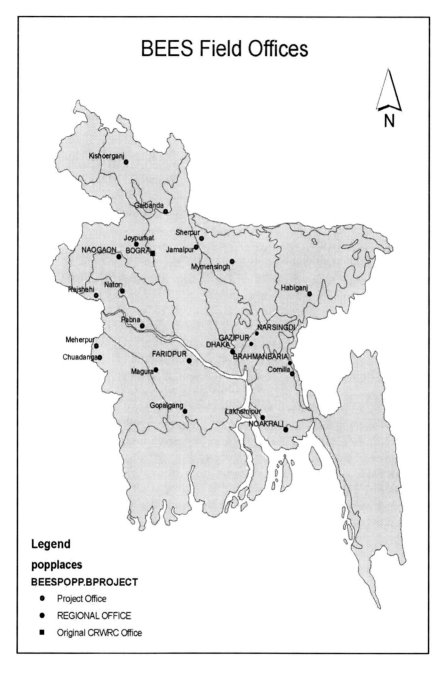

Figure 6.3.   Location of BEES regional and project offices as well as the original CRWRC office in Bogra.

the success it had in Bogra to more than 20 additional districts. The core management team included staff members who had been with the organization over 20 years. The emphasis on measurable results, initiated by DeHaan and VanderMeulen in the late 1970s has not gone away.

The former parent, CRWRC pursued a different strategy, based on development of small church groups in other districts. The relationship is no longer a strong one, although former expatriates who worked in Bogra stay in contact whenever they can and feel more allegiance to BEES than they do to the current CRWRC project.

The six innovations that BEES diffused have served it well over the years, but they may not be enough. As Borden (2003) points out, microcredit lending requires very high interest rates that essentially charge the poor for the services they are provided. Even though nominal rates are in the 15% range, effective interest rates can be over thirty percent. If BEES could afford to lower its nominal interest rate to just 8%, charged up front before the loan was dispersed, the effective interest rate would go down to just eighteen percent (USAID, 1995). If they made such a change, their income from lending would be reduced by 50%. They would have to make larger loans or reduce their overhead substantially to afford such a change. In 2004-2005, BEES received just 37% of its income from microcredit. The previous year, it received over 60% if its income from the same source (Report on BEES, 2006). A small amount of external aid reversed the percentages from 1 year to the next. These data suggest that BEES is still not completely self-sufficient, but dependent on both internal and external funding sources in somewhat unpredictable ways.

Does strategic management have an impact on poverty reduction? The experience of Bangladesh Extension Education Services suggests that it can and does, but not necessarily in ways that we can predict before hand. The strategic management practices ingrained in the top management team at BEES starting in the late 1970s have allowed it to adapt and grow. BEES still does not have a donor base that is local and must rely on a combination of user fees and interest plus international largess to fund its programs. It continues to search for ways to improve the physical well being of their clients and has grown to be the tenth largest NGO in Bangladesh. Their next challenge will be to train and put in place the next generation of leaders who will replace the founders and take them into their fourth decade of success.

NOTE

1.   When Spee returned to the United States, he took classes from Drucker and received his MBA and PhD from the Claremont Graduate University where Drucker was a faculty member from 1971 until his death in 2005.

REFERENCES

Borden, K. (2003, October). Microenterprise lending at the Grameen Bank: Effective lending rates on a sample loan portfolio. Paper presented at the Business & Economics Research Conference, Las Vegas, Nevada.

Drucker, P. F. (1974) *Management: Tasks, responsibilities, practices.* New York: Harper and Row.

Report on BEES. (2006). Retrieved June 29, 2007, from http://www.bees-bd.org/annualreport/Bees%20Report.pdf

Target Group of BEES. (2005). Retrieved June 29, 2007, from http://www.bees-bd.org/terget.html

USAID. (1995). Calculating effective interest rates on microcredit loans. *Microenterprise Development Brief Number, 12.* September. Retrieved April 12, 2007, from http://www.microfinancegateway.org/files/1505_1505.pdf

Part III

**FOR-PROFIT ORGANIZATIONS REDUCING POVERTY—
"DOING WELL AND DOING GOOD"**

CHAPTER 7

REDUCING POVERTY THROUGH SUCCESSFUL BUSINESS

The Role of Social Capital

Peter S Heslam

ABSTRACT

Business holds a vital key to positive social, material, and spiritual transformation in the contemporary world. This situation exists largely because of business's potential to increase social capital (including its relational, moral, institutional, and spiritual elements) as it pursues its commercial objectives. This chapter offers a framework to help business strategists make decisions that will be successful both in terms of profit and in terms of contribution to one of the world's greatest needs for transformation—the need to reduce global poverty. In doing so, the chapter lays out a fresh research agenda focusing on the links between social capital and the core operations of business. These links are crucial to the expertise rich nations have accumulated on how to run businesses that are socially and commercially successful. As such there are primary ways in which Western nations can exercise soft power to meet pressing human needs within today's globalized yet divided world.

Innovative Approaches to Reducing Global Poverty
pp. 131–152

If we learn anything from the history of economic development, it is that culture makes all the difference. (Landes, 1998, p. 513).

The overall achievements of the market are deeply contingent on political and social arrangements. (Sen, 2004, p. 142).

INTRODUCTION

Commercial enterprise faces unprecedented opportunities to be an agent of positive social, material, and spiritual transformation in the contemporary world. This is partly because under the impact of globalization, business is becoming the predominant form of global culture as people all over the world belong to the same community of work. It is also because global business enterprise demonstrates an ability to lift people out of poverty. This is not obvious to many. During 2005, the plight of the world's poor reached the top of the international agenda. This was largely due to the mobilization of a huge conglomeration of nongovernmental organizations (NGOs), campaign groups, trade unions, celebrities, and faith groups under the banner "Make Poverty History." The emphasis was on aid, debt relief, and the reform of global trade rules. While the last of these gave tacit recognition to the importance of commerce, the campaign as a whole largely ignored the potential of business to help in the fight.

Ignoring the role business can play in reducing poverty is a major oversight. Foreign direct investment has become the largest source of funding in the developing world. Whereas annual Official Development Assistance to developing nations remained flat at U.S.$53 billion between 1990 and 2000, net private capital inflows to developing nations nearly quadrupled, from $44 billion to $154 billion over the same period (Institute for International Finance, 2007).

After 50 years and more than a trillion dollars spent on international development, nearly half the world's population live on less than U.S.$2 per day. Part of the reason why commercial enterprise promises greater effectiveness in development outcomes is that it gives people hope for the future and a vision of dignity and well being that can be achieved through their own honest endeavor. Without such a vision, people perish as they resign themselves to a life-sentence of poverty once the aid flows dry up. There is no conceivable way to banish poverty long term, therefore, than through the vigorous growth of enterprise. This has been true for every rich country, and it is true for every poor one now.

Business alone is not enough, of course. To really prosper, a nation requires the social institutions that characterise free societies, such as property rights and the rule of law. It also needs the cultivation of norms and the exercise of virtues beyond the requirements of the law. These norms and virtues are instilled, nurtured, shaped, inspired, and sustained through strong relationships, and through social institutions and networks (including religious ones) that are built on trust. Business thrives in such conditions, as it does so driving poverty and its ugly history toward their final end.

Norms, virtues, relationships, trust, social institutions, and networks—these are all aspects of what social scientists now call "social capital." We cannot, therefore, regard the wealth creation that is needed for poverty alleviation along narrowly economic lines. Indeed, "capital" cannot be restricted to investments, factories, and equipment. Effective poverty reduction will only take place when proper regard is given to other types of capital, such as:

- Human capital (labor, skill, intelligence, knowledge);
- Social capital (social networks, attitudes, trust and norms); and
- Natural capital (natural resources, living systems, the services of the ecosystem).

Even though it has not received adequate attention in scholarly research, the second of these, social capital, is of particular importance for reducing poverty, not least because of the way the global economy is developing within a volatile environment some describe as the clash of civilizations. While skills, knowledge, machinery, and money can be transferred relatively easily across borders, the same is not true for social capital. This has to be carefully built if the trust that is needed for effective wealth creation is to develop and grow.

This chapter will therefore explore the development potential of business' contribution to social capital, which it makes in pursuit of its commercial objectives. Social capital is, however, a broad category. For this reason it is helpful to break it down into some of its key elements, even though these elements interact and overlap with each other:

- relational capital;
- institutional capital;
- moral capital; and
- spiritual capital.

In discussing these types of capital, the aim will be to offer a framework that will help entrepreneurs, company directors and business strategists make decisions that will be successful both in terms of profit and in terms of reducing poverty. The focus will be on core business activities, rather than on corporate social responsibility (CSR) projects. This is partly because there has been disproportionably little informed debate about what the opportunities, rather than responsibilities, of companies are in addressing the scourge of poverty. Often it is assumed—if business is thought to have any positive role to play—that its contribution to development is restricted to CSR or corporate philanthropy. However, expenditure on CSR projects by the largest companies is only around $13.5 billion per annum in the United States and $1.5 billion in the United Kingdom. While these are sizeable sums, they almost pale into insignificance compared to the turnover of these companies. The resulting irony is that the positive impact business could have on poverty through its core activities, which is generally much greater than that through its CSR initiatives, is overlooked.

This accounts in part for the fact that, while much has been written about the ill-effects of large companies operating in low-income countries, remarkably little research has been carried out into how effective multinational companies (MNCs) are in helping to reduce poverty. And while a significant body of literature now exists about the relationship between social capital and individuals, countries and communities, very little work has been done on the links between social capital and business (Jones, Pollitt, & Bek, 2007). This is a serious imbalance and threatens to undermine the usefulness of the concept, given the seismic changes business and society have been undergoing in recent years. It also represents a serious blind spot in the search for enterprise solutions to poverty, in view of the contribution social capital can make to improvements in health and education, lowering crime levels, more active citizenship and greater social cohesion.

Against this background, this chapter seeks to sketch out the contours of a fresh research agenda. Much development research focuses on definitions and causes of *poverty*. It is questionable, however, how useful this knowledge is compared to the question "what causes *wealth*?" In a forthcoming book to be published by the Acton Institute, I argue that it was mainly Pope John Paul II's willingness to ask this question that makes his encyclical *Centesimus Annus* of 1991 distinctive in Catholic social teaching. If nearly half the world's population live on less than $2 dollars per day, the crucial question this statistic should raise, but hardly ever does, is "what happened to the other half?" Seeking to answer this question implies a solutions orientated approach. The generation of material wealth is, after all, the solution to material poverty. This is why, contrary to popular perception, wealth creation is generally a greater preoccupation of the poor than of the rich.

The concern of this chapter is primarily with MNCs. This emphasis does not seek to overlook the fact that in developing countries small to medium sized enterprises (SMEs) often account for 90% of gross domestic product. However, MNCs are the key agents of globalization, responsible for the vast majority of international trade. Their operations and investments in developing countries have helped millions of people to escape from poverty and their actions can greatly influence SMEs and all other parts of host countries.

WHAT IS CAPITAL?

There is an ancient parable, thought to have originated in China: Three blind men are asked to describe an elephant. One man, grasping the trunk, says, "An elephant is like a large snake." Another, holding the trail, claims the elephant is more like a rope. The third man, his arms wrapped around the leg, observes, "An elephant is like a tree." Trying to define social capital can often seem as confusing as the blind men's dilemma, which is why it is helpful to break the concept down into more manageable parts. Social capital is generally taken to mean the way groups of people contribute to the well-being of the societies in which they live. This, however, pays insufficient attention to the second half of the term – "capital." This word must be properly understood by anyone wanting to investigate the role of the capitalist economy in resolving global poverty.

A good way to unpack the meaning of "capital" is to contrast it with "money," with which it is often confused. Fundamentally, capital is not about money but about know-how. Whereas money is static, know-how is dynamic, productive, social, and spiritual. This is because it is geared towards meeting human needs and desires. Money can only become capital if it placed in a social context where it is exposed to the risk, initiative and creativity that generate returns. That is why money is never a sustainable solution to poverty, as reflected in the case of Saudi Arabia, which may have sufficient money but has insufficient capital.

Capital has the transformative power to generate wealth out of virtually nothing. That power is given to it though human relationships. Understanding capital as money leads to an inert and materialistic view of the market, which inevitably leads to inert and materialistic solutions. Such solutions are ineffective because they fail to acknowledge what it means to be fully human. Charities and voluntary associations (including religious ones) often understand development in these terms, showing a propensity to view the market is an inanimate machine fuelled by "profit" and to prioritize overseas aid above overseas investment. For a discussion on Christian attitudes toward business and globalization, see Heslam (2007) and Heslam (2004) respectively.

An economy based on capital, rather than money, is an economy bursting with the opportunity that comes when people trade with each other in pursuit of their vision of human flourishing (Blank & McGurn, 2004, p. 72). This involves habits, outlooks, attitudes, aspirations and relationships. It is, therefore, inseparable from all that makes up social capital, including its spiritual components.

This understanding of capital appears to find support in the work of the Peruvian economist Hernando de Soto. He points out that, in developing countries, assets generally serve immediate physical uses: houses for shelter, land for farming, and so forth. In developed countries, by contrast, such assets also lead a parallel life as "capital outside the physical world." They can, for instance, be used to facilitate more production by serving as collateral for a loan (De Soto, 2000, p. 39). The poor do not lack assets, De Soto contends, but they are only able to use them, however modest, in a material sense and they are only able to sell them in their immediate vicinity.

Hopefully, the implication of this understanding of capital is clear as to the meaning of institutional, relational, moral and spiritual capital; they denote the economic value of institutions, relationships, morality and spirituality. Whereas a married man and woman have a relationship, relational capital is about the value their marriage has to the economy. A woman's spirituality may mean she loves her neighbor and has a sense of purpose in life. But it becomes spiritual capital when these things inspire her to run her business in such a way that she can be of greatest service to her customers and colleagues. A tribal society may have a particular culture, but if that culture plays a role in increasing the tribe's general level of material prosperity, it is functioning, at least in part, as social capital. Some may wish to dismiss all this as an attempt to impose a "hard" utilitarian economic framework on "soft" human and spiritual realities. But to do so would be to overlook the fact that such realities have multiple implications, including economic ones. Using the term "capital" as a suffix is merely a means of referring to these economic implications. No reduction is implied—institutions, relationships, morals and spirituality all have intrinsic value, entirely independent of their economic value. But in considering enterprise solutions to poverty their economic value is of critical importance, as we shall see.

RELATIONAL CAPITAL

Previously considered a marginal issue, relationships have come to be regarded as a key component of business success, due to their impact on morale, motivation, and productivity. Although their economic value defies precise measurement, staff retention and career development provide a rudimentary indication of a company's relational health. Research carried out by Tomorrow's Company, a leading U.K. business think tank, has revealed that many companies regard relational measures as predictive of business performance. The report concluded, however, that "more work is needed to find robust measures for the full range of key relationships" (Tomorrow's Company, 1995, p. 11). More recently, the Cambridge think tank The Relationships Foundation has devised a "relational health audit" as a measurement and management tool (www.relationshipsfoundation.org).

Many of the most admired companies drawn up by *Fortune* magazine calibrate these kinds of measurements. (See, for example, www.money.cnn.com/magazines/fortune/mostadmired.) The best companies to work for, it seems, are those that provide a supportive environment in which good communication is encouraged and ingenuity rewarded, overseen by managers who are both visible and accessible. Some companies go as far as to measure progress on their "people" targets on a quarterly basis, the targets including qualitative performance measures such as innovation, mutual trust, respect, teamwork, and respect for diversity

The impact of relationships on business success is sufficient to indicate their importance to the role of business in development. But there are some more specific reasons for this importance, including the following.

Competitive Advantage

Most leading MNCs with significant operations in developing countries are in fierce competition with each other. Naturally the focus in maintaining competitive advantage tends to be on the quality and pricing of products and services. But the network of relationships a company develops with employees, customers, suppliers and local communities is crucial to developing strategic competitive advantage. This is largely for two reasons. First, as markets are flooded with products and services that are very similar, it becomes increasingly difficult for clients and customers to differentiate between them. It is often, therefore, the quality of relationships that becomes the unique selling point that commends a particular brand over against its competitors. Gauging this quality vis-à-vis the way a company treats those at the beginning of the supply chain, who are often producers in developing countries, has been significantly enabled through recent advances in communication and information technology. Second, a company's "relational architecture" is complex, built over time and is unique to the particular circumstances of the company and its operational context. It is thereby impossible to patent or replicate, meaning the incentive to excel in this area, in an effort to secure competitive edge, is kept at a premium.

One company that has self-consciously championed this area is Starbucks. It has been persistent in seeking to develop good relationships with its key constituencies, including producers (Gulati, Huffman, & Neilson, 2002, pp. 3-6). Stimulated in part by Starbucks' success, "relationships management" has risen to a place of importance in executive training, the key emphasis in which is developing trust. A recent study by McKinsey of 231 global companies identified three management practices as essential for business performance, all of which have important relational implications: clear roles, an inspiring vision, and an open and trusting culture (Leslie, Loch, & Schaninger, 2006).

Market Culture

Relationships of trust lie at the heart of cultures that can support flourishing markets. This is partly because of the rapid pace of change involved. National cultures resistant to change almost always reveal weak relationships and low levels of trust. The same is true of business culture, in which maintaining the pace of change is crucial to success. The challenge, therefore, is to understand better how corporations that are relationally and commercially successful can impact the culture of host countries in ways that help build levels of trust. This investigation is bound to challenge the way markets are assessed using the Marxist "labor verses capital" construct. The primary relationships in market economies, as the economy of Hong Kong exemplifies, are not those between capital and labor but between a mass of social networks that capital both creates and depends on. Indeed, markets are best regarded in terms of the relational networks between and among people rather than the goods and services transacted. It is partly for this reason that, for the poor, the real danger is rarely markets but frequently the absence of them. Although the market economy is often blamed for the rise of individualism, it actually presumes networks of human relationships.

Peace Building

Conflict, warfare, violence, and terrorism represent the most extreme form of relational breakdown. The causes of conflict are generally complex and as yet it is unclear what direct role poverty plays. There is no doubt, however, that violent conflict thwarts economic growth. Indeed, such conflict represents the greatest deterrent for MNCs deciding to begin or expand operations in a particular country. It is, therefore, another Marxist fallacy that capitalism inevitably leads to war. As the market is based on relationships, it relies on peace to survive. In the 1990s the *New Times* columnist Thomas Friedman captured the link between peace and business in his well-known "Golden Arches Theory" of conflict prevention, according to which, no two countries with at least one McDonalds restaurant have ever gone to war with each other. While this observation oversimplifies the role of business in peace building, and may indeed no longer be true, the contribution of commercial enterprise to peace and security has to be part of any investigation into the role of enterprise in alleviating poverty.

Endorsement of this suggestion appears to come from Pope John Paul II, who established a clear link not only between poverty and violence but also between development and peace:

> At the root of war there are usually real and serious grievances [such as] ... poverty.... For this reason, another name for peace is development. Just as there is a collective responsibility for avoiding war, so too there is a collective responsibility for promoting development.... This is the culture which is hoped for, one which fosters trust in the human potential of the poor, and consequently in their ability to improve their condition through work or to make a positive contribution to economic prosperity.... Creating such conditions calls for a concerted worldwide effort to promote development. (John Paul II, 1991)

The Pope is clear—to promote peace is to promote development. A similar vision helped inspire the best impulses of the seventeenth century Dutch seaborne empire. Indeed, *Commercium et Pax*, commerce and peace, was the proud motto of seventeenth century Amsterdam, reflected in the vast number of foreign shipping vessels that graced its harbor. When people are at peace, they trade; when they trade, they promote peace. Trade forges the strong relationships it demands, converting them into the relational capital that builds and sustains prosperity.

MORAL CAPITAL

As the world becomes more prosperous, and more closely connected, the alleviation of poverty is becoming an increasingly important issue in global moral discourse. Business is an active partner in this dialogue. Indeed, the moral dimensions of operating in developing countries are attracting growing attention amongst MNCs. This is good news, for the private path to prosperity can only be sustained if the thinking and actions of business are infused with norms, values and virtue. A commercially successful company so infused is a company that is high in moral capital and has the potential to disseminate that capital within the communities in which it operates, while strengthening the moral capital that already resides there. Some participants in the discourse argue, however, that the market is the least likely instrument to be an effective carrier of virtue. It appeals, they say, to some of the lowest human motives—greed, the quest for profit, and the service of self—all of which dissolve the moral fabric of society. It is, therefore, the duty of the state to impose ethical behavior on business, by means of regulation.

The state does indeed have a regulatory role. It must try to prevent certain markets emerging (such as those in dangerous drugs, prostitution and slavery), and to keep business away from those areas of human life in which is has neither legitimate role nor competence. Regulation is necessary for human beings to be able to exercise freedom, including the freedom the market brings. There are good reasons, however, why regulation is unable to secure an ethical market economy and why it *is* possible to look to business as a valid agent of the moral capital required to achieve and sustain prosperity, some of which are summarized here.

Profit is Moral

The quest for profit, rather than disqualifying business from moral agency, is its first and foremost moral obligation—business' role is to generate wealth, on which the whole of society turns. Indeed, it is only if this obligation is fulfilled that business can make any further contribution to moral capital, or to any other kind of capital. Whereas many virtues are recognized as such because the source of their authority is clearly based in moral or religious tradition, the specific virtues necessary for good business success are no less moral because they have to do with satisfying customers, promoting innovation and generating new wealth, all with an eye to turning a profit. While profit is not an end in itself, it is a vitally important means of serving what *is* the end of all economic activity, which is the human person. It can therefore act as a valid measure of how well this end has been served. Profit is neither immoral nor amoral. Because it is gained through human relationships, results from certain choices, serves as a measure of stewardship, and has the potential to service human needs, it is intensely moral.

Enterprise Encourages Ethics

The free market cannot be blamed for the moral evils with which it is often associated, such as rampant consumerism, environmental destruction, and marital infidelity. Such things merely reflect the fact that market freedom, like any other freedom, gives people opportunities both for virtue and for vice. As Lord Acton famously argued, "liberty is not the power of doing what we like, but the right of being able to do what we ought." This is why not all young people exposed to tobacco advertising start smoking, or why, though the entertainment industry may constantly expose them to the glamour of sexual promiscuity, some decide on one partner for life.

Freedom, the very destiny of humanity, contains an inbuilt moral challenge. So too, by extension, does the free market. Business faces this challenge on a daily basis, and needs to be inspired, incentivized and resourced in order to meet it. Substituting this for legal coercion is misguided not because it imposes too much on business, but too little. It also assumes that business cannot be a moral agent without such coercion. But companies can and do provide a fertile context for people to acquire and convey moral competence. Such competence is more important than the law as a source of justice, reflected in the fact that businesses frequently will not do things which are legal but are not moral, even when this may not appear to serve their best financial interests.

The moral role of business is revealed in particular, however, in the relationship between economic growth and moral development. Benjamin Friedman has recently provided a rigorous analysis of this relationship. A growing economy, he argues, has the potential to improve the environment, reduce poverty, and promote democracy, openness and tolerance (Friedman, 2005). The extent to which he considers this impact to be inevitable is, however, unclear. If the social capital framework for analyzing enterprise solutions to poverty proposed in this chapter is sound, economic growth can certainly be expected to foster growth in moral capital, but this is most likely to happen if there is a corresponding growth in relational, spiritual and institutional capital. Much more detailed research is needed in this area. In the meantime, Friedman's core thesis is plausible and indeed has precedents in the work of the Nobel Prize-winning economist Simon Kuznets. It may even find support in the writings of Pope John Paul II, who wrote: "The advancement of the poor constitutes a great opportunity for the moral, cultural and even economic growth of all humanity (John Paul II, 1991)." This perspective represents not only a departure from the zero-sum economics that typifies ecclesiastic perspectives on economics but also a recognition that economic and moral growth go together. This is borne out later in the same encyclical, where John Paul II makes clear that he sees "the training of competent business leaders who are conscious of their responsibilities" as a way in which rich countries can help poor ones (John Paul II, 1991).

Trust is Paramount

Trust, as noted above, is a quality of relationship. It is also, however, a moral virtue and one that is of particular importance to the ways in which business can contribute to the moral capital required for economic development. Indeed, this virtue helps explain why so many countries have failed to develop a full market economy. If trust is limited or confined to familial or tribal relationships, trading opportunities are lost and the need for state regulation increases, thus raising transaction costs. High levels of trust, on the other hand, such as is exist in the United States, Sweden, and Japan, encourage strong private sectors in which large companies are able to grow. Such companies are often wary about doing business in low trust societies, due to the associated risks and costs of doing business. The consequences for economic development are serious, given the important role played by large companies in tackling poverty, noted above.

This is why it is so important to gain a better understanding of the role of business in promoting trust, as was noted in the previous section. Communication methods must be central to this investigation, given that recent research indicates that the top performing companies are those that are most effective in communicating the company's moral values and guiding principles (Leslie et al., 2006). It is also important to explore how a company can ensure its operations reinforce whatever indigenous networks of trust there are that extend beyond familial and tribal loyalties. What mechanisms can be put in place to ensure that infringements of ethical behavior are met with the social disapproval and peer pressure that come from within the host community, rather than relying on legal pressure imposed from outside? Addressing such questions will help business live up to its potential as a purveyor of moral virtue through its core operations. The analysis has to shift, however, from the constraints ethical behavior imposes to the market opportunities it creates. Where the opportunities are limited, due perhaps to pressure from shareholders or competitors, the possibilities companies have to cut the costs of ethical behavior need to be explored.

INSTITUTIONAL CAPITAL

When a company, of whatever size, contemplates the possibility of beginning operations in a particular low-income country, it looks not only at the relational and moral context but also for certain institutional features such as private property, the rule of law and a limited state. Without them, firms lack the assurance they need that their property rights will be upheld, the honoring of contracts can be enforced and that their freedom to operate will not be unduly hampered through either poor or excessive regulation.

This fact alone holds out the promise that the expansion of the global market into developing countries will drive the development of institutional capital, which in turn will encourage further commercial investment, spurring further growth—a "virtuous circle" of ever increasing institutional development and economic prosperity. The problem, however, is how to get this circle turning. For without at least some institutional capital, the only kind of economy that can survive is the informal economy, in which cheating, broken promises and criminal behavior is rife and in which a rich élite profits at the expense of the poor.

Opinions are divided, however, as to whether economic growth leads to institutional growth, or visa versa. There is no space here to engage with this debate but the evidence does seem to suggest that making investment conditional on too many institutional reforms may not help economic development. It appears, in fact, that significant institutional improvements tend to occur when society grows richer, partly because institutional development becomes more attractive to people whose income is rising and that such development is less likely to be reversed once a country has passed a level of economic development amounting to around $6,000 per capita gross domestic product (Przeworski & Limongi, 2000). This emphasis on the importance of economic growth does suggest that economic growth is *sufficient* to create the institutional conditions favorable to growth, only that it appears to be *necessary*. Over the long-term, economic and institutional growth are nearly always codevelopments.

This relationship calls attention to the fact that other sectors of society, besides business, have a role to play in institutional development. Indeed, it is often when business works in partnership with government and civil society that each side of the partnership find it can maximize leverage. And leverage is all important, as the people who are in the best position to tackle corruption and other failures of governance are generally the very people who benefit from it the most. Efforts to stimulate institutional development therefore have to strive toward conditions in which public and private agents consider it to be in their own interests to shun bad governance. These conditions will almost certainly include an independent judiciary that protects human rights and property rights, enforces contracts, upholds order and acts as a check on the power of the state; an effective and impartial police and prison system; a range of financial and regulatory systems such as central banks, land registries and bodies to administer ports and customs posts; a free press and media industry that can hold the government to account and expose corruption and inefficiency; and a reduction in red tape, which hampers business development and increases opportunity for corruption.

Again, not all these conditions have to be perfect before growth can occur. Uganda is an example of what is possible when institutional and economic development begin to reinforce each other. Since the early 1990s, that country's investment and governance conditions have grown considerably, enabling economic growth in excess of 4% per annum over the last decade. This growth has allowed the proportion of people living in poverty to drop from 56% at the start of the 1990s to 35% in 2000 (Department of International Development, 2006).

Such results are encouraging. But while it is well established that institutional development facilitates economic development, much more research is needed into how business can stimulate institutional development. The fact that Transparency International's corruption scale indicates that the freer and more open the market, the less corruption there is, should serve as a spur to this research (www.transparency.org).

The following areas need to be included in investigations of how business can stimulate institutional development.

Corporate Culture

Through its corporate culture, an MNC can significantly impact the way business is done more broadly in a country because of its capacity to act as a catalyst for the emergence and growth of indigenous businesses. Particularly where there are inadequate laws to govern the actions of foreign companies, MNCs are increasingly adopting voluntary codes and standards of practice that guide their behavior and hold them accountable to shareholders, customers and civil society groups. When a company drives up standards of accountability in this way, these standards function as standard-bearers for other companies and represent an alternative to the traditional regulatory approach. Although anticorporate critics often dismiss such a process as merely a means by which corporations seek to avoid binding regulation, it is better understood as a response to the dysfunctional regulatory frameworks that typify many developing economies.

Business Associations

Business networks and associations such as chambers of commerce are often very effective in encouraging their members to develop standards of corporate governance to protect shareholders and other constituencies. Examples include Responsible Care in the chemical industry and the

Global Mining Initiative. The partnerships and research efforts that have flowed from these initiatives continue through the International Council on Mining and Metals, the World Business Council for Sustainable Development, and other industry associations that share experience in promoting local growth through agreed principles and standards. Such associations are a means by which a MNC can collaborate with its competitors to tackle governance challenges that it could not address on its own. Some MNCs are also developing a type of association known as a business "ecosystem." These are designed to enhance the governance capacities of local SMEs. Whereas many of the relevant governance principles can be disseminated through normal market interactions, some forward looking MNCs are pioneering business ecosystems as a way of being more actively involved, mentoring indigenous entrepreneurs, organizing enterprise incubators, carrying out relevant research, and offering policy advice.

Improvements in Finance

Financial and professional service firms can play a particularly important role in building institutional capital. Firms such as KPMG, PricewaterhouseCoopers, McKinsey, Citigroup, and Morgan Stanley are well placed to support governments in their efforts to modernize financial institutions and improve the effectiveness and efficiency of regulatory and governance frameworks. In certain circumstances, they can also help train government officials, build the capacity of government bodies and help restructure financial and economic institutions. Of particular importance is improving electronic payment methods, which allow greater security and transparency.

Public-Private Partnerships

Public-private partnerships can be strategic in implementing development objectives. This possibility is reflected both in the United Nation's Global Compact and in the International Finance Corporation's Equator Principles, which are voluntary codes of responsible behavior drawn up, supported and "owned" by both public and private spheres. Export credit agencies are also effective in this area. These are bodies backed by the governments of rich countries that provide loans, guarantees, credits, and insurance to private companies that invest or engage in trade with developing countries and comply with anticorruption measures. Another initiative worthy of special mention is the Extractive Industries Transparency Initiative (EITI), which is being implemented in a number of African countries. Under the scheme, oil, gas, and mining companies publicly disclose all payments they make to governments. Governments, in turn, publish what they receive from these companies. Individual citizens and civil society groups can then scrutinize these reports. The initiative has been endorsed by the World Bank and is currently supported by a growing number of leading MNCs.

SPIRITUAL CAPITAL

Capitalism is often considered good for the bottom line but spiritually empty. Capitalism is not, however, solely about things but also about the human spirit. That is why it is appropriate to speak about spiritual capital, which is primarily about meaning and purpose. As such it is aligned to, and dependent on, a broad definition of wealth that encompasses the enrichment not only of the body and mind but also of the spirit—a notion of wealth that inspires people to give of their best in creating it because it is about ultimate concerns. There are all sorts of factors that contribute to the vehement reactions to capitalism that have been seen in recent years on the streets of London, Seattle, Davos, and Genoa, and to the hatred that fuels anticapitalist and anti-Western terrorism. But one significant factor is a narrow and prohibitive understanding of wealth that Westerners are often apt to convey. The strength of the reaction against this phenomenon highlights the importance of spiritual capital in today's globalized economy.

Spiritual capital is concerned with what human life is all about and how it can be improved. In business it is generally expressed in the overall aim of a company, its vision, ethos, values and how business objectives are worked out in relation to broader and deeper goals to which most humans aspire. It is about what some companies and business writers refer to as the "spirit," or even, "soul" of a company (Batstone, 2003; Pollard, 1996; Ressler & Mitchell Ressler, 2007). Giving serious attention to this matter is now seen as important to the recruitment and retention of a motivated and high performance workforce. It reflects the fact that more and more people seek meaning and purpose in their lives through their work. Going to work merely to perform a function is increasingly understood to lack a sense of wholeness, or integrity, the likely result being alienation from the work itself and low motivation. If people's work is to be an opportunity for personal learning and growth, they must be allowed to express their vision for meaning in life in and through their work.

Many businesses have sought to meet this need by hiring holistic consultants who offer classes, seminars, and workshops on topics such as yoga, meditation, emotional intelligence, improving communications,

and balancing work and home life. Increasing CSR, commitments to philanthropic activities and volunteering programmes also partly reflect this
response. The aim has been to reach and develop employees at a deeper
level, to engage more of workers' total selves in an effort to develop staff
that are more satisfied, productive, and innovative.

Whatever methods are used, increasing the spiritual capital of a company invariably helps the other types of capital covered in this chapter to
develop and grow. Relational capital grows when, for instance, workers
are helped to utilize spiritual capacities such as gratitude, or those that
are generally regarded as "feminine," such as nurture, cooperation and
intuition. Likewise, when companies seek to develop a sense of higher
purpose and become more intensely and consciously values-based, the
contributions of the company in building moral and institutional capital
are likely to improve.

Much work still needs to be done in this area. Indeed, the study of well-
being or "happiness," to which spiritual capital closely relates, is a science
in its infancy (Layard, 2005). The particular challenge, again, is one of
measurement, although many components of well-being are relatively
easy to quantify, such as caloric intake, child labor, education, access to
safe water and life expectancy. There is good evidence that where market
reforms have been implemented, levels in all these indices have risen
(Goklany, 2002).

Further research is also needed into the nature of "spiritual intelligence," that aspect of human intelligence that some have associated, since
the work of Victor Frankl, with the "God-spot" area of the brain. It is often
referred to as SQ, to correlate with IQ, the Intelligence Quotient, and EQ,
"Emotional Intelligence" (Goleman, 1995). Although further scientific
analysis is needed to bring greater rigour and clarity to this area, the findings of neurology, neuroscience, and psychology may be particularly
important. The emerging discipline of neuro economics also promises
insights that could be helpful to the role of business in spiritual development.

This is not, therefore, a field of investigation in which theology or religious studies has a monopoly of insight. Indeed, the way the word spiritual is understood in this chapter has no necessary connection with
organized religion. A person can be high in SQ, for instance, but have no
religious faith. And a person may be very religious but have very little SQ.
SQ is about the innate capacity of the brain that gives us the basic ability
to form meanings, values, and beliefs in the first place. SQ is therefore
precultural, and more primary than religion. It may possibly be construed
as a form of intelligence that allows humans to imagine situations and
possibilities that do not yet exist—to recontextualize problems and situa-

tions, to see them from a wider point of view and thus to draw on the best of their impulses and motivations.

There is, therefore, an intimate connection between spirituality and business, which if severed can have damaging consequences. Spirituality is the root of humanity's moral convictions and of its aspirations for the personal and common good. It is partly for this reason that business is a powerful transformative force in human society. Infused with spiritual values about purpose and meaning—along with moral values about right and wrong—business is a major force in the development of peoples and cultures.

It is true, of course, that the spirituality of most human beings takes religious form and preliminary research into religious capital has started (see, for example, Furbey, 2006, and Baker & Skinner, 2006.) Religious teaching, inspiration, motivation and support can play a very significant role in the contribution individual business people can make to a company's spiritual capital. Although it is perfectly valid for some specialized businesses, such as religious publishing companies, to seek to build religious capital, in most cases it is inappropriate for business to assume this role. This is not to suggest that faith and business occupy separate realms—the sacred-secular divide is an Enlightenment mirage that is fast fading from the intellectual landscape. Moreover, data from the World Values Survey suggests that religion correlates closely with high rates of economic growth and this is likely to be due to the positive role of religion in the generation of social capital (Putnam, 2000).

This relationship has been explored by several social scientists, who have recently pointed out that it is particularly religion in its less hierarchical form (such as in Protestant Christianity) that positively affects economic performance (Treisman, 2000, and Lipset & Lenz, 2000, pp. 120-122). According to the Index of Economic Freedom produced by the Heritage Foundation, the higher the percentage of Protestants, the greater the degree of economic freedom (www.heritage.org/index). These findings confirm, in part, the work of Max Weber a century ago.

But a business is in the first instance a business, whatever religious affiliations its workers have, just as a religious organization is a religious organization, whatever business affiliations its members have. In other words, social institutions enjoy a certain level of autonomy and competence within their own sphere which is not transferable to other spheres.

The crucial area of enquiry is how MNCs can not only increase their own spiritual capital but actively contribute to its development in low income countries. Central to this issue is the question of how MNCs can help develop indigenous workers who have not only the knowledge and skills that are necessary for wealth creation but also the norms, dispositions, beliefs, sensibilities, temperament and sense of purpose that are required. One of the key challenges to overcome is an attitude of dependence and the accompanying erosion of confidence, dignity, and determination. Largely the unintended consequence of development aid, this attitude has diminished many people's ability to make effective use of their own capacities and to be prepared to take initiative and risk. MNCs have a unique opportunity to influence the prevailing mindset to become supportive of hard work, ingenuity, initiative, creativity and innovation, and help create a conductive environment for these attributes to emerge. Low levels of motivation and accountability have allowed a culture that admires "effortless" success to emerge. This attitude has to be overcome, as the greatest potential for economic development lies within a country's own people and is grounded in their sense of purpose and their aspirations for well-being. Successful commerce with high levels of spiritual capital can be effective in unlocking these powerful drivers of positive change. For the spiritual capital of business finds expression in the creative dynamism that propels it forward. Implicit in this dynamism is a commitment to make things better. If a religious assumption needs to be behind this dynamism, it is that the creator did not make the world finished but *to be* finished. In this view, human beings are made in God's image and are drawn into God's creative work as cocreators. This task, which involves the building of spiritual capital, is common to all people, not just religious believers. Once again, Pope John Paul II appears to endorse this view:

> Solving serious national and international problems is not just a matter of economic production or of juridical or social organization, but also calls for specific ethical and religious values, as well as changes of mentality, behaviour and structures. The Church feels a particular responsibility to offer this contribution and … there is a reasonable hope that the many people who profess no religion will also contribute to providing the social question with the necessary ethical foundation.… I am convinced that the various religions, now and in the future, will have a preeminent role in preserving peace and in building a society worthy of humanity. Indeed, openness to dialogue and to cooperation is required of all people of good will. (John Paul, 1991)

CONCLUSION

International business is crucial to the exercise of soft power by Western nations in the world today. In contrast to the hard power of military might, soft power is about the positive attractiveness of Western society, particularly in terms of its relational, moral, institutional, and spiritual components. The social capital of developing countries is built up when

MNCs inspire and lead in these areas. It is partly due to insufficient regard for soft power that Western countries have sometimes relied too heavily on military solutions in furthering the cause of freedom, democracy, peace, and security around the world. Much of the social capital these countries enjoy has been built through economic activity—the United States in particular is a country built on commerce—and in turn it has stimulated economic growth that has brought prosperity on an unprecedented scale to many people. In the process, rich nations have accumulated vast amounts of knowledge and experience about how the conditions that are necessary for economic growth can be created, and about how to run businesses that are successful in both ethical and commercial terms.

Globalization holds the promise that this body of expertise can be disseminated to those areas of the world where it is needed most. MNCs are the primary means through which this can be achieved, though businesses of all sizes have a role. Together they are the key agents of soft power. Business leaders need therefore to ignore the condescending attitudes society often expresses toward them. These are reflected, for instance, in the fact that, in many countries a career in the military enjoys immense prestige, while business is barely recognized as a profession. These attitudes are ironic in a global situation in which commercial power has overtaken military power as the chief means of social transformation. Business is the institution to which the world is becoming increasingly committed. It is the social form distinctive of an increasing amount of cooperative activity outside the family, government, and personal friendships. While nation-states have been on the defensive and voluntary associations, political parties, and trade unions have been in decline, business has been gaining in strength. Its potential to act on the world stage not only as an ambassador but as an agent of social good has never been greater.

This chapter has been written out of a desire to see that potential realized. Given the size of the challenge, however, it has sought to do little more than call attention to some of the key research fields and questions that will need to be addressed. The hope is that, in doing so, it will stimulate not only those who conduct academic research but also those who are business strategists and leaders to think creatively about the role of business in today's world. While the development case for business has been the main theme, the business case for development has been a subtheme and one that is of no less importance in the search for effective enterprise solutions to poverty. Attempts to improve living standards and quality of life issues without the involvement of the private sector are bound to fail, just as attempts to grow successful business without concern for living standards and quality of life will be disappointing in the long run. In this sense, although the relational, moral, institutional, and spiritual aspects of business may be referred to collectively as soft power, they are no longer the soft issues they have generally been thought to be. In a fragile and divided world they are becoming the hard issues, essential not only for reducing poverty but also for successful business enterprise.

ACKNOWLEDGMENT

The author wishes to thank Simon Deakin, Ian Jones, Michael Pollitt and William Yu of Cambridge University 's Centre for Business Research, Judge Business School, for their helpful discussions in this area.

REFERENCES

Baker, C., & Skinner, H. (2006). *Faith in action: The dynamic connection between spiritual and religious capital*. Manchester, United Kingdom: William Temple Foundation.

Batstone, D. (2003). *The soul of a company*. San Francisco: Jossey-Bass.

Blank, R. M., & McGurn, W. (2004). *Is the market moral?: A dialogue on religion, economics and justice*. Washington, DC: Brookings Institution Press.

De Soto, H. (2000). *The mystery of capital: Why capitalism triumphs in the west but fails everywhere else*. New York: Basic Books.

Department for International Development. (2006). *Eliminating world poverty: Making governance work for the poor*. London: Stationary Office.

Friedman, B. M. (2005). *The moral consequences of economic growth*. New York: Knopf.

Furbey, R. (2006). *Faith as social capital: Connecting or dividing?* Bristol, United Kingdom: Policy Press/Joseph Rowntree Foundation.

Goklany, I.M. (2002). *The globalization of human well-being* (Cato Policy Analysis 447). Washington: Cato Institute.

Goleman, D. (1995). *Emotional intelligence*. New York: Bantam.

Gulati, R., Huffman, S., & Neilson, G. (2002). *The Barista principle: Starbucks and the rise of relational capital*. New York: Booz Allen Hamilton.

Heslam, P. S. (Ed.). (2004). *Globalization and the good*. Grand Rapids, MI: Eerdmans.

Heslam, P. S. (2007). Purposeful wealth creation: Eradicating poverty through enterprise. In J. Atherton & H. Skinner (Eds.), *Through the eye of a needle: Theological conversations over political economy* (pp. 121-136). Peterborough, United Kingdom: Epworth.

The Institute of International Finance. (2007). *Capital flows to emerging market economies*. Retrieved June 28, 2007 from http://www.iif.com/download.php?id= IlAmw15v7Jk=

John Paul II. (1991). Centesimus Annus. Available: www.vatican.va/phome_en.htm

Jones, I. W., Pollitt, M. G. & Bek, D. (2007). Multinationals in their communities: A social capital approach to corporate citizenship projects, Basingstoke, UK: Palgrave Macmillan.

Landes, D. (1998). *The wealth and poverty of nations*. London: Little, Brown.

Layard, R. 2005. *Happiness: Lessons from a new science*. London: Penguin.

Leslie, K., Loch, M. A., & Schaninger, W. (2006). Managing your organization by the evidence. *The McKinsey Quarterly*, 3.

Lipset, S., & Lenz, G. (2000). Corruption, culture and markets. In L. Harrison & S. Huntingdon (Eds), *Culture matters: How values shape human progress* (pp. 112-124). New York: Basic Books.

Pollard, W. (1996). *The soul of the firm*. New York: HarperCollins.

Przeworski, A., & Limongi, F. (2000). *Democracy and development: Political institutions and material well-being in the world, 1950-1990*. Cambridge, United Kingdom: Cambridge University Press.

Putnam, R. (2000). *Bowling alone: The collapse and revival of American community*. New York: Simon & Schuster.

Ressler, P., & Mitchell Ressler, M. (2007). *Spiritual capitalism*. New York: Chilmark Books.

Sen, A. (2004). *Development as freedom*. Oxford, Enland: Oxford University Press.

Tomorrow's Company. (1995). *The role of business in a changing world*. London: RSA.

Treisman, D. (2000). The causes of corruption: A cross-national study. *Journal of Public Economics, 76*, 399-457.

CHAPTER 8

CREATING MARKET SIZE

Regional Strategies for Use in the Least Developed Areas of the World

Scott A. Hipsher

ABSTRACT

Considerable research has focused on macroeconomic policies and the role of the not-for-profit sector in poverty reduction, However, at the micro-level, little attention has been paid to assisting the private sector in discovering innovative approaches that can provide employment opportunities and efficiently produced products and services for individuals living in "the bottom of the pyramid" markets. A three-tiered regional framework is proposed that international for-profit organizations can use to increase the market size of some of the least developed areas of the world in ways that will help the organizations reduce global poverty. The framework involves using a regional approach at the strategic level, a national/local approach at the tactical level, and a global approach at the operational level to create win-win scenarios that help reduce poverty while contributing to shareholder value.

Innovative Approaches to Reducing Global Poverty
pp. 153–173

153

IMPORTANCE OF INTERNATIONAL TRADE
AND INVESTMENT IN REDUCING POVERTY

Research and other evidence strongly support the concept that investment and trade by foreign firms into lesser economically developed
regions can have a positive impact on relieving poverty. However, academic work on poverty reduction has in general concentrated on the
effects of government policies and the work of not-for-profit nongovernmental organizations (NGOs). Although the macroeconomic effects of
international trade and investment on economic growth and poverty
reduction have been studied extensively, there has been a lack of research
aimed at producing practical strategies for use by individual for-profit
firms interested in creating win-win scenarios where firms can contribute
to poverty reduction without having to sacrifice shareholder value. The
importance of government policies and the work of NGOs on poverty
reduction are well established, however "A dynamic private sector is crucial for sustainable economic growth, a necessary condition for poverty
reduction" (Chino, 2004, p. 10). International trade and the introduction
of business practices developed outside the host country can contribute to
creating an environment where economic growth and poverty reduction is
possible (Lin, 2004). De Valk (2003) suggested that the transfer of existing
knowledge can be more important than the creation of new knowledge in
fostering increased productivity and improved economic growth in the
least developed countries (LDCs). International trade and investment by
private for-profit firms can play a vital role in transferring existing business and technical knowledge to locations where this knowledge can be
used to create employment and job skills—important factors in fostering
environments favorable for sustainable poverty reduction.

The relationship between international trade and investment and economic growth and poverty reduction is complex and multilayered (Bardouille, 2005). However Langenfeld and Nieberding (2005) reported
economists have been studying the relationship between trade and economic growth for an extended period of time and the balance of the evidence overwhelmingly supports the likelihood that increased levels of
international trade and investment have a positive effect on increasing
economic growth and reducing poverty. The correlation between
increased levels of international trade and economic growth has been well
established (Anderson, 2005; Arora & Varnvakidis, 2005; Becker, 2003;
Berggren & Jordahl, 2005; Farrell, 2004; Masson, 2001; Ramirez, 2005;
Sen, 2002; Stark, 2005; Stevens, 2003; Winters, 2006; Yao, 2006). Walde
& Wood (2004, p. 275) summed up the general consensus of the academic
community that has studied this issue by stating, "Existing literature
repeatedly documented a strong correlation between trade and growth."

In addition to increased international trade being a force in economic growth and poverty reduction in the developing world, there is also considerable evidence that cross border trade and investment is beneficial to citizens of the more economically developed countries from where much of the trade is initiated (Broda & Weinstein, 2005; Desai, Foley, & Hines, 2005; Wooster, 2006). Therefore international trade between developed and developing economics can produce a complimentary effect and in general creates sustainable win-win situations.

Increased international trade and investment can also act as a catalyst for improvements in the institutional environments in developing countries which can lower levels of corruption and transaction costs. These improvements create spillover effects which improve the efficiency of the entire economy (Kwok & Tadesse, 2006). Furthermore, international trade, and specifically foreign direct investment (FDI), often creates other positive spillover effects through increasing the overall knowledge of employees, suppliers, competitors, and others; thus contributing to overall economic growth in the host country. However, Banga (2006) discovered that FDI from different geographical regions have differing impacts on improving the productivity of the manufacturing sector in India through spillover effects. Wei and Liu (2006) found similar results in China; some types of investment seemed to produce more spillover effects than others. These results suggest that not only is the quantity of international trade and investment important in achieving economic growth and poverty reduction, but the "quality" of the trade and investment also matters.

Alfaro, Chanda, Kalemli-Ozcan, and Sayek (2006) found the nature of the financial markets in a host country will affect the spillover effects and the overall benefits that come from foreign direct investment. This finding suggests that the institutional environment of the host country also has an impact on the effectiveness of increasing levels of international trade on poverty reduction. These findings suggest both foreign and domestic organizations have a role to play in lessening the grip poverty has over so many individuals in LDCs.

When looking at poverty reduction, it makes sense to look at past successes as well as current problems. There has been a lot of success in poverty reduction in recent years, and this success has been especially evident in Asia. The percent of the population in Vietnam living in extreme poverty has fallen from around 80% in 1990 to under 50% today. It has been reported that 156 million people in China were able to lift themselves out of extreme poverty in the years from 2001 to 2005 (World Bank, 2006, p. 10). Simultaneously there have been substantial increases in levels of international trade and moves toward more market-based economies in the areas which have seen success in reducing poverty. In Asia, there has been a strong correlation between increasing quantities of international trade and poverty reduction. It should also be noted that this reduction in poverty in China and Vietnam does not appear to be correlated to a significant extent with an increase in foreign aid. Furthermore, research by Mahadevon (2006) in Malaysia suggests economic growth does not automatically result in other undesirable effects, such as increasing inequalities in income over the long term.

Comparisons have been made in the post-World War II era between the rapid growth and progress in poverty reduction in Asia and the less successful economic performance of nations of Central and South America. It appears differences in levels of international trade between those regions have played a part in the differences in their success in lowering the rates of poverty (Elson, 2006; Frankema & Smits, 2005). Economies in Central and South America have been less successful in increasing integration with the global economy than have Asian economies in recent years. Additionally, it should be noted the nations of Africa have received extensive amounts of foreign aid, while at the same time receiving very little foreign investment into the private sector. The results don't show African nations in general have significantly reduced the percentage of citizens living in extreme poverty while receiving large sums of aid and limited amounts of investment. Meanwhile, the nations of Asia have received lower levels of foreign aid but have been the recipients of much of the world's private sector investment into developing economies and have experienced in recent years the greatest success the world has ever seen in reducing poverty.

While the general effect of market-based economic reforms has been positive in the developing world, the effect does not appear to of a consistent or linear nature (Zagha, Nankani, & Gill, 2006). Other factors in addition to economic liberalization and increases in international trade appear to play important roles in poverty reduction. Harrison (2006), Lin and Wong (1997), and Sui (2003) found gaining substantial benefits from increased international trade was dependent on other factors such as education and infrastructure creation. These findings suggest that foreign aid from governments and NGOs that goes into building infrastructure and building up educational systems can be important components of laying the ground work for poverty reduction. However, new roads contribute little to economic growth if there are no products to transport and education without employment opportunities leads to dissatisfaction and migration.

The literature shows international organizations, national governments, and aid agencies all have important roles to play in reducing poverty in the least developed nations. Furthermore, there is a general agreement amongst development specialists that private for-profit firms can do more in the fight against poverty. Operating a business profitably in LDCs is difficult and the benefits for large multinational corporations (MNCs) are limited. However, by looking for innovative approaches, MNCs can contribute to economic growth and poverty reduction in LDCs without sacrificing shareholder value. The purpose of this paper is to explore a strategy MNCs and other firms can use in some of the smaller LDCs to create profits as well as employment and professional development opportunities for people from these regions.

PROBLEM: SIZE MATTERS IN INTERNATIONAL BUSINESS

Research indicates that size of the market can be a significant factor influencing location decisions for investment into developing markets by international companies (Alon, 2006; Bevan & Estrin, 2004; Chakrabarti, 2001; Tahir & Larimo, 2005, 2006; Tarzi, 2005). Not surprisingly, MNCs and international business (IB) scholars have been paying particular attention to some of the largest and fastest growing markets, while ignoring others. In Asia, the emergence of China from its years of isolation from the global economy is resulting in China attracting a large amount of FDI, which many claim is coming at the expense of the smaller economies of the region (Felker, 2003; Shapiro, Gedaijlovis, & Erdener, 2003). Although the evidence appears to indicate China's growth and attraction of FDI on balance is a benefit to the other economies of Asia (Weiss, 2004), the smallest and least developed Asian economies, for example, Laos, Nepal, and Cambodia, could be overlooked by MNCs as locations for investments due to their small populations and low levels of purchasing power. Similar situations are likely to be replicated in other developing areas of the world, especially in Africa where there are a number of countries with small populations having limited purchasing power.

Traditionally, businesses leaders and scholars have used national boundaries to separate markets and measure market size. However, the lowering of trade barriers and transportation costs worldwide allow for the drawing of various boundary lines around markets that both cut and cross national borders, at times yielding much larger markets than might be suggested by traditional methods. It is proposed that the use of innovative regional strategies that expand the concept of market size in LDCs will decrease the chances that smaller countries miss out on the benefits of being integrated into the global economy.

THREE TIERED REGIONAL APPROACH

In order to be successful, all firms need to create strategies and operational practices that are aligned with the environment. There is a substantial amount of compelling evidence showing convergence of business activities and environments around the world (e.g, see D'Artigues & Vignolo, 2005; Holmes, 2005; Ugeux, 2004) and also compelling evidence showing convergence of business practices is not happening, or at least not happening consistently or rapidly (e.g, see Kolk, 2005; Stamatakis & Petrakis, 2005; Tregaskis & Brewster, 2006). This seemingly conflicting evidence fuels the ongoing localization versus globalization of business strategies and practices debate.

The topic of finding the correct mix of localization and globalization of various business practices has been a widely studied topic (i.e., see Geppart & Williams, 2006; Husted & Allen, 2006; Shimoni & Bergmann, 2006). Bartlett and Ghosal (1989) proposed that multinationals should simultaneously use global and locally responsive practices without resorting to a compromise solution, a strategy they referred to as a transnational strategy. However, there may be limitations of costs and effectiveness in actually implementing this strategy and there are specific situations that require choosing either a local or "global' international business practice (Paik & Sohn, 2004; Wasilewski, 2002). Furthermore, it has been proposed a transnational strategy may not be the optimal solution for MNCs to use in order to be successful in the "bottom of the pyramid markets" (London & Hart, 2004). It has been claimed that success in these different environments will require innovative approaches that take into account the environmental conditions found in these areas as opposed to adjusting existing global strategies to take into account the "deficiencies' found in these markets (London & Hart, 2004; Ricart, Enright, Ghemawat, Hart, & Khanna, 2004).

Building on the concept of employing a transnational strategy that uses universal best practices alongside local responsiveness (Barlett & Ghosal, 1989) and the need for innovative ground up approaches to conducting business in LDCs (London & Hart, 2004), it is proposed that a three-tired regional framework can be used by MNCs and other companies to better align their business strategies with the local environments found in LDCs.

We are all members of the human race, and therefore have similar capabilities, needs, and desires. Each and every person on the planet is a unique individual. One can accept either of these seemingly contradictory statements without rejecting the other. In between these two extremes, there are an unlimited number of methods one can use to define groups of people that have similar characteristics. The concept of grouping people by similarities so that they can then be targeted by businesses (market segmentation) has long been a key component of marketing research and practice (Grapentine & Boomgaarden, 2003; Kumar & Nagal, 2001).

The most common border for the grouping of people and organizations used in studying IB strategies is the nation-state, and this framework is a very useful one to use. However, it does not preclude the use of other frameworks for use as the basis for innovative IB strategies. Regional groups that cross national boundaries are another option. Research has shown that the majority of international trade is of a regional nature as opposed to being global (Chortareas & Pelagidis, 2004; O'Neil, 2004; Rugman, 2001; Rugman & Brain, 2003, 2004a, 2004b; Rugman & Moore, 2001; Rugman & Verbeke, 2004, 2005). Transportation costs is one factor limiting much international trade to a regional basis, but a case can be made that similarity of economic, political-legal, and sociocultural environments add to the relative ease of doing business regionally as opposed to globally. Therefore a regional approach to conducting business in the least developed economies of the world is a viable alternative to focusing on each individual country as a distinctly different market or using a global approach that does not take into account local differences.

The regional approach being proposed is not simply a compromise between using a global or multi-domestic strategy. It is an approach that looks at the global standardization versus local responsiveness issue separately at all three levels—the strategic, the tactical, and the operational.

Strategic Level

Business strategy is about making choices and acknowledging the necessity of tradeoffs (Peng, 2002; Porter, 1996). In making strategic decisions, a firm identifies its boundaries and a single set of best strategic practices for all firms in all environments can not be found. Fast-food restaurants and restaurants at five star hotels choose very different strategies, and both types of strategies can be successful. Porter (1985) proposed there are three generic types of strategy a company can pursue, cost-leadership, differentiation, and focus, and all three of these strategies attempt to create separation between a company and its competitors as a primary objective. The strategic level of decision making is often considered the level of decision making that has a long term influence on a firm and involves the firm as a whole The strategic level is where the decisions about what products to develop and sell and what positioning strategy should be used can be found.

Choosing a particular strategy is influenced by a multitude of environmental factors. Social-cultural, technological, and political-legal aspects of the environment all play a role in strategy formulation. However, as strategies are primarily about choices, a case can be made that the economic environment is the single most influential environmental consideration that is taken into account when strategy is created. Increasing economic development creates increased strategic options for firms.

Strategy is designed to have consumers and business customers voluntarily exchange money for goods and services. Where there is more money available, there are more strategic options available to make mutually profitable exchanges. The options available to the average American consumer in the shopping malls and grocery stores continue to grow as American consumers continue to become more affluent. This wide range of product and service options for consumers is created by a large number of diverse companies following very diverse strategies. On the other hand, when one travels into the least developed regions of the world, there is limited diversity in the types of goods and services offered and a limited number of business strategies being employed.

As the economic development of the world is extremely diverse, the possibility of a single global strategy that encompasses both developed and developing regions is problematic. London and Hart (2004) discovered most MNCs were using strategies designed for the use in the developed world and the exclusive "top of the pyramid" segment of the markets in developing countries. For the most part these companies were ignoring the majority of the population of the planet. London and Hart believed that MNCs should craft strategies specifically tailored to the conditions found in the LDCs. However, the low levels of development and low population numbers in the smaller economies in some areas make the potential market size too small for profitable tailoring of strategies to those areas. The entire purchasing power of the country of Laos is lower than that of a medium-sized city in the domestic market of MNCs from the United States, Western Europe, or Japan. The challenges of crafting strategy by executives from developed countries in the very different environments found in small and poorly developed countries in far off lands with very different cultures are great. The benefits gained from success, from the standpoint of financial profits, is minuscule. It is not surprising that instead of "exploiting" workers and consumers in the bottom of the pyramid markets, most MNCs are ignoring those markets.

Economic development between nations within a region is usually much less diverse than what is found on a global scale. For example, El Salvador's per capita gross domestic product (GDP) of around $2,300 ($4,980 purchasing power parity (PPP)) makes its market a very different one from Denmark's with its per capita GDP of around $40,650 ($31,550, PPP). However, within the region, the economic development of El Salvador is much closer to that of its neighbors Guatemala with a per capita GDP of around $2,130 ($4,140, PPP) and Honduras with a per capita GDP of approximately $1,030 ($2,710 PPP) (World Bank, 2005). This example is intended to show regional areas tend to be more economically homogeneous than the world is as a whole and therefore regional strategies on selecting products, pricing, and positioning would appear to be often more feasible than global strategies.

Furthermore, there are often some similar social and cultural factors, such as language and religion, among regional neighbors. These similarities, along with the geographical proximity that lessens transportation costs, can contribute to the effectiveness of using a regional approach at the strategic level of decision making. Strategic decision making is primarily the domain of top managers, and using a regional framework for strategic decision making in the LDCs will allow for busy executives to formulate business strategies that can contribute to further integrating marginalized people into the world economic system and enjoy the benefits from this integration without the executives having to spend excessive time on areas of the world where the potential to gain profits or sales is limited.

Due to extreme differences in economic development in the LDCs compared to the more developed nations where the vast majority of MNCs originate, basic positioning and product strategies of a single company can take on very different forms. Many products or brands that are positioned as value-priced products for the masses in developed economies may have to be positioned and promoted quite differently in the developing world where the average purchasing power of the consumers is significantly lower.

Additionally, the market for a very low priced stripped down model of a particular product, for example a mobile phone or radio, may be very limited in the more developed economies and not economically feasible to produce, but this stripped down product may attract strong demand in areas where the purchasing power of the consumers is comparatively lower. Creating a separate positioning or product strategy for each individual country in the developing areas of the globe may be cost prohibitive, but redrawing the boundaries for strategy creation from a national to a regional level may increase the market size to a level that becomes more attractive for MNCs.

Tactical Level

There is no clear separation between the strategic, tactical, and operational business practices of an organization. In this chapter, the term "tactical business practices" refers to those practices that fall somewhere between long-term strategic and day-to-day operational practices. Putting together strategic business practices and strategic planning are primarily the responsibility of top managers and generalists. Tactical business practices are mostly the responsibility of middle managers and specialists. As

Lewis notes: "Strategy changes how you think about something; tactics change how you do something" (1998, p. 153). Examples of tactical-level business practices include launching a marketing campaign; implementing specific human resource management practices for hiring, retention, promotion, and training; and using specific styles of management and leadership.

The part of the environment that appears to have the most effect on the selection of tactical level business practices is the sociocultural aspect of the external environment. In deciding "how you do something" it is vitally important to take into account the cultural context in which the work is being carried out. Hofstede (1980, 1983) made the case that the basic elements of cultures do not rapidly change despite surface appearances. Therefore, from a theoretical standpoint, it would seem that diverse and slowly changing cultural environments would not be significantly pressuring business practices to converge.

Research appears to indicate there continues to be a divergence in tactical business practices across national boundaries. For example, tactical approaches to marketing do not appear to be converging across cultures. Suh and Kwon (2002) found local differences in consumer tastes and spending patterns are not swayed to any great extent by the global marketing efforts of large multinationals, which suggests that successful tactical marketing approaches will continue to be responsive to local conditions. Tactical marketing practices are pressured to converge to some extent by the legal-political and technological environments; however the differences in economic development and especially the differences in cultures and languages across borders limit the amount of marketing convergence at the tactical level. Research by Lu and Lee (2005) reported distinct differences in consumer patterns from different countries within the Asian region, which supports the proposition that tactical marketing activities will need to be adjusted to the environment found in each nation within a region.

In a similar vein, it appears that firms will have difficulty using a regional or global approach to tactical human resource management practices. Even with political integration within the EU, there has not been substantial convergence of human resource (HR) practices in Europe (Mayrhofer, Muller-Camen, Ledolter, Strunk, & Erten, 2004). This result supports the proposition that it is the slower moving cultural environment that has the most effect on some tactical HR business practices. This situation also appears to apply in Asia as the evidence does not appear to show HR business practices in Asia are becoming less localized to any significant extent (Beer & Katz, 2003; Chen & Wilson, 2003; Chew & Goh, 1997; McGrath-Champ & Carter, 2001). The tactical HR practices of hiring, retaining, and training employees may be equally important for businesses around the world; however, how these practices are done appears to be influenced to a great extent by the cultural context in which they take place.

The notion of management and leadership styles and the universality and convergence of these styles has been widely discussed and studied. Management and leadership styles are more closely associated with how to do something as opposed to what to do, and therefore fit closer to the tactical-level than other levels. Hofstede (1980, p. 63) believed attempting to foster universal leadership or management styles was misguided and claimed the possibility of convergence was limited. Empirical evidence appears to support Hofstede's position that basic practices, attitudes, and underlying assumption of what constitutes management are very diverse and are culturally bound. Existing research does not suggest that worldwide convergence of the tactical aspects of management is occurring (Chong & Thomas, 1997; Javidan & Carl, 2005; Kanungo & Wright, 1983; Michailova, 2000; Neelankavil, Mathur, & Zhang, 2000; Suutari, Raharjo, & Riikkila, 2002; Zagorsek, Jaklic, & Stough, 2004).

MNCs and other firms using a regional three-tiered strategy to create market size in less developed regions of the world will need to use locally responsive business practices at the tactical level. Firms will need to adjust their advertising campaigns, hiring practices, and management styles to take into account the individual sociocultural environments found in each nation. Furthermore, the legal requirements that firms operate in usually extend only to a nation's borders. And regulations, especially in the tactical marketing, finance, and human resource areas, will require the use of various tactical practices to ensure legal compliance. Therefore while the regional strategic decisions can be made by the top executives, it would probably be most productive to delegate the formulation of tactical business practices in LDCs to managers (both expatriate and local) familiar with local conditions.

Operational Level Business Practices

The operational level of business practices is the level where all the grand strategic plans and more detailed tactical plans are put into practice. The selection of a particular operational level practice is primarily driven by costs. Costs are affected to a significant extent by the use of operational techniques and technology. The strategic and tactical levels primarily focus on effectiveness while the focus at the operational level is more likely to be on efficiency. There are no best practices as far as strategy goes, using a cost leadership strategy is not automatically more or less effective than using a differentiation strategy, even within a single industry. However, there can be best practices at the operational level that are more efficient in nearly every situation; for example, the use of containers in transportation that involves both sea and land travel has proven more efficient and effective than other types of shipping in nearly all environments regardless of culture or industry.

Technology and technique are often less context specific than strategy and tactics. A single operational business practice can be used for a variety of strategic and tactical purposes. The business letter that today is most likely produced using a standardized operational level tool and technique (computer and word processor) can have countless tactical or strategic purposes. Changes in operational level business practices can often be incorporated into a company without having to change the organizational structure, strategic intent, tactical frameworks, or organizational culture. It is normally much easier and effective to make the transfer of operational business practices across industries and geographical locations than it is to transfer strategic and tactical business practices.

From an intuitive point of view, there appears to be a fairly large amount of worldwide convergence of business and personal activities at the operational level. The tools and techniques used in both daily life and in the professional world appear to becoming more and more alike across regions. For example, in many parts of the world, the computer and the mobile phone have become the main tools used to communicate, regardless of language used or types of messages exchanged. The operational level is the most visible level and it is at this level much discussion of "globalization" focuses. Furthermore, the dissemination of technology across the planet moves much quicker than in the past and it also appears new technology moves across income levels at a faster rate than seen before The convergence of the world wide technological environment is contributing to a convergence of operational business practices. Moreover, while firms do not need to share structures, strategies, or tactical approaches to conduct business transactions with each other, a certain level of standardization of operational procedures is almost always required. Shared communication channels, accounting procedures, transportation linkages, common weights and measurements, and other standardized operational procedures facilitate trade. As international trade increases, pressures to standardize operational procedures internationally will also increase.

There appear to be worldwide convergence in many operational areas of business. Studies show some level of international convergence in accounting and auditing (Brackney & Witmer, 2005; Herrmann & Hague, 2006; Horstmann, 2005), use of information technology (Kauffman & Techatassanasoontorn, 2005; Van Ark & Piatkowski, 2004; Zhang & Jeckle, 2004), and production technology (Frantzen, 2004). However, managers need to guard against assuming that all operational business practices are universal, since an elimination of national differences in all operational practices has not been seen and some of the national differences in operational business practices can be attributed to culture (Pagell, Katz, & Sheu 2005). Nevertheless, many best practices at the operational level are not as dependent upon the economic, socioculture, or political-legal environment as are business practices at the strategic or tactical level. Therefore it is proposed that firms using a three tiered regional approach primarily make use of global best practices at the operational level.

CONCLUSION

The issue of poverty reduction is one of the most important issues of our time, however, instead of being a uniting issue that left and right, religious and secular, and rich and poor work together to solve, the issue has often been used in attempt to gain political advantage against perceived opponents and the empirical evidence on poverty reduction has often been ignored (Eskew, 2005; Hipsher, 2006a). Cairns (2005) outlined how much of the discussion about conditions in the developing world is conducted through a hierarchal lens. It is not uncommon to read about how "we" should address the issue of poverty reduction (without clearly defining who is we and who is they). For an example, see Karnani (2006). Such a we-they framing often ignores the ability of individuals in LDCs to choose for themselves what is in their best interest when confronted with additional employment or purchasing opportunities. The empirical evidence is clear that there has been an amazing amount of poverty reduction throughout East Asia in recent times and this reduction has happened at the same time as economic liberalization and increased integration of East Asian economies into the global marketplace (World Bank 2006). In areas of the world where international trade remains limited there has been little reduction in poverty. Nobel laureate Sen (2002, p. 12) astutely summed up the outlook of most devolvement economists:

The economic predicament of the poor across the world cannot be reversed by withholding from them the great advantages of contemporary technology, the well-established efficiency of international trade and exchange, and the social as well as economic merits of living in open rather than closed societies.

While this chapter has focused on the role of MNCs in poverty reduction, it should be realized that large MNCs are accountable for only a small percentage of the business transactions in developing countries and LDCs. Over 80% of the FDI driving the phenomenal growth in China comes from within the Asian region with American and European firms having made relatively minor investments into the country contrary to what is often reported in the popular press (Breslin, 2004; Yin & Choi, 2005). In Southeast Asia, Vietnam has experienced both rapid growth in recent times as well as substantial increases in investment. However more investment comes into the country from Singapore than from Japan. In Lao PDR, the majority of the investment into the country does not come from the European Union, but from neighboring Thailand, while in Cambodia, Malaysia is the country where the largest amount of investment originates (Freeman, 2002). IB should not be thought of as being synonymous with business conducted by MNCs. Economic liberalization in many developing countries has not brought about huge amounts of investment by the world's largest corporations, but has brought about a significant increase in regional business transactions that have assisted in improving the efficiencies of the economies, bringing in turn greater economic growth and poverty reduction.

What the MNCs from developed economies lack in quantity of investment may be made up by quality of investment. Investment by MNCs from developed countries into LDCs often bring new technologies, knowledge and training of operational business practices that create an impact beyond what would be created by investment of a similar size by firms from developing economies. MNCs often work with local suppliers to improve the effectiveness and efficiency of operations, provide training and quality employment opportunities for local workers, many of whom later use the experience and training gained to become entrepreneurs. The MNCs often increase the overall level of knowledge in the total business environment, which includes customers and competitors, therefore improving the overall efficiency of the economy. Simply exporting into LDCs appears to have the fewest spillover effects. Therefore, to maximize impact on poverty reduction, MNCs might want to contemplate using a more integrated regional strategy where products and services are produced, distributed, and sold as much as possible within a single region.

The three-tiered regional strategy proposed in this chapter includes breaking down business practices into three distinct layers. At the strategic level, it is proposed to use a regional strategy as the economic environments are usually less diverse at the regional level than at the global level. At the tactical level, it is proposed that practices be adjusted for each country individually due to differing cultural and political-legal environments encountered. At the operational level, universal best practices, or operational business practices similar to ones used in the MNC's country of origin may often be the most efficient and effective ones to use.

An example of using this three-tier strategy was found while studying I-Apple, a Thai owned audio and video production company operating across the Greater-Mekong Subregion (Hipsher, 2006b). At the strategic level, I-Apple positions itself as a full service company where the entire process, including both creative and business activities, is handled by the company at a value price and with a reasonable level of quality. The economic conditions and business environments across the regions are somewhat similar. The positioning as a full service company makes sense as most potential business customers operating in the region lack the size, experience, and sophistication to develop their own advertising campaigns, and due to the relatively low level of monetary value of business transactions in the region, keeping costs down is a necessity.

At the tactical level, I-Apple makes adjustments for each national market where it operates. In Laos the company attempts to use images, symbols, and dress associated with traditional Laotian culture in its productions, in accordance with the wishes of the Lao government. In Cambodia, cultural sensitivity requires the firm to refrain from using more risqué types of promotion such as those sometimes used in Thailand. Also, as the language of each country the firms operates in is different, commercials and advertisements need to be custom made for each country. In addition, in LDCs, personal relationship contracting is often more important than written contracts (Carney, 2004), and therefore the owner of the company, Mr. Rittirong Kotophan works hard to establish and maintain personal and professional relationships with government officials and managers of TV and radio stations, as well as with his core customers in each location where the company operates. Other tactical practices, such as hiring staff, are adjusted for conditions within each country as each country has a supply of labor with differing levels of skills and education, different government regulations, and differing norms for business practices.

At the operational level, I-Apple uses the same basic technology as used throughout the world, with some limited adjustments due to cost factors. The techniques and equipment used to edit video commercials would be familiar to those working in the industry in developed countries. Kotophan learned the operational business practices the company uses while studying and working in Thailand, a country known for the quality of its movie and audio productions while relying on similar techniques and technology used in developed economies. He took these universal operational best practices and added a regional strategic positioning strategy along with a tactical local-responsive approach at the national level to create a successful company that is making profits and working toward improving the efficiency of the economies in countries such as Cambodia and Laos.

The proposed strategy in this chapter is only one of many possible innovative strategies that private companies from developed economies can use to make a positive impact on the lives of people who are unable to achieve their full potential due to the limitations imposed on them by poverty. For example, Karnani (2006) advocated buying from producers in LDCs as a way to improve living conditions in LDCs. This strategy proposed by Karnani as well as other strategies can have a positive effect on reducing poverty. Scholars and business practitioners interested in contributing to the reduction of poverty around the world should not be looking for a single strategy to be used by every company in every country; instead we (business practitioners, government officials, scholars, and others interested in poverty reduction from all areas of the world) should be working on finding a multitude of innovative strategies that will move us closer to achieving the United Nation's Millennium Goals on poverty reduction.

REFERENCES

Alfaro, L., Chanda, A., Kalemli-Ozcan, S., & Sayek, S. (2006). How does foreign direct investment promote economic growth? (Working paper No. 15222, National Bureau of Economic Research). Cambridge, Massachusetts.

Alon, I. (2006). Executive insight: Evaluating the market size for service franchising in emerging markets. *International Journal of Emerging Markets, 1*, 9-20.

Anderson, K. (2005). On the virtues of multilateral trade negotiations. *Economic Record, 81*(255), 414-438.

Arora, V., & Varnvakidis, A. (2005). How much do trading partners matter for economic growth? *IMF Staff Papers, 52*, 24-40.

Banga, R. (2006). The export-diversifying impact of Japanese and US foreign direct investments in the Indian manufacturing sector. *Journal of International Business Studies, 37*, 558-568.

Bardouille, N. C. (2005). Globalization and the WTO; Reconciling "development" in global trade talks. *Journal of Eastern Caribbean Studies, 30*(1), 108-120.

Bartlett, C. A., & Ghosal, S. (1989). *Managing across borders: The transnational solution.* Boston: Harvard Business School Press.

Becker, G. S. (2003, March 16). When globalization suffers, the poor take the heat. *Business Week*, 28.

Beer, M., & Katz, N. (2003). Do incentives work? The perceptions of a worldwide sample of senior executives. *HR: Human Resource Planning, 26*(3), 30-44.

Berggren, N., & Jordahl, H. (2005). Does free trade really reduce growth? Further testing using the economic freedom index. *Public Choice, 122*(1-2), 99-114.

Bevan, A. A., & Estrin, S. (2004). The determinants of foreign direct investment into European transition economies. *Journal of Comparative Economics, 32*, 775-787.

Brackney, K. S., & Witmer, P. R. (2005). The European Union's role in international standards setting. *The CPA Journal, 75*(11), 18-27.

Breslin, S. (2004). Greater China and the political economy of regionalisation. *East Asia, 21*(1), 7-23.

Broda, C., & Weinstein, D. (2005). Are we underestimating the gains from global-ization for the United States? *Current Issues in Economics and Finance, 11*(4), 1-7.

Cairns, G. (2005). Perspectives on a personal critique of international business. *Critical Perspectives on International Business, 1*(1), 43-55.

Carney, M. (2004). The institutions of industrial restructuring in Southeast Asia. *Asia Pacific Journal of Management, 21*, 171-188.

Chakrabarti, A. (2001). The determinants of foreign direct investment: Sensitivity analysis of cross-country regressions. *Kyklos: International Review of Social Sciences, 54*, 89-114.

Chen, S., & Wilson, M. (2003. Standardization and localization of human resource management in Sino-joint ventures. *Asia-Pacific Journal of Management, 20*, 397-408.

Chew, I., & Goh, M. (1997. Some future directions of human resources practices in Singapore. *Career Development International, 2*, 238-253.

Chino, T. (2004). President's address. *Asian Development Bank Review, 36*(4), 9-12.

Chong, L. M., & Thomas, D. C. (1997). Leadership perceptions in cross-cultural context: Pakeha and Pacific Islanders in New Zealand. *Leadership Quarterly, 8*, 275-293.

Chortareas, G. E., & Pelagidis, T. (2004). Trade flows: A facet of regionalism or globalization? *Cambridge Journal of Economics, 28*, 253-271.

Desai, M. A., Foley, C. F., & Hines, J. R., Jr. (2005). *Foreign direct investment and domestic economic activity* (Working paper No. 11717). National Bureau of Economic Research, Cambridge, MA.

De Valk, P. (2003). *How do firms learn? With case studies from Lao PDR* (Working paper series No. 385). Institute of Social Studies, The Hague.

D'Artigues, A., & Vignolo, T. (2005. An evolutionary theory of the convergence towards low inflation rates. *Journal of Evolutionary Economics, 15*, 51-64.

Elson, A. (2006). What Happened? *Finance and Development, 43*(2), 22-27.

Eskew, M. (2005). Are we losing the globalization debate? *Chief Executive, 207*, 14

Farrell, D. (2004). The case for globalization. *The International Economy, 18*(1), 52-55.

Felker, G. B. (2003). Southeast Asian industrialisation and the changing global production system. *Third World Quarterly, 24*, 255–282.

Frankema, E., & Smits, J. P. (2005). Exploring the historical roots of Eastern Asia's post war catch-up growth: A trade perspective. *Journal of the Asia Pacific Economy, 10*(2), 178-194.

Frantzen, D. (2004). Technological diffusion and productivity convergence: A study for manufacturing in the OECD. *Southern Economic Journal, 71*, 352-376.

Freeman, N. J. (2002). *Foreign direct investment in Cambodia, Laos and Vietnam.* Paper presented at the Conference on Foreign Direct Investment Opportunities and Challenges for Cambodia, Laos and Vietnam, Hanoi, Vietnam.

Geppart, M., & Williams, K. (2006). Global, national and local practices in multi-national corporations: Towards a sociopolitical framework. *International Journal of Human Resource Management, 17*(1), 49-69.

Grapentine, T., & Boomgaarden, R. (2003). Maladies of market segmentation. *Marketing Research, 15*(1), 27-30.

Harrison, A. (2006. *Globalization and poverty* (Working paper No. 12347). National Bureau of Economic Research, Cambridge MA.

Herrmann, D., & Hague, I. (2006. Convergence: In search of the best. *Journal of Accountancy, 201*(1), 69-73.

Hipsher, S. A. (2006a). Re-evaluation of underlying assumptions and refocusing of objectives in criticisms of international business. *Critical Perspectives on International Business, 2,* 114-127.

Hipsher, S. A. (2006b). *Regional internationalization strategies of firms originating from the Greater Mekong Sub-region: An exploratory case study.* Unpublished doctoral dissertation, Capella University, Minneapolis.

Hofstede, G. (1980). Motivation, leadership, and organization: Do American theories apply abroad. *Organizational Dynamics, 9*(1), 42-63.

Hofstede, G. (1983). The cultural relativity of organizational practices and theories. *Journal of International Business Studies, 14,* 75-89.

Holmes, M. J. (2005). New evidence on long-run output convergence among Latin American countries. *Journal of Applied Economics, 8,* 299-319.

Horstmann, C. A. (2005). Playing a leadership role in international convergence. *Journal of Accountancy, 200*(4), 98-99.

Husted, B. W., & Allen, D. B. (2006). Corporate social responsibility in the multinational enterprise: Strategic and institutional approaches. *Journal of International Business Studies, 37,* 838-849.

Javidan, M., & Carl, D. E. (2005). Leadership across cultures: A study of Canadian and Taiwanese executives. *Management International Review, 45*(1), 23-44.

Karnani, A. (2006). *Fortune at the bottom of the pyramid: A mirage. How the private sector can help alleviate poverty* (Working paper No. 1035). Ross School of Business Working Paper Series, University of Michigan, Ann Arbor.

Kanungo, R. N., & Wright, R. W. (1983). A cross-cultural comparative study of managerial job attitudes. *Journal of International Business Studies, 14,* 115-129.

Kauffman, R. J., & Techatassanasoontorn, A. A. (2005). International diffusion of digital mobile technology: A coupled-hazard state-based approach. *Information Technology and Management, 6,* 253-292.

Kolk, A. (2005). Environmental reporting by multinationals from the triad: Convergence or divergence? *Management International Review, 45,* 145-166.

Kumar, V., & Nagal, A. (2001). Segmenting global markets: Look before you leap. *Marketing Research, 13*(1), 8-13.

Kwok, C., & Tadesse, S. (2006). The MNC as an agent of change for host-country institutions: FDI and corruption. *Journal of International Business Studies, 37,* 767-785.

Langenfeld, J., & Nieberding, J. (2005). The benefits of free trade to U.S. consumers. *Business Economics, 4*(3), 41-51.

Lin, C. W., & Wong, K. Y. (1997). *Economic growth and international trade, the case of Hong Kong.* Paper presented at the Dynamics, Economic Growth, and International Trade conference, Hong Kong.

Lin, J. Y. (2004). Development strategies for inclusive growth in developing Asia. *Asian Development Review, 21*(2), 1-27.

Lewis, B. (1998). Your integrated plan can translate your company's strategic goals into action. *InfoWorld, 20*(24), 153.

London, T., & Hart, S. T. (2004). Perspective: Reinventing strategies for emerging markets: Beyond the transnational model. *Journal of International Business Studies, 35,* 350-370.

Lu, L. T., & Lee, Y. H. (2005). The effect of culture on the management style and performance of international joint ventures in China: The perspective of foreign parent firms. *International Journal of Management, 22,* 452-463.

Mahadevon, R. (2006). Growth with equity: The Malaysian case. *Asia Pacific Development Journal, 27*(10), 27-52.

Masson, P. (2001). *Globalization: Facts and figures.* IMF policy discussion paper No. PDP/01/04: International Monetary Fund, Washington D.C.

Mayrhofer, W., Muller-Camen, M., Ledolter, J., Strunk, G., & Erten, C. (2004). Devolving responsibilities for human resources to line management? An empirical study about convergence in Europe. *Journal for East European Management Studies, 9,* 123-146.

McGrath-Champ, S., & Carter, S. (2001. The art of selling corporate culture: Management and human resources in Australian construction companies operating in Malaysia. *International Journal of Manpower, 22,* 349-368.

Michailova, S. (2000). Contrasts in culture: Russian and Western perspectives on organizational change. *Academy of Management Executive, 14,* 99-112.

Neelankavil, J. P., Mathur, A., & Zhang, Y. (2000). Determinants of managerial performance: A cross-cultural comparison of the perceptions of middle-level managers in four countries. *Journal of International Business Studies, 31,* 121-140.

O'Neil, T. (2004). Globalization: Fads, fiction and facts. *Business Economics, 39*(1), 16-27.

Pagell, M., Katz, J. P., & Sheu, C. (2005). The importance of national culture in operations management research. *International Journal of Operations & Production Management, 25,* 371-394.

Paik, Y., & Sohn, D. (2004). Striking a balance between global integration and local responsiveness. *Organizational Analysis, 12,* 347-359.

Peng, M. W. (2002). Towards an institution-based view of business strategy. *Asia Pacific Journal of Management, 19,* 251-267.

Porter, M. E. (1985). *Competitive advantage: Creating and sustaining superior performance.* Free Press: New York.

Porter, M. E. (1996). What is strategy? *Harvard Business Review, 74*(6), 61-78.

Ramirez, M. D. (2005). Did institutional factors enhance FDI flows to Chile during the 1985-2001 Period?: An error correction analysis. *Journal of Emerging Markets, 10*(1), 18-29.

Ricart, J. E., Enright, M. J., Ghemawat, P., Hart, S. L., & Khanna, T. (2004). Perspective: New frontiers in international strategy. *Journal of International Business Studies, 35,* 175–200.

Rugman, A. M. (2001). Viewpoint: The myth of global strategy. *International Marketing Review, 18,* 583-588.

Rugman, A. M., & Brain, C. (2003). Multinational enterprises are regional, not global. *Multinational Business Review, 11*(1), 3-12.

Rugman, A. M., & Brain, C. (2004a). Regional strategies of multinational pharmaceutical firms. *Management International Review, 44*(3), 7-25.

Rugman, A. M., & Brain, C. (2004b). The regional nature of the world's banking sector. *Multinational Business Review, 12*(3), 5-22.

Rugman, A. M., & Moore, K. (2001). The myths of globalization. *Ivey Business Journal, 66*(1), 64-68.

Rugman, A. M., & Verbeke, A. (2004). A perspective on regional and global strategies of multinational enterprises. *Journal of International Business Studies, 35*, 3-18.

Rugman, A. M., & Verbeke, A. (2005). Towards a theory of regional multinationals: A transaction cost economics approach. *Management International Review, 45*, 5-17.

Sen, A. (2002). Globalization, inequality and global protest. *Development, 45*(2), 11-16.

Shapiro, D. M., Gedaijlovis, E., & Erdener, C. (2003). The Chinese family firm as a multinational enterprise. *International Journal of Organizational Analysis, 11*(2), 105-122.

Shimoni, B., & Bergmann, H. (2006). Managing in a changing world: From multiculturalism to hybridization—The production of hybrid management cultures in Israel, Thailand, and Mexico. *Academy of Management Perspectives, 20*(3), 76-89.

Stamatakis, D., & Petrakis, P. E. (2005). Human capital convergence: A cross country empirical investigation. *The Business Review, Cambridge, 3*, 310-321.

Stark, J. (2005). The state of globalization. *The International Economy, 19*(2), 52-56.

Stevens, J. (2003). *The role of import substitution and export orientation strategies on Thailand's economic growth*. Doctoral dissertation, Argosy University, UMI Number 3127039.

Suh, T., & Kwon, I. G. (2002). Globalization and reluctant buyers. *International Marketing Review, 19*, 663-680.

Sui, Z. (2003). *Essays on economic development and international economics*. Doctoral dissertation, University of Oklahoma: UMI No 3109060.

Suutari, V., Raharjo, K., & Riikkila, T. (2002). The challenge of cross-cultural leadership interaction: Finnish expatriates in Indonesia. *Career Development International, 7*: 415-429.

Tahir, R., & Larimo, J. (2005. Understanding the strategic motivations of Finnish manufacturing FDIs in emerging Asian economies. *Asian Business & Management, 4*: 293-313.

Tahir, R. & Larimo, J. (2006. Strategic motivations of Finnish FDIs in Asian countries. *Cross Cultural Management, 13*, 244-256.

Tarzi, S. (2005). Foreign direct investment flows into developing countries: Impact of location and government policy. *The Journal of Social, Political and Economic Studies, 30*, 497-515.

Tregaskis, O., & Brewster, C. (2006). Converging or diverging? A comparative analysis of trends in contingent employment practice in Europe over a decade. *Journal of International Business Studies, 37*, 111-126.

Ugeux, G. (2004). Towards global convergence in corporate governance: An assessment of the current situation. *International Journal of Disclosure and Governance, 1*, 339-354.

Van Ark, B., & Piatkowski, M. (2004). Productivity, innovation and ICT in old and new Europe. *International Economics and Economic Policy, 1*, 215-246.

Walde, K., & Wood, C. (2004). The empirics of trade and growth: Where are the policy recommendations? *International Economics and Economic Policy, 1*, 275-292.

Wasilewski, N. (2002). An empirical study of the desirability and challenges of implementing transnational marketing strategies. *Advances in Competitiveness Research, 10*(1), 123-149.

Wei, Y., & Liu, X. (2006). Productivity spillovers from R&D, exports and FDI in China's manufacturing sector. *Journal of International Business Studies, 37*, 544-557.

Weiss, J. (2004). *People's Republic of China and its neighbors: Partners of competitors for trade and investment?* (Discussion paper No. 13). Asian Development Bank Institute, Manila.

Winters, A. L. (2006). International trade and poverty: Cause or cure? *Australian Economic Review, 39*(4), 347-358.

Wooster, R. B. (2006). US companies in transition economics: wealth effects from expansion between 1987 and 1999. *Journal of International Business Studies, 37*, 179-195.

World Bank. (2005, July 15). World Development Indicators Database, Washington, DC.

World Bank. (2006). *East Asia Update.* Washington, DC: Author.

Yao, S. (2006). On economic growth, FDI and exports in China. *Applied Economics, 38*, 339-351.

Yin, E., & Choi, C. J. (2005). The globalization myth: The case of China. *Management International Review, 45*, 103-120.

Zagha, R., Nankani, G., & Gill, I. (2006). Rethinking growth. *Finance and Development, 43*(1), 7-11.

Zagorsek, H., Jaklic, M., & Stough, S. J. (2004). Comparing leadership practices between the United States, Nigeria, and Slovenia: Does culture matter? *Cross Cultural Management, 11*(2), 16-34.

Zhang, L. J., & Jeckle, M. (2004). Convergence of web services and grid computing. *International Journal of Web Services Research, 1*(3), 1-4.

CHAPTER 9

MEASURING THE CONTRIBUTION OF SMALL FIRMS TO REDUCING POVERTY AND INCREASING SOCIAL INCLUSION IN THE UNITED KINGDOM

Fergus Lyon and Marcello Bertotti

ABSTRACT

While enterprise policies are a strong feature of economic development in the United Kingdom, there is paucity of research on the impact of firms and their innovation on poverty in both urban and rural deprived areas. This chapter proposes and applies an innovative methodology to measure the impact of different types of enterprise in deprived areas emphasizing the need for more attention to qualitative, social aspects of impact evaluation. Drawing on a review of literature and methods of measuring impacts on poverty, a framework is set out that is tested in 2 contrasting locations. The innovative behavior of small enterprises in deprived areas is shown to have varying impacts on poverty. Innovations in policy and research methodology for impact assessments are also identified.

Innovative Approaches to Reducing Global Poverty
pp. 175–202
Copyright © 2007 by Information Age Publishing

While entrepreneurship and small enterprises are considered to be important players in reducing poverty, little is known of the impact of these organizations, and the way in which innovation and entrepreneurial strategies can affect social inclusion in areas of concentrated poverty. This chapter develops a framework for measuring the impact of small firms on poverty. The framework includes a range of economic and social indicators drawing on a social audit approach, multiplier effect studies, business community relationships and other impact assessment studies. A case study survey of 30 enterprises is used to examine the impact on owner/managers, staff, customers, suppliers, competitors, investors, and the local community. Implications are drawn for ways in which policies for reducing poverty can build on entrepreneurship and small enterprises, and how larger companies can engage with smaller businesses to have a greater impact on poverty reduction.

There has been a growing interest among U.K. policymakers concerning the role of enterprise development and innovation by entrepreneurs in poverty reduction. At present there is a lack of robust empirical evidence to demonstrate the actual contribution of enterprises to the reduction of poverty and deprivation. While many existing studies rely on measuring the number of jobs created, this chapter presents alternative methodologies for measuring the contribution of different types of enterprises to poverty reduction using a wide range of economic and social indicators. Particularly innovative in terms of impact evaluation is the attention paid by this chapter to identifying social capital and inter-business links as well as the contribution of businesses and employees to the local community. This broader view of measuring the impact on poverty, is reflected in wider debates in development studies that look beyond the economic impacts to include a more comprehensive view related to access to resources, opportunities and social inclusion (Mkandawire, 2004)

The chapter addresses this broader view by tackling three main questions: what are the social and economic indicators that describe best the contribution of different types of enterprises (social or mainstream) to reducing poverty? What types of survey data can be collected on these indicators? What are the impacts found in two case study areas?

There has been a growing interest around the world on the role of small enterprises in poverty reduction. Much attention has been focused in less developed countries by national governments, NGOs and aid donors. In more advanced economies, there is also growing interest, particularly with regard to concentrations of poverty in deprived areas (Blackburn & Ram, 2006; Porter, 1995). In the United Kingdom, the issue of enterprise success in deprived areas offers the promise of uniting the New Labor Government's interests of economic competitiveness, social inclusion and neighborhood renewal (HM Treasury, 1999). In addition to a wide range of local and regional government policy-based initiatives, national policy on enterprise and innovation in deprived areas is carried forward in many ways. These include the Small Business Services' Business Link support services, the Phoenix Fund, the Department for Education and Skills' New Entrepreneur Scholarship scheme, the Department for Work and Pensions' New Deal for the Self-employed, H.M. Treasury's Stamp Duty Relief, Business Improvement Districts, Local Enterprise Growth Initiative, City Growth Strategies, the Enterprise Areas measures, and the Department for Environment, Food and Rural Affairs' support for rural businesses as well as many other nongovernmental initiatives aimed at enterprise development in deprived areas.

DEVELOPING A METHODOLOGY FOR MEASURING THE CONTRIBUTION OF SMALL FIRMS

Following a review of the different types of impact assessment studies, a conceptual framework was established that recognizes the range of impacts received by a wide range of stakeholders. This framework is shown in Figure 9.1.

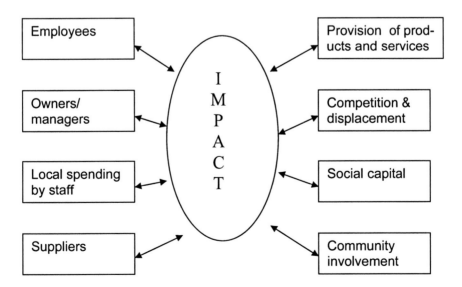

Figure 9.1.   The multiple impact and stakeholder model.

Employees

Enterprises have a direct impact on those employed by providing income as well as providing training and nonfinancial benefits. These businesses may be located in areas of concentrated poverty, or in neighboring areas but employing people living in disadvantaged areas. A challenge facing studies on the impact of enterprise in poverty reduction is measuring the extent to which the employees are from the deprived area itself and are drawn from disadvantaged groups.

The "employment deprived" (Department of the Environment, Transport and the Regions, 2000), are those who want to work but are unable to do so through unemployment, sickness or disability. Employment deprivation is seen as separate from the domain of income deprivation to which the lack of work may of course often lead (and lead quite quickly). The issue of sickness and disability makes it important that impact studies seek to gauge the importance of social firms (those whose explicit aim is to recruit from the ranks of such individuals).

Less skilled workers in deprived areas are often, almost by definition, in the very worst positions in the labor market. Growth of innovative knowledge based firms may exclude the less skilled living locally (O'Sullivan, 2002). If there *are* jobs for unskilled workers on their doorstep the deprived area residents are not guaranteed to get them as more skilled workers will often travel in to take such jobs. Furthermore, as small firms follow a "word of mouth" recruitment method, disadvantaged residents are excluded from the process as they often do not belong to such networks (Rosenfeld, 2002). Thus, it is important to look at methods of recruitment employed by firms in these areas and the "exclusivity" of networks. However, the extent of recruitment by these firms will also depend on other job opportunities and therefore will be influenced by employment opportunities in the local subregion. The policy consequences of this are that any exercise to see business-led regeneration and poverty reduction may be a forlorn exercise unless it occurs alongside a wider renaissance in the urban and regional labor market. The extent of demand for the less skilled also differs dramatically according to sector.

Clearly there are *some* jobs where being local is at a premium—for example where there are night shifts, where public transport is inaccessible and costly, and, even sometimes, where firms feel that employing locally reduces crime against them and provides better staff recruitment channels. Varying combinations of transport costs, childcare and low wages also mean that many workers will not be prepared/able to travel far. Indeed, research from the Social Exclusion Unit (Office of the Deputy Prime Minister [ODPM], 2004) found that London's deprived locations have a high number of workless lone parents, and a higher proportion of people in part time employment in low paying sectors. Low waged groups are found to spend a disproportionate amount of their income on getting to work, and longer commuting times can have wider environmental side effects of congestion and pollution.

Employment is not only a source of income, but also an opportunity to acquire skills and a source of various forms of occupational welfare. The role of enterprise in building human capital differs between firms with different types of contracts and conditions. There is some evidence that the wage levels and formal training opportunities are limited in smaller firms (Atkinson & Storey, 1993), although many employees state that they prefer the flexibility and personalised relations with such employers (Johnson, 1991). Flexibility is particularly important to individuals with childcare responsibilities, who are returning to work or are combining several part time jobs.

Employment can affect participation in various formal and informal social networks and can provide an individual with skills that can be used outside the workplace. Ways in which companies encourage staff to mix (e.g. company away-days, shared eating facilities/spaces, etc.) can also determine workers' friendship networks (which may also have implications for cohesion). However, community activities (both formal and informal) may be disrupted if unemployed people central to these networks' operation are forced off benefits into work. Furthermore the number and patterns of hours worked can affect the quality of life especially if it is shift work with unsociable hours.

Owners and Managers

Existing enterprises create income for owners and managers and new enterprises can increase income for business owners (if they are currently unemployed or in low income jobs), as well as for any managers they may employ. Starting enterprises can also increase access to opportunities for making a living for groups that are otherwise disadvantaged or excluded (London Regeneration Network [LRN], 2001). Indeed, disadvantage or discrimination in the labor market is one of the factors influencing some members of ethnic minorities to set up businesses (Blackburn & Ram, 2006). Although some may prefer salaried employment, starting a business may be a viable option for disadvantaged residents (Gavron, Holtham, & Westall, 1998). Startups can also benefit women reentering work since they can provide more flexible working conditions, such as part time work. These opportunities can be attractive to women with child-care responsibilities, who may otherwise be excluded from the labor market.

At the same time, studies of the startup rate show that rates of new firm formation are lower in most deprived areas although there are exceptions to this (Westall, Ramsden, & Foley, 2000) especially in London (ODPM, 2004). The current contribution of self-employment from new enterprises to reducing poverty is limited. Those starting up in business are more likely to do so because of "push factors" rather than "pull factors," and those pushed into self-employment are less likely to employ anyone else (Gray, 1998). It also needs to be recognised that self-employment is risky and not necessarily better than waged labor especially for the socially excluded. Moreover, the survival of businesses set up by those who have been unemployed has been shown to be lower than for those coming from employment (Smallbone, 1990).

Local Spending

Increased incomes of employees and owners are likely to contribute to a greater demand for local services (LRN, 2001). However, the scale of this impact is affected by the spending patterns of those in receipt of higher incomes and their ability to buy locally. If new consumer service firms allow/encourage residents to use local rather than nonlocal services, the flow of income within the locality will be increased with positive multiplier benefits (Westall et al., 2000).

However, the extent to which purchases will be local varies and multiplier effects are less where spending is concentrated on companies that source from outside of the locality. However, local spending can be greater amongst poorer households that have insufficient funds to travel elsewhere to make their purchases.

Suppliers

Businesses can impact other businesses through buying from or selling to them. However, Curran and Blackburn (1994) found that the types of small firms that have been increasing since the 1980s tend to be the least reliant on local markets. Firms that provide retail and personal services for local people and businesses allow greater amounts of money to be spent in the locality, which increases the multiplier effect and reduces the flows of resources out of deprived areas (Westall, Ramsden, & Foleyl, 2000; LRN, 2001). Before deciding how to treat the issue of firms' impacts upon local suppliers, and customers it is again necessary to question the extent to which businesses of any size have their suppliers, or markets within the *same* ward (the basic unit for measuring deprivation in the U.K.) or a larger local area. Impact measures also need to consider the extent to which the suppliers are employing people from deprived areas.

Provision of Products and Services

Innovative businesses can also produce social benefits through offering goods and services for sale. Indeed, the issue of "underserved" markets has been a major policy discussion in the United Statesin recent years (see Porter, 1997) and has attracted some attention in the United Kingdom (see Business in the Community, 2002). Underserved market areas are characterised by a lack of an adequate and often expensive retail offer of products and services. However, the significant overall purchasing power of local residents coupled with the "distinctive needs" of the significant ethnic mix of these areas creates the conditions for companies to invest in these areas based on the exploitation of niche markets (Porter, 1997). Thus, the lack of retail investment in deprived urban areas is explained by the inaccurate "perception" that the private sector holds about these areas. In the last few years, some alternative ways of assessing the potential of these areas emerged from U.S. based experience (Social Compact, 2001).

It is, however, important to note that there needs to be careful investigation of the extent of the existing business base and potential displacement before large retailers are "persuaded" to locate in these areas. There is increasing and contradictory evidence (Dixon, 2005) about the impact of large retailers—and especially food retailers at least in the United Kingdom—entering the locality. Beyond the direct employment creation, which can be substantial, large food retailers can provide positive spill over effects including increased attraction of customers to street shops, (Dunford, 2006).

Disadvantages may overcome these positive effects if such large retailers make use of existing supply chain relationships with companies located outside the immediate area and if the displacement effect on local shops that sell similar products is taken into account (Arnold & Luthra, 2000). In the case of large food retailers in the United Kingdom, the displacement effect may be great as such chains offer an increasingly wider range of products (e.g. clothes, eectrical appliances, flowers, etc). Over time, these expanded offerings may have a negatlive impact on a growing number of local companies but without some of the benefits mentioned above in terms of a further increase in the flow of customers to local shops.

Large retailers can also offer low prices (sometimes they may engage in price dumping to eliminate competition) to which people on low incomes are very sensitive. The other alternative for local retailers to compete (i.e. product differentiation) proposed by Porter (1995) may attract some customers that have specific needs and in this case the ethnic mix of such areas may play a role in terms of different tastes and needs. The evidence in relation to the impact of large retailers on the locality is very limited (Dunford, 2006), therefore the answer to this question should be the object of empirical investigation.

Social enterprises (defined as organisations trading for social aims and not for personal profit) might well be expected to make a particular contribution to inclusion within disadvantaged communities and localities (Leadbetter & Christie, 1999; Pearce, 1993). This contribution may be made by filling gaps in service delivery, improving employability and giving people experience of enterprise. However, the small number and scale of existing social enterprises at present suggests that their contribution is limited (Amin, Cameron, & Hudson, 2002).

It is also worth pointing out that certain forms of business activities (particularly shops, shopping parades/centers, pubs and clubs of varying descriptions) offer an arena for people to meet—over and above the purchases that they may or may not make when there. In this context the presence of such social infrastructures increases the opportunities for face to face social interaction that may lead to increasing referrals between companies and more generally the sharing of knowledge and information.

Competition and Displacement

The work of Michael Porter has stressed the virtues of strong local competition to keep business' performance high—that is to encourage the sorts of constant innovation that characterise the clusters of competitive advantage on which he focuses (Porter, 1995). Local competition is of course less obviously beneficial, to employment in a locality, where one company's gains come at the expense of another (referred to as displacement). Displacement is problematic in relation to government policies that have been criticised for creating displacement by favoring enterprise creation in low entry threshold activities that copy and undercut existing businesses. Where businesses are innovating and offering new services, there may be greater gains that do not come at the expense of others.

Robson, Bradford, and Deas (1999) have explained that displacement by innovative firms can be seen positively as constituting the invasion of new and more buoyant economic activity surplanting less competitive enterprises. This approach is taken by a range of recent government publications emphasising the "productive churn" as a market-force driven process that enables worse performing businesses to be replaced by new businesses that have higher productivity—the shift of market share from businesses with lower to those with higher productivity (e.g., HM Treasury, 2003).

In those instances where firms are overly concentrated in similar types of low-entry-threshold activities in a constrained local market (hairdressing, car repairs, etc.) competition can lead to high rates of displacement, contributing little to a diversification of the local economy (Atkinson & Storey, 1993; Mole, Green & Storey, 2002; Storey & Johnson, 1987; Storey & Strange, 1992; Turok & Richardson, 1991). New or growing firms may also encourage job switching which adds no benefit if the jobs are similar and in the same labor market.

Displacement can be low in conditions of buoyant local demand, and high in conditions of overall macroeconomic downturn. Thus, examination of displacement needs to control for the influence of macroeconomic conditions, otherwise investigation may yield different results in different periods of upturn or downturn.

Displacement is measured by looking at the location of competition, the extent of the geographic market and the uniqueness of the product/service (Hughes, 1991). Conventional studies of enterprise have only looked at displacement of jobs, although there can be displacement of other indicators such as services provided, money circulating in the local economy and community involvement. Displacement can be measured for a range of domains: within a ward/neighborhood, within a local authority area, within a region, nationally or even internationally. Most studies ignore the displacement at an international level and concentrate on other domains. Research on this topic is limited because the assessment of displacement can be problematic because the displaced firms may no longer in business.

Social Capital and Interbusiness Link

Business can also have a positive impact through working with partners to develop local collaborative links on research and development, training, infrastructure, marketing, purchasing, and supplies. The extent to which these forms of collaboration can stimulate improved performance from firms that employ un/low-skilled workers and/or serve deprived areas/groups needs to be assessed. In the research on "innovative milieu," the notion of there being a "learning dynamic" (a culture of continuous innovation, an enthusiasm for technology and ongoing dialogue about current/future products between user and producer) is prominent. Similarly, in the clusters approach of Porter (1997) the role of supply and technological linkages between companies increases the flow of information that ultimately has positive effects on the competitiveness of the area. Evaluations of these linkages have emerged in recent years from a number of studies (e.g. Lundequist & Power, 2002; Raines, 2002).

Much has been made in the literature on successful regional economies (notably the innovative milieu and new industrial districts work) about trust relationships between firms. In addition to making companies ready to trade and collaborate it may allow discussion of commercially sensitive information (with suppliers, buyers and collaborators, etc.) without recourse to a formal (costly) contractual/legalistic approach. Trust ties can perform an informal social control function against unethical business practices such as deliberate sale of defective goods/services, hostile (zero-sum) worker-poaching, late/nonpayment; poaching not training; overpricing, reneging on informal agreements (confidentiality concerning technical or commercial information) and so forth. Clearly, many firms have legal agreements to protect them against most forms of malpractice—the point is that some degree of trust is needed before firms will even enter into such agreements in the first instance. And it is a costly and time consuming process to make sure that contractual agreements are respected.

Businesses play a role in building trust-based networks within communities through collaboration and increasing the amount of interaction and transactions. They can be an important part of the intra community linkages that allow sharing of information and encouragement to entrepreneurs. However, defining trust and social capital is notoriously difficult. The difficulties of defining, operationalizing and measuring social capital are well documented however (see Concise, 2002). The economic terms the benefits of social capital are mainly identified in terms of reduced transaction costs and the appropriateness of the accumulated social capital in groups (Woolcock, 1998, 2001).

Community Involvement by Businesses and Employees

Business support for local good causes (community engagement) is also another way, perhaps the most commonly recognized way, in which businesses enhance the local social fabric. Examples here include: donations to, and sponsorship of, local good causes; apprenticeships, student placements, and mentoring; and participation in and managing community activities (Atherton & Sear, 2001). However, Curran and Blackburn (1994) found little evidence of a "local consciousness" among business owners, over and above a necessity to trade locally.

As well as economic multipliers, enterprise activity can produce social, cultural and psychological multipliers. These multipliers include investor, resident and business confidence from local business success stories as well as peer support and encouragement through the demonstration effect and through personal contact with entrepreneurs. These influences are particularly important for those parts of society where there are low startup rates (particular ethnic groups, women, particular localities such as coalfields). Flora, Sharp, and Flora (1997) refer to these influences as part of the entrepreneurial social infrastructure.

Enterprises can clearly play a key role in shaping the image of neighborhoods. While businesses that invest in local infrastructure and provide services can increase the attractiveness of an area, impacts can also be negative—for example, the impact of steel processors and scrap dealers in parts of Sheffield (Dabinett & Ramsden 1999).

METHODOLOGY FOR TESTING THE FRAMEWORK

The following approaches were drawn upon in developing the methodology used in this study:

- Economic approaches: Conventional impact assessment studies concentrate on quantifiable indicators such as jobs created, increases in income and turn over of businesses (Cowling & Hayward, 2000, Storey & Strange, 1992). Much attention has been given to measuring job displacement (i.e. how new jobs are created at the cost of displacing existing jobs).

- Social audit approaches: These approaches measure the wider impact on the stakeholders shown in the figure above (including local communities and employees). Indicators of business community relations include measures of explicit impacts such as donations, sponsorship, and so forth, and the less obvious impacts such as community cohesion, trust and supporting people from a diverse range of groups. There has been growing interest in these approaches among the private sector as consumers and investors are putting pressure on larger firms to consider their impact on the local communities where they operate and to ensure they have beneficial impacts.

- Monitoring local money flows: Multiplier effect studies aim to provide information on where money coming into a community goes and the extent to which it circulates within the local economy. Three types of effects can be measured: the direct effect of the firm's spending, the indirect effect of the spending by the firms' suppliers and the induced effect of the spending by employees.

Following the review of the different approaches to measuring impacts, a set of questions was developed and tested empirically. The study involved a total of 30 semistructured face-to-face interviews with members of companies of different sizes and operating in quite varied sectors, including manufacturing, retail, agriculture, and social enterprises. These organizations were selected to represent as many business typologies as possible. In order to be able to grasp potential differences between rural and urban economies, two disadvantaged areas of Boston in Lincolnshire and Luton in Bedfordshire were examined. In addition, six key informants were interviewed in each area to collect useful information on the economic and social profiles of the wards.

FINDINGS FROM THE CASE STUDIES OF THE IMPACT OF SMALL FIRMS ON POVERTY AND SOCIAL EXCLUSION IN TWO DEPRIVED AREAS

Employees and Jobs

The impact on employees depends on the extent to which enterprises employ those from the deprived areas and in particular people from disadvantaged or socially excluded groups within such areas. This study found that on average, half of all employees of enterprises in deprived wards live outside the area although the extent to which people in deprived areas travel elsewhere for work is not known. It is important to gain a greater understanding of the distance socially excluded people are willing to travel and, if necessary, what can be done to encourage them to look for opportunities further away. While 47% of the population in Dallow (Luton) are from ethnic minorities, 10 out of 15 firms were recruiting less than 10% of their employees from ethnic minorities.

The methodology developed in this study can be used to assess whether the needs of the socially excluded are best met by encouraging firms to establish themselves in deprived areas or to set up in a location where they perceive that they will grow faster and therefore employ more people. The benefits of having local jobs (in terms of reduced travel times, less congestion, access for those without access to cars or public transport, and helping those who want to be near childcare) should also be recognized. This methodology can also be used to assess which types of firms create more jobs for the socially excluded, and therefore should be supported in deprived areas. For example the growth of innovative "knowledge intensive" firms may not help those with few skills. There is some evidence that in deprived areas some high-tech sectors (e.g., ICT) have been targeted to comply with government (i.e., DTI) priorities (Tully & Berkley, 2004; Woodward, 2005). Public sector support should therefore concentrate on innovative firms that provide additional employment for those on lower incomes rather than displacing jobs.

The quality of the job depends on the salary and other benefits derived by staff. The survey found that salaries in rural areas were approximately 10% lower and were also lower in social enterprises, in part because of the greater extent of part time work. Perks such as company cars, houses, and bonuses are hard to quantify and are not included in this survey.

Quality of employment also depends on the levels of stress, working conditions, health and safety risks, and the satisfaction a person gets from the job. An indicator of staff satisfaction is the number of staff who have left in the past year (staff turnover). The survey found that the staff turnover rates were higher in the more menial, less skilled types of work such as manual factory work, restaurant work, and shop assistants.

Building skills is also a benefit commonly reported by employees. The types of training reported fit into the following categories:

- In-house mentoring and apprenticeships;
- Internal training courses;
- External short training programs; and
- External long-term education, such as day release building up to a qualification.

Seven social enterprises were interviewed and it was found that they had more part-time workers, women, young, and ethnic minorities. These types of organizations are also offering innovative approaches to meeting social needs of those in poverty, building on a range of different business models. In addition to creating jobs, social enterprises can have the objective of building up the skills and confidence of their staff.

For example, one manager who works part time as a volunteer when not caring for her father-in-law gave her story:

Twenty-six years ago I stopped work. But over the last ten years my sister kept saying … that I should try and go back to work. I kept saying how, when, where? Although I've never done a computer course, I've gone on to the computer, and I'm self taught, and it's given me great … it's built up … as soon as my father-in-law dies, [this organisation] will be at a loss, because I will be going for a job. Which I know I will get … I'm confident enough to know.

Owners and Managers

The main impact on owners and managers is the change in income. Incomes may have increased if the enterprise has become profitable or decreased if the firm is less successful or the individual decided to move from paid employment for lifestyle reasons or redundancy. The survey found 14 of the 30 owners and managers interviewed were not resident in the deprived wards selected for the pilot study. However, a greater proportion of smaller businesses and those located in rural areas have owners living in the deprived areas and therefore contributing to the locality. As mentioned earlier, starting a business may be a useful option for disadvantaged individuals who are excluded from the labor market. However, only 3 of the 30 enterprise owners/managers were previously unemployed or economically inactive.

Respondents were also found to have come from previous employment where they had been made redundant, so although they never became unemployed they might have if they had not started the business.

> I was a housewife bringing up the children and my husband was working at … as a mechanic, they went through a rocky patch, … So when he was made redundant he decided to set up repairing sewing machines and he was doing that for the domestic market at first and then we found that there was a need for people to do agricultural sewing machines that sew up potato bags. And so that was what got us into the industrial market and on onwards into the rest of the packaging line.

The above quote also demonstrates the importance of looking at the impact of enterprise on household incomes rather than individuals. This issue is particularly important when household labor is involved in the enterprise.

In addition to changing incomes, self-employment has both positive and negative effects on people's quality of life. The survey asked an open question and a large proportion of the respondents referred to the greater satisfaction but the pressure on nonwork parts of their lives. As one manager of a credit union put it, "I've no life left, no life … with the credit union and all the other things I have to do … but I get great satisfaction." Another reported that stress had reduced compared to his previous work in a large firm with its politics and rivalries.

An owner of a growing business stated:

> I think working for yourself is either brilliant or terrible, it's very rarely anything in between. It's either going really well, or it's about to fall off a cliff. It's never average, never ok. Overall, we've had a good life. I think our life-

style's been fine, we have had some very lean years in that, and we've had some very good, years. We're still here!

There are particular pressures on women who have other responsibilities: "I think being a mum and a wife, it does mount up at the end of the day. It is very hard to manage running a business … running the home, running the children, and everything."

For those businesses facing difficulties, the costs of self-employment can be high. One farmer reported:

> I don't mind working for myself at all. The problem is that we're getting less and less free time. The kids are getting grown up, and I've hardly seen them grow up, and … er … as you get older you begin to see what you've missed in trying to grow or build up a larger business all the time. This weekend was the first weekend I've been away in July since 1976 … when you see your profit diminishing, or even going the other way to a negative, you wonder why on earth you're putting these sorts of hours in, to be honest. It is getting to that stage, where you wonder why you continue to carry on doing it, really.

Negative effects on owner managers are more likely to be reported by those who have not continued the business, either through forced closure or deciding to work for others. One owner related the story of a competitor who had eventually committed suicide due to financial and personal difficulties.

The survey also explored how running an enterprise had affected people "personally" resulting in changes in skills, confidence, participation in community activities, and aspirations. People referred to a range of skills they had developed, using terms such as communication, research, negotiating, and organizational skills. Others referred to "knowing how to deal with a situation," "being able to bang heads together," "it teaches you an awful lot about people," "I'm confident about meeting new people and professionals," and "it teaches you to be diplomatic with people."

Local Spending (by Employees and Owners)

Two thirds of expenditure by employees and owner/managers was in their wards or within a 10-mile radius. The proportion spent locally was greater in urban areas, although the extent to which this money is recirculated in the locality through these retailers buying locally is not known.

Supply Chains and Subcontractors

Some sectors and types of firms are more "embedded" in local supply chains than others resulting in more of their expenditure circulating and a greater multiplier effect for their contribution. Identification of these types of firms is required in order to target support that has the greatest impact. It is hypothesized that the less specialized products and services will source more locally and have more local customers. This possible relationship suggests that more innovative and knowledge intensive firms may have less impact on poverty reduction on this dimension. An exception may be clusters of specialized companies that gain competitive advantage through working closely together and using "Just in time" approaches. An average of the 30 enterprises interviewed shows that less than half of all supplies come from the ward or locally (within 10 miles), although the seven social enterprises sourced on average three quarters of supplies locally.

In the sample of rural firms, a third of the interviewees reported that they have a policy of buying locally where possible in order to support local firms as well as to have the service they require.

> Well, we are a big advocator of trying to support local businesses, because obviously it's in our interest to have service close to hand so we don't have a loss of too long a down time, then obviously we get a quicker turn around of any problems that we should have.

An important part of expenditure on supplies can be in the form of casual labor. Employment agency labor was found to be particularly important in the horticultural sector of the Boston area. The "gang masters" as they are referred to locally may be local businesses themselves but draw on labor from neighboring counties (particular those urban areas with concentrations of deprivation, or from eastern European countries.) The working conditions and benefits to those working for these agencies vary although respondents felt that recent stringent checks on company operations have reduced the risk that workers will be exploited. The impact of this system of importing casual labor is also felt in the urban areas from which this labor is recruited.

> The agencies can bring them from anywhere—from Birmingham, from Rotherham, from Mansfield.... Well there's an awful lot of eastern Europeans now residing in Boston, ... knowing there's plenty of seasonal work available ... Bulgarians and Poles and Russians ... they get work in pack houses ... there's a lot of processing lines in the Boston area, whether it's for packing fruit or prepacking vegetables, or processing industries.

Provision of Products and Services

Enterprises can make a particular contribution to deprived areas if they provide services such as shops, transport or leisure. Enterprises in disadvantaged areas play a key role in providing services to local people. The impact on customers who are the final consumers (rather than businesses) is greater in the retail sector and among social enterprises. Indeed, many social enterprises have as their primary goal the provision of social and economic benefits to a defined particular locality. In many deprived areas, retail outlets have closed, a problem that is particularly acute in rural areas. In one of the wards in Boston there were no retail outlets at all.

The extent of the benefit depends on the objectives of the enterprise. The small sample for this survey does not allow an analysis of this impact. The survey does show that a third of sales are in the wards with differences according to sectors and type of enterprise. A very small proportion of sales of the manufacturing sector is directed to the local economy while a majority of social enterprise customers operate in the same ward.

Competition and Displacement

The positve impact of enterprises on a deprived area can be negated if they crowd out other enterprises that are already involved in their activity (i.e. displacement). Where services are very similar, the growth of one firm will result in declining market shares for others and hence will yield no increase in employment for the area. There is less displacement when innovative firms can identify new markets in deprived areas. To measure displacement it is therefore necessary to measure the extent of geographic markets, the levels of competition, and the uniqueness of the product or service. The first of these factors is measured in the previous section, and the second and third factors can be measured by collecting data on the number of competitors and the percentage of competitors in the ward or local area.

Competitors will not only attempt to take some of the market from other enterprises but may attempt to poach staff. One social enterprise was particularly concerned when a similar organization was established in the same rural area: "we did consider our position [location] when xxx were formed, because it's a small town and a small pool of ... we were concerned about whether it was big enough for both of us in the sense of being able to draw upon a limited employment pool."

The pilot survey found that service firms have more customers in local markets and may therefore be displacing other local firms serving the local market. However, there is a need to break down the category of services to assess the uniqueness of the service, and the extent to which there is a local gap in the service delivery in the locality. Cowling and Hayward (2000) found that business services can have the lowest level of displacement while household trades and retail can have high displacement.

Social Capital and Interbusiness Links

Enterprises build relationships with suppliers, customers and other businesses as part of their day to day activities. These networks are an important part of a community's social capital and can be an important resource in terms of encouraging new enterprises to start and allowing others to grow. Through participation in some of these networks, socially excluded groups can have better access to resources and hence an impact on poverty reduction. The types of relationships can be bilateral (i.e., one to one) or multilateral (i.e., a group of enterprises in an association). Relationships can also be formalized or informal.

The types of collaboration mentioned by the 30 organizations in the study interviewed can be classified into the following categories:

• Sharing equipment, space, staff (e.g., farmers borrow equipment and exchange fields for a year, lend out forklift trucks and trailers);

• Sharing ideas knowledge and information (e.g. talking to other enterprises involved in marketing at social events in the village, farmers discuss which crops to use or the quality of different consultants);

• Referrals (e.g., "we put work their way," get new markets through referrals from others); and

• Joint projects/alliances (e.g., a garage works with a car dealership to do their MOTs, a flooring company gives a preferential deal to an estate agent and pub who can demonstrate its products, a group of farmers share equipment).

Reducing Poaching of Staff

Behind all the relationships is an element of trust that is built up over time, through reciprocal dealings or through relying on a third party trusted by both parties in the relationship. In most cases there is no contract and people rely on "word of mouth" and "a gentleman's agreement." The reasons for the relationships are not always in terms of immediate benefit. Some relationships are built up so that they can be used in the future for unpredictable reasons. In such cases social capital is linked to serendipitous outcomes and is considered as a "bank of goodwill" that can be drawn on later. In many cases, the relationships are seen as friendships rather than as a calculated investment of time and resources with a clear expectation of a return.

> It's as much about making friends than anything else. You tend to do business with people you like, I mean if you don't like them, then you, for the best reasons in the world, tend to end up not dealing with them, so yeah I think it is about making friendships and relationships, really.

Some relationships are built up subconsciously or tacitly. The quote below demonstrates that tacit relationships can be identified when interviewees pause to reflect. After indicating that they had not really thought about the issue, they may see things they had not seen before:

> Q: "Do you help other firms?"
> A: "No, we don't help others although it does happen in an informal way. Just by talking to people you build up relationships with people so it does happen but in an informal way.… I suppose it is everyone we deal with regularly. If you are talking to people regularly you build up a relationship and exchange ideas."

The extent to which these relationships are beneficial is debatable in some circumstances. Cartels are made of strong relationships and can have negative consequences for the wider public. One enterprise was quite frank about this: "we are trying to collaborate with our competitors in Leicester to rig the price, to stay away from his customers, to do this, to do that … it is a straightforward dog-eat-dog … how you want to interpret that, of course, is entirely up to you." The impact of these relationships depends on the importance of the networks to the performance of the enterprise or the amount that is put at stake and at risk.

Business networks or clubs were defined as a networks or formal associations involving more than five other enterprises. Examples of networks include sector specific bodies, local regeneration committees and the chamber of commerce. The latter is the most commonly reported group although most of those reporting it felt that they were a net giver rather than a net receiver of support. However, it was seen as being important for sourcing local services.

Community Involvement by Businesses and Employees

Business support for local good causes (community engagement) is also another way, perhaps the most overt way, in which businesses can enhance the local social fabric. While "corporate social responsibility" has received much discussion in relation to larger businesses, this study shows how information on smaller businesses, and their impacts within their communities, can be collected. While many firms had a fund for on-going sponsorships and charitable activities, others decided to donate money for particular causes. Many enterprises gave their products free of charge such as a game of golf or a crate of bananas. The selection of recipients is made by owner/managers of small firms or the public relations managers of larger firms. Some sponsorship is considered as a form of advertising or public image management, while other types are more philanthropic.

Allowing the use of company resources or property was frequently reported with examples such as a housing association allowing a charity to have offices in their buildings, allowing a play group to use buildings when not in use, and a farm hosting a ploughing match. Contributions to local churches were mentioned by five of the interviewees.

Apprenticeships were found in only one enterprise: a horse stud business where there were people with an interest in horses willing to learn to be a stable manager. Almost half the interviewees were involved in short term placements for school children. This was done as a purely philanthropic act: "Really they are here to look at all aspects of what we do and just give them some understanding. I think really it's to give them some work ethos."

As well as economic multipliers, enterprise activity can produce social, cultural and psychological multipliers. These include investor, resident and business confidence from local business success stories as well as peer support and encouragement through the demonstration effect and knowing entrepreneurs. This factor is particularly important for those parts of society where there are low startup rates (particular ethnic groups, women, particular localities such as former coal-fields where there are concentrations of poverty). Very few of the enterprises interviewed could think of examples of mentoring other businesses and encouraging people to start up, despite the fact that mentoring and advice from other businesses is frequently mentioned as an important encouraging factor by people who have started up a business. This type of impact may come about without the owner/manager realizing it, as part of everyday life, rather than a conscious action. After some thought one owner said:

> "Er yes I think there is a bit of a networking thing happens. People come to you and think you have all the answers. You have made it look so easy so they can do it.... Yes but informally.... mostly from people in the village because we live here, people we have contact with. But wherever you go people think you are a font of information.

One enterprise gave advice and mentoring to others under a formal mentoring scheme ("Partners in Leadership" that links teachers to other businesses), and a manager of a social enterprise was involved in a community business development program. Owner/managers can contribute to a local community by participating in and taking a managing role in activities. A third of the firms had owner/managers on community related committees. All social enterprise owner/managers were also on other committees compared to less than a half of manufacturing firms and less than one third of service firms.

The types of community involvement can be classified into the following categories:

- Charitable: trustee of various charities, on board of directors of charity or other social enterprise;
- Church/religious group: on Parochial Church Council for the parish church;
- School: school governor, PTA;
- Civic: local council, parish council, local regeneration board, community playing fields committee; and
- Specialist interest group: sports club, horse show jumping society, ploughing competition.

Examples of involvement in activities for improving the reputation of an area included restoration of buildings by a housing association, building offices that would attract other businesses, and building an art gallery to attract people to come to the community. A firm that had recently moved felt that their decision was a good statement: "Well, we're here—I think that's raising the reputation of the area.... We could've chosen the whole country but we picked this one."

The significant amount of community involvement found in this small sample challenges the assertion of Curran and Blackburn (1994) in the study cited earlier that found little evidence of a "local consciousness" among business owners, over and above a necessity to trade locally.

CONCLUSIONS

This chapter has examined the ways in which enterprise can have an impact on poverty reduction. The issue of innovation is addressed from three directions. First in terms of innovation in enterprises and the impact on poverty reduction, second in terms of innovation in public policy related to increasing the impact of enterprise on poverty reduction, and finally in terms of innovation in research and impact assessment methodologies.

Innovation in enterprises can have considerable impacts on poverty reduction when it leads to business growth. However, there is a need to assess the extent to which this growth "trickles down" to the poorest. Provision of jobs is the most direct effect of business growth, although this study has made a distinction between those types of firms that help reduce poverty by providing jobs for the poor, and other businesses that might exclude poorer people (especially those that are unemployed) because they do not have the required skills and experience. There is initial evidence that knowledge intensive and innovative firms located in areas of concentrated poverty may not employ people from those areas, especially when they require highly skilled people (O'Sullivan, 2002). These firms may also have international supply chains and source less from local firms, thereby having a small multiplier effect.

The types of firms that can employ the less skilled and do source more locally are, however, often found to be less innovative. These enterprises may mimic existing firms in the locality, and new business startups may displace existing businesses operating in the area. The greatest impacts on poverty reduction occur when businesses can develop new innovative markets, employing less skilled people and creating "escalator jobs" that increase skill levels. There are also opportunities for firms in areas of concentrated deprivation to tap into markets in more affluent areas. In such cases innovation may have to overcome barriers related to the insular networks that can arise in deprived areas. Social capital is a crucial ingredient and there is a need for both bonding social capital within communities and bridging social capital that opens up innovative opportunities.

This study has also shown that poverty-reducing innovation in enterprises does not relate only to providing jobs, products and services. Firms may also be innovative in terms of human resource development, increasing job quality, training and community involvement, all of which can contribute to poverty reduction.

With regard to poverty-reducing innovation by policymakers, this chapter has identified factors that need to be assessed in the design of policy. In particular there is a need to ensure that any initiatives are adapted to local specificities and the needs of the poor. Innovative policies are needed that ensure that benefits are received by poor people resident in deprived areas and from disadvantaged groups rather than simply assuming that firms located in deprived areas will automatically benefit those in poverty. These assumptions are widespread with the U.K.'s Department of Trade and Industry having a public service agreement target to "generate more sustainable enterprise in the 20% most disadvantaged local authority wards." The impact of enterprises upon poverty comes both from firms located in deprived areas *and* from firms outside those areas that employ deprived area residents.

Understanding local contexts and behavior is crucial. One key aspect is the extent to which people are willing to travel outside their local area for work. Innovative policy requires the integration of employment and transport policies and a refocus of policy support toward employment creation from a local to a subregional level.

Finally, this chapter offers insights into innovation in means of carrying out research and measuring the impact of enterprises on poverty reduction. Such research and measurement requires going beyond simple economic indicators like jobs created, to include a wide range of indicators as set out in this chapter. In addition to jobs created, other impacts include provision of services, local money flows, benefits to supply chains, building social capital and community contributions. While some indicators can be quantified, qualitative impacts such as job satisfaction, quality of life and personal development are also important indicators of impact. These are summarized in Table 9.1.

Innovative research methods are needed to challenge policy assumptions about the relationship between enterprise and poverty reduction. In particular, research should consider where people living in deprived areas are working or willing to work and not assume that the poor will benefit when a firm is established or grows close to where they live.

Despite the large number of public sector initiatives supporting small enterprises, there is still little detailed study of the impacts of these firms on poverty. There is also very little evidence of the poverty-reducing impact of public sector support for small enterprises. Blackburn and Ram (2006) suggest that there is an overoptimism among policymakers with the associated risk of a backlash against the promotion of business ownership when negative evidence emerges. Research on the impacts of small enterprise on disadvantaged areas and research on the impact of policies for the support of entrepreneurship need to be undertaken over time via a longitudinal examination of such localities.

This study has examined the impact of small firms on poverty. However, the methodology could also be used to assess large firm contribution to deprived locations. Such assessment would be particularly important in the context of less developed economies where debates on development often revolve around the attractiveness or dangers of investment from multinational companies. Little is actually known about the social and economic impact of those firms.

ACKNOWLEDGMENTS

This chapter is developed from a paper "Measuring the Impact of Enterprise in Deprived Areas" presented at the Small Business and Entrepre-

Table 9.1.   The Multiple Impact of Enterprise Framework

Types of impact	Types of indicators	Specific indicators
Jobs for people from deprived areas	The types of employment currently available to people in deprived areas	• Location of employment for people in deprived areas • Quality of employment opportunities (see below)
	Number of employees and extent to which staff needs match local labor market and disadvantaged groups	• Number of jobs (full and part time) • Number of full time equivalent jobs • Proportion of socially excluded /low skilled among recruited staff • Proportion from different ethnic groups • Proportion of men and women • Proportion from different age groups • Methods of recruitment • Proportion of employees that are casual / seasonal labor
Quality of jobs	Wage levels	• Wages of different levels of staff (managerial, professional, artisanal/ skilled, less skilled)
	Skill development and learning	• Amount of formal training provided • Percentage of staff claiming to have gained skills and earning potential • Perceived change in specific skill aspects including technical, communications, negotiation, research, organisational and managerial skills
	Job satisfaction	• Staff turnover in past 3 years • Perception of satisfaction
	Changes in quality of life	• Perception of quality of life
	Workplaces as arenas for social cohesion	• Extent of intra firm mixing and examples of how this has had an impact
Impacts on owners, managers	Avoiding unemployment and low wages	• What they were doing before starting
	Change in income	• Percentage change in income for past 12 months compared to before starting
	Change in quality of life	• Increase or decrease in income, stress, leisure time, family time, and general perception of quality of life
	Skill development and learning	• Amount of formal training gained • Perceived change in specific skill aspects including technical, communications, negotiation, research, organizational and managerial skills

(Table continues on next page)

Table 9.1.   (Continued)

Types of impact	Types of indicators	Specific indicators
	Personal development	• Perceived changes in confidence, self esteem and ability
Supply chains and subcontractors	Local purchasing and generating local business	• Extent of enterprise's spending in locality • Extent of use of local business support services • Extent to which local suppliers purchase locally
Competition	Potential for displacement	• Number of direct competitors in locality • Extent to which market for goods or services is saturated
Social capital and interbusiness links	Helping other local firms	• Number of collaborative links • Examples of helping each other
	Participating in business networks and clubs	• Membership of business networks and clubs • Extent of involvement
Community involvement by businesses and employees	Donations and sponsorship	• Amount of donations and sponsorship for deprived areas • Use of company resources (time, space, equipment, vehicles, etc.)for deprived areas
	Participation in and managing community activities	• What types of activities • What management roles or committee membership
	Apprenticeships, student placements	• Number and length of apprenticeships over past three years • Number of student placements over past three years
	Improving the image of a locality	• Whether enterprise is involved in promoting image • What kind of involvement
	Encouraging people to move into the locality	• Examples of cases where others were encouraged to move
	Encouraging people to start, sustain or grow a business through advice and mentoring	• Examples of cases where encouragement was given to other businesses • Types of support

neurship Development Conference, in 2003. The authors are grateful for the input from David Smallbone, Mel Evans, Gareth Potts, and Peter Ramsden in the design of the original research. All views expressed are those of the authors.

REFERENCES

Amin, A., Cameron, A., & Hudson, R. (2002). *Placing the social economy.* London: Routledge.

Arnold, S. J., & Luthra, M. N. (2000). Market entry effects of large format retailers: a stakeholder analysis. *International Journal of Retail & Distribution Management, 28*(4/5), 139-145.

Atherton, A., & Sear, L. (2001). *Are you one of us? An analysis of the interactions and linkages between small businesses and their local communities.* Paper presented at the 24th ISBA National Small Firms Policy and Research Conference, Centre for Enterprise, Leicestershire, United Kingdom.

Atkinson, J., & Storey, D. (1993). *Employment, the small firm and the labour market*, London: Routledge.

Business in the Community. (2002). *Business investment in under-served markets.* London: Author.

Blackburn, R., & Ram, M. (2006). Fix or fixation? The contributions and limitations of entrepreneurship and small firms to combating social exclusion. *Entrepreneurship and Regional Development, 18*(1), 73-89.

Centre for Enterprise and Economic Development Research & New Economics Foundation. (2003). *The impact of different forms of entrepreneurship on local economies in disadvantaged areas.* A report for the Small Business Service, Department for Trade and Industry, United Kingdom.

Conscise. (2002). *The contribution of social capital in the social economy to local economic development in Western Europe, Report 6: Local socio-economic profiles: Consolidated report.* Available at: www.conscise.mdx.ac.uk

Cowling, M., & Hayward, R. (2000). *Out of unemployment.* Birmingham, United Kingdom: Research Centre for Industrial Strategy.

Curran, J., & Blackburn, R. (1994). *Small firms and local economic networks: The death of the local economy?* London: Paul Chapman.

Dabinett, G., & Ramsden, P. (1999). Urban policy in Sheffield: Regeneration, partnerships and people. In R. Imrie & H. Thomas (Eds.), *British urban policy and the urban development corporations.* London: Sage.

Department of the Environment, Transport and the Regions. (2000). Indices of deprivation. *Regeneration Research Summary* (31). London: Author.

Dixon, T. J. (2005). The role of Retailing in urban regeneration. *Local Economy, 20*(2), 168-182.

Department of Trade and Industry. (2002). *Engaging SMEs in community and social issues*, London: Author.

Dunford, J. (2006). Under-served markets. *Local Economy, 21*(1), 73-77.

Flora, J., Sharp, J., & Flora, C. (1997). Entrepreneurial social infrastruture and locally initiated economic development in the non-metropolitan United States. *Sociological Quarterly, 38*(4), 623-644.

Gavron, R., Cowling, M., Holtham, G., & Westall, A. (1998). *The entrepreneurial society.* London: IPPR.

Gray, C. (1998). *Enterprise and culture.* London: Routledge.

HM Treasury. (1999). *Enterprise and social exclusion. National strategy for neighbourhood renewal: Policy Action Team 3.*

HM Treasury. (2003). *Productivity in the UK: 4 – The local dimension*. United Kingdom: Her Majesty Treasury and the ODPM (Office for the Deputy Prime Minister).

Hughes, J. (1991). Evaluation of local economic development: A challenge for policy research. *Urban Studies, 28*(6), 909-918.

Johnson S. (1991). *Small firms and the UK labour market: Prospects for the 1990s*. London: MacMillan.

Leadbetter, C., & Christie, I. (1999). *To our mutual advantage*. London: Demos.

London Regeneration Network. (2001). *Enterprising neighbourhoods ... the role of micro-businesses in revitalising neighbourhoods*. London: LVSC.

Lundequist, P., & Power, D. (2002). Putting Porter into practice? Practices of regional cluster building: Evidence from Sweden. *European Planning Studies, 10*(6), 685-704.

Mkandawire, T. (Ed.). (2004). Social policy in a development context: Introduction. In *Social policy in a development context* (pp. 1-18). Houndmills, United Kingdom: Palgrave Macmillan.

Mole, K., Greene, F., & Storey, D. (2002). *Entrepreneurship in three English counties*. Paper presented at the 25th ISBA National Small Firms Policy and Research Conference: Competing Perspectives of Small Business and Entrepreneurship.

Office of the Deputy Prime Minister. (2004). *Jobs and enterprise in deprived areas* (Social Exclusion Unit Report). England: Author.

O'Sullivan, F. (2002). *Dot com clusters and local economic development: The case of new media development in London's city fringe* (London Regeneration paper 5). Middlesex, United Kingdom: CEEDR Middlesex University.

Pearce, J. (1993). *At the heart of the community economy: Community enterprise in a changing world*. London: Calouste Gulbenkian Foundation.

Porter, M. (1995). The competitive advantage of inner cities. *Harvard Business Review, 73*(3), 1279-1312.

Porter, M. (1997, February). New strategies for inner city economic development. *Economic Development Quarterly, 11*(1), 11-27.

Raines, P. (2002, May). *The challenge of evaluating cluster behavior in economic eevelopment policy*. Paper presented at the International RSA Conference "Evaluation and EU Regional Policy: New Questions and Challenges," Aix-en-Prrovence.

Robson, B., Bradford, M., & Deas, I. A. (1999). Beyond the boundaries: Vacancy chains and the evaluation of urban development corporations. *Environment and Planning, A*(21), 647-664.

Rosenfeld, S. A. (2002). *Just clusters: Economic development strategies that reach more people and places*. Carrboro, NC: Regional Technology Strategies.

Social Compact. (2001). Harlem neighborhood market drilldown. Social Compact, submitted to the Fleet Community Banking Group, in http://socialcompact.org/pdfs/Harlem_ Neighborhood_Market_DrillDown_Report.pdf

Smallbone, D. (1990). Success and failure in small business start ups. *International Small Business Journal, 8*(2), 34-47.

Storey, D., & Johnson S. (1987). *Job generation and labour market change*. London: Macmillan.

Storey, D. J., & Strange, A. (1992). New players in the enterprise culture? In K. Caley, E. Chell, F. Chittenden, & C. Mason (Eds.), *Small enterprise development: Policy and practice in action*. London: Paul Chapman.

Tully, J., & Berkley, N. (2004). Visualising the operating behaviour of SMEs in sector and cCluster: Evidence from the West Midlands. *Local Economy, 19*(1), 38-54.

Turok, I., & Richardson, P. (1991). New firms and local economic development: evidence from West Lothian. *Regional Studies, 25*(1), 71-83.

Westall, A., Ramsden, P., & Foley, J. (2000). *Micro-entrepreneurs: Creating enterprising communities*. London: IPPR/NEF.

Woodward, D. (2005, December). *Porter's cluster strategy versus industrial targeting*. Paper based on a presentation at the ICIT Workshop, Orlando, Florida.

Woolcock, M. (1998, April 27). Social capital and economic development: Toward a theoretical synthesis and policy framework. *Theory and Society, 2*, 151-208.

Woolcock, M. (2001). Microenterprise and social capital: A framework for theory, research and policy. *Journal of Socio-Economics, 30*(2), 193-198.

CHAPTER 10

REDUCING POVERTY THROUGH RETAIL-LED REGENERATION IN DISADVANTAGED NEIGHBORHOODS

A BRITISH PERSPECTIVE

Paul Whysall

ABSTRACT

Traditional urban base theory sees retailing as largely irrelevant to economic regeneration of disadvantaged areas, overlooking the contributions retailing can make to reducing poverty and increasing social inclusion. However, a shift in attitudes has occurred in recent years. In both Britain and the United States retailing is now being seen as a key driver in economic regeneration and social revitalization. The process of rethinking the role of retailing is traced in the British context as a response to several interacting agendas: the failure of "traditional" policies, the evolution of eco-

Innovative Approaches to Reducing Global Poverty
pp. 203–235

nomic base theory, the rise of the sustainability agenda, concern for declining traditional retail centres, health and dietary concerns, and so forth. These various influences are discussed and recent studies in British retail-led regeneration are reviewed. The chapter concludes by exploring challenges and barriers still faced by retail-led regeneration.

Relationships between retailing and policies to reduce poverty, combat disadvantage and regenerate economies have shifted markedly. Traditionally retailing seemed largely irrelevant to these goals, indeed even detrimental to such poverty reducing approaches as "export-led" economic development. More recently notions of retail-led regeneration and the role it can play in pursuing such important goals as reducing poverty and combating disadvantage have gained widespread support in North America and, subsequently, Britain. However retail-led regeneration itself contains a number of problematic issues which remain disputed and unresolved.

Retail-led regeneration in Britain represents a convergence of interacting agendas: the evolution of economic base theory, failures of "traditional" urban planning, changing attitudes to retailing, shifting priorities within public policy frameworks, property market pressures, and international comparisons. The ensuing discussions explore and illustrate those processes, before the emergent model of retail-led regeneration is appraised in terms of its sustainability and the challenges that remain to be confronted.

Attitudes to retailing's potential contribution to regeneration of disadvantaged areas in Britain shifted completely over time, from negative to positive. This occurred as a result of a sequence of innovations. It starts with changes in thinking pertaining to economic base theory, a conceptual innovation that rejected the previous view of retailing as generally not contributing to economic development and began seeing retailing's potential for positive economic benefits in deprived areas. Most notably it was Michael Porter who gave that view momentum and credibility in his 1995 article in the Harvard Business Review. In Britain, there was a reworking of the retail planning regulations that represented a shift to a more restrictive attitude to decentralized retailing, but more innovatively, identified a positive view of retailing as a core function in regeneration strategies. In the face of this changing regulatory environment and other contextual shifts, leading British retailers were forced to react and adapt, and they did so by focusing on regeneration as a theme within their wider social responsibility agendas.

ECONOMIC BASE THEORY AND RETAILING

Discussions of the economy of cities half a century ago were substantially predicated on a distinction between basic and nonbasic activities (Alexander, 1954; Tiebout, 1956). Alexander (1954) traced the concept back to academic work by Aurousseau (1921) and policy researches for the New York Regional Planning Committee's *Regional Survey* of 1927. Basic (city forming) activities bring income to the city from beyond. Nonbasic (city serving) activities serve the needs of the city's own population. Cities cannot be self sufficient and must generate income from basic "exports" to fund required imports of food and raw materials. As Hoover and Giarratani (1984) observed:

> A ... region cannot get richer by simply "taking in its own washing"; it must sell something to others in order to get more income. Consequently, exports are viewed as providing the economic base of a region's growth. (http://www.rri.wvu.edu/WebBook/Giarratani/chaptereleven.htm)

In metropolitan centres with extensive catchments, or places with a strong tourist trade, retailing might bring significant wealth from outside the city, but most often urban retailing was seen as nonbasic and city serving.

Retailing was therefore not seen as having potential for regenerating ailing economies, and its expansion was seen as diverting capital and labour away from more valued basic sectors of the economy. Thus, in 1966 the U.K. government introduced the selective employment tax "with the aim of diverting labour away from service industry to manufacturing" (Hall, 1974, p. 149).

Doubts over retailing's contribution to regeneration resurfaced in Britain's enterprise zone policies of the 1980s. While some have drawn attention to those zones where significant retail presences developed (Lowe, 1998, 2005a; Thomas & Bromley, 1987), the more general picture was of a presumption against retail development. Others concluded that enterprise zone policies generally did not favour retail developments, largely because of perceived threats to existing shopping:

> The idea of total freedom for retail development has been tempered by local authority pressures to limit any development and to protect existing investment.... The enterprise zones have continued the policy ... of protecting the existing retail hierarchy. (Dawson & Sparks, 1982, p. 46)

Sparks (1987, p. 42) identified Swansea's enterprise zone retail developments as exceptional, noting "nervousness towards retailing in Enterprise Zones." Sparks suggested the wider picture reinforced "traditional attitudes of the planning system towards retailing, i.e., restrictive and reactive rather than proactive and positive" (Spark, 1987, p. 42). Interestingly, the U.K.'s enterprise zone model would resurface in the United States several years later in the form of empowerment zones, a model that would contribute to the reappraisal of retailing's contribution to regenerating disadvantaged urban communities (Lavin & Whysall, 2004).

By the early 1980s there were calls to recognize the importance of retailing in Britain's economy and its potential in inner city area regeneration. Sparks (1983, p. 24) observed: "There is now a need to obtain government acceptance that retailing plays a major part in economic life and is a large-scale employer." Strong statements like that one were complemented by a view that strong retail centres were important elements of the urban fabric, not least in communities suffering economic and environmental deterioration. However in 1988 commentators could still highlight the absence of attention to retailing in reports on urban regeneration (Fitch Benoy Shopping Centre Consortium, 1988).

THE EVOLVING POLICY CONTEXT OF REAILING AND COMMUNITY REGERATION

Figure 10.1 provides structure for ensuing discussions and conceptualizes changing British attitudes toward retailing and disadvantaged communities over recent decades. This diagram should not be interpreted in historical-evolutionary terms, however, as many elements coexited.

The Failure of "Traditional" Regeneration Policies

Lloyd, McCarthy, and McGreal (2003) see a shift in regeneration policies with the election of Tony Blair's "New Labour" in 1997, bringing "a synthesis of social democratic interventionism and neo-liberal market ideas" (Lloyd et al., 2003, p. 295) and a "wider and more imaginative search for policy innovation in urban regeneration" (Lloyd et al., 2003, p. 299). The "urban problem" had not been overcome and, despite geographical notions of spatially concentrated deprivation, it was realized that social and economic exclusion is thematic, impacting on particular groups.

The failure of traditional regeneration policies is well documented:

- Carley (2000, p. 279) suggested that since the 1960s there had been "an almost bewildering number of short-term initiatives," and, despite some local successes, areas persisted with pressing problems of job losses and deprivation: "What progress there is seems insufficient to the task" (Carley, 2000, p. 274). Failure was attributed to a

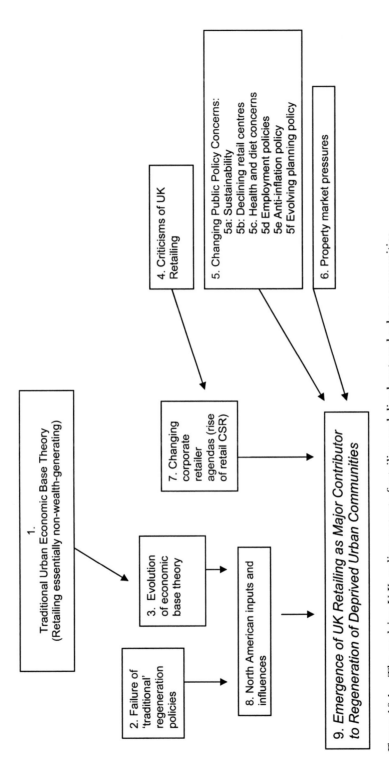

Figure 10.1. The evolving U.K. policy context of retailing and disadvantaged urban communities.

tendency to short-term "solutions", failures to learn, compartmen-
talization of initiatives, and a lack of integration. Partnerships,
notably with business, offered promise, although many were
already in place with key stakeholders suffering "partnership
fatigue" (Carley, Kirk, & McIntosh, 2001, p. 68).

- Baldock (1998) reviewed impacts of the urban program on London's small businesses to conclude it had been underfunded and
had little impact beyond small "niche" market enterprises.

- Ramsden, Potts, Mayo, and Raymond (2001, p. 2) classified policy
initiatives over 36 years and suggested:
  Policy reactions to inner city problems were preoccupied first with social
  pathology, then physical redevelopment and prestige projects. Until
  very recently little attention has been paid to the economics of the inner
  city and the potential for local enterprise to contribute to regeneration.

- Community involvement was fundamental to urban policy through
the last quarter of the twentieth century. Ball (2004) examined
community involvement in urban regeneration partnerships to
detect tendencies to "policy over-optimism" and a need for greater
realism of what community consultation and empowerment could
achieve.

Unemployment dominated regeneration policies, but "hidden unemployment," meaning those effectively unemployed yet not appearing in official statistics, remained deeply entrenched. Existing policies did not
address this phenomenon (Beatty, Fothergill, Gore, & Green, 2002). An
official study concluded worklessness was increasingly concentrated
among multidisadvantaged groups and neighborhoods, and concluded
"existing policies, while reducing worklessness overall, have not worked as
well for those who are least competitive in the labour market" (Department for Communities and Local Government, 2006, p. 11).

Research from the office of the deputy prime minister (2003a) emphasized linking "place-based business strategies" with "place-based people
strategies" and targeting by business sector. Retailing attracted interest.
Dixon (2005, p. 171) suggests manufacturing decline and trends to a ser-
vice-based economy "led policy makers in the UK to champion the
importance of retailing as a potential creator of jobs, and economic vital-
ity, not only nationally, but more locally in local regeneration projects,
especially in disadvantaged, inner city areas" (p. 171). Lowe (2005a) suggests urban development corporations "found it expedient to use retail
development to "kick start" urban regeneration" and "from the 1990s ...
links between retailing and urban regeneration became increasingly more
prominent" (p. 450).

The Evolution of Economic Base Theory

Williams (1997) reviewed retailing's role in economic development, noting from economic base theory:

> Conventional discourse understands retailing as a "parasitic" activity which lives off the endeavours of other sectors and contributes little.... During the past decade, however, this view ... has been conclusively discredited. (pp. 206-207)

For:

> the retail sector has been revealed to be able to contribute to the development of economies not only in its much neglected role as a basic sector activity which attracts external income but also in its non-basic inward-looking role of preventing the leakage of income out of an area. (pp. 217-218)

Ward and Lewis (2002) developed the "leaky bucket" model of a local economy to support local regeneration initiatives. This reworking of urban base theory emphasized retaining wealth within communities over "exports," taking its lead from a National Strategy for Neighbourhood Renewal official report that stated that the problem is not whether money is flowing into a neighborhood but rather what is done with such money by consumers, businesses, and public services. Drawing on frequent retailing examples, such as spending shifts to an edge-of-town multiple supermarket from locally based town center stores and an anti-Wal-Mart campaign in Massachusetts, Ward and Lewis derived multipliers to show the benefits of shopping locally.

Criticisms of U.K. Retailing

If a British "retail revolution" had occurred by the early 1990s (Dunham, Berkeley, Healey, & Noon, 1994), its effects were unwelcome to many (Blythman, 2005). Benefits of retail change apparently accrued mostly to mobile higher-status groups. In areas without large supermarkets, traditional retailing often continued to contract. Those with cars became "outshoppers," using larger stores further away, leaving the less mobile with reduced local shopping of poorer quality (Bromley & Thomas, 1995). The decline of smaller, independent shops was often seen as socially undesirable: independent retailers "provide a social shopping experience for their customers ... which is not easily replicated by the competing multiple retailers" (Baron, Harris, Leaver, & Oldfield, 2001). Large retailers could be socially divisive, as Hillman (1973) had suggested they might be. Food retailers were particularly criticized. Cummins and Macintyre (2002a, p. 2116) observe: "The prevailing analysis in the UK is that the market practices of large retail organizations have contributed to the production and maintenance of (these) spatial inequalities in food access."

From an employment perspective Dunham et al. (1994) saw the "retail revolution" generating low pay, deskilling, casual and insecure employment, and eroding employment rights. Raven, Lang, and Dumonteil (1995) leveled criticisms against the larger supermarket operators including confusing and inadequate labelling, high "real" transport costs, excessive packaging, poor environmental and ecological performance, and negative impacts on town centres, alongside the social exclusion argument.

Grassroots Action on Food and Farming (2005) typify critics of U.K. supermarkets. A large new supermarket would cause smaller shop closures in towns. Unlike smaller shops which are integrated into the local economy, supermarkets would leach wealth from the area:

> Very little of the wealth generated by the supermarkets stays within the local economy.... Supermarkets are vacuum cleaners sucking money out of the community to corporate head offices and to shareholders around the world.

Training in regeneration projects was too job specific, and innovations such as self-scanning were seen within a long-term strategy to reduce labour costs. Supermarkets' claimed job creation was challenged: Tesco had outsourced jobs to India and imported Polish distribution workers. Lang (1997) was especially scathing:

> Retailers are the power brokers of the modern food economy.... This is a new baronial class.... The hypermarket chains should be broken up. They are too powerful and have outlived their usefulness.

Retailers eventually responded:

> Supermarkets ... have traditionally been labelled the corporate bad boys, but have been forced to adapt their business models. (Bashford, 2002, p. 19)

Those responses will be considered subsequently.

Changing Public Policy Concerns in the United Kingdom

Several contemporaneous and interacting concerns were changing the retail business environment.

Sustainability

Criticisms of retailers' environmental performance paralleled increasing pressures toward sustainability. Distances travelled by supermarket foods—notions of "food miles," and sourcing of "designer foods" from developing countries—became public concerns (Blythman, 2005; Clarke, Hallsworth, Jackson, De Kervenoael, & Perez del Aguila, 2003; "Retailers Face," 2006). British commitments given at the 1992 Rio Earth Summit prompted revisions to planning policies which would impact retailers' locational policies (Adams, Disberry, Hutchison, & Munjoma, 2002). The European Commission emphasized sustainable urban development, with retailing being key in many European examples of renewing and regenerating centres (Court, 2002). Sustainability and balance with nature were promoted as core design principles in retail regeneration (Building Design Partnership, 2002).

Carley, Kirk, and McIntosh (2001) related car based shopping to climate change claiming "nearly incontrovertible" evidence linking CO_2 emissions to global warming; however evidence of sustainability considerations in regeneration policies was scant. Yet support for more sustainable shopping might not necessarily mean halting retail decentralization, with some planners arguing regional centres in dense urban locations represented sustainable regeneration (Rhodes & Bashford, 2002).

Declining Retail Centers and Disadvantaged Consumers

The decline of older shopping areas and independent retailing in Britain has long been seen to have social and economic implications. Westlake (1993) traced concern for disadvantaged consumers from the 1970s, focusing particularly on women, the disabled and elderly. Poorer consumers' reliance on smaller shops with higher prices raises a dilemma:

> It could be argued that, because small shops have higher prices, their decline is entirely to be welcomed. But the personal, indeed social, service they provide cannot be measured in terms of price. (Piachaud, 1974, p. 21)

Large-scale retailing left the disadvantaged with reduced access to cheaper goods and consequent social costs (Hillman, 1973).

The emergent dominance of large multiple retailers raised the spectre of local monopolies. Poole, Clarke, and Clarke (2002, p. 658) concluded "concerns over the existence of regional monopolies are well founded." That growth of large stores caused smaller outlets to close leading to higher prices in deprived neighborhoods became accepted by Governmental bodies:

> Poor access to food shops reflects the growth of out-of-town shopping centres and supermarkets at the expense of smaller, more local shops:

- The number of small shops fell by 40% between 1986 and 1997 (with the probability that reduced local competition has resulted in higher prices being charged by surviving shops). (Social Exclusion Unit, 2003, para. 1.21)

Bell, Davies, and Howard (1997) saw declining local shopping adversely impacting disadvantaged consumers as a pan-European phenomenon:

Paradoxically it is the low income groups that are most interested in the low prices offered by supermarket chains, but are least able to avail themselves of these. (p. 858)

Williams and Hubbard (2001, p. 276) derived support for "the widespread assertion that there are certain types of household whose socioeconomic status leads them to use a restricted range of stores," confirming that retail change was impacting negatively on disadvantaged groups. Yet those with limited shopping options did not necessarily see that as a poorer alternative; some disadvantaged consumers actively avoided destinations patronized by more advantaged consumers. It seemed "problems of retail disadvantage are not as clear cut as has been previously suggested" (Williams & Hubbard, 2001, p. 284). Woodliffe (1998) had suggested similarly that "a consumer who lives in a low income household, is disabled or in ill health, or does not have access to personal transport for grocery shopping does not necessarily face consumer disadvantage" (p. 530).

While large retail developments may destabilize neighborhood shopping, they may also be its saviour. Cummins, Findlay, Petticrew, and Sparks (2005a) disputed the assumption that opening a hypermarket would always have deleterious effects on an area's retail structure, although the regenerative effects of retail developments in inner cities are unproven (Whysall, 1995). Nonetheless, Lowe (2005a, p. 451) notes how "a strong social inclusion rationale was marshalled by the major retailers to support large-store based redevelopment of rapidly degenerating district centres," providing a case study of retail-led regeneration in a major city centre as representative of a several such developments. Lowe (2005b) details positive impacts of that scheme. Government policy shifted to emphasis commitment to traditional centres, an "urban renaissance," and a "retail planning policy to provide access to shopping for all" (Raynsford, 2000, p. 6).

Health and Diet Concerns

Concerns for health and diet among low income households became linked to retail food provision. Caraher, Dixon, Lang, and Carr-Hill (1998) perceived less concern for a healthy diet among lower income groups, who rather choose foods on the basis of cost and taste.

Festing (1998) noted that grocers in poorer areas stocked a relatively limited array of food, on occasion not selling fresh fruit and vegetables even. Improving shopping access in deprived neighborhoods was a key theme in the government's "healthy neighborhoods/healthier nation" initiative, resulting in the report of Policy Action Team 13 (Department of Health, 1999). Significantly that report reiterated many arguments which the "new" approach to retail-led regeneration would dispute:

- Multiple retailers found neighborhoods too small support "conventional supermarkets".
- Population densities were too low.
- Insufficient parking existed to attract custom from other areas.
- "large multiples have decimated small shops" (p. 28).

Emphasis was placed on local strategies, proactive planning and regeneration, addressing crime and the fear of crime, supporting smaller retailers and easing business burdens. Access to healthy food was also addressed by the Competition Commission (2000) and the Social Exclusion Unit (2003):

> This lack of choice in the food that is within reach of people from disadvantaged communities can result in poor dietary habits and, consequently, poor health. (para. 1.24)

Despite skilful budgeting, financial pressures on low income families encouraged consumption of a diet low in fresh fruit and high in fat (Kempson, 1996). Several studies appeared linking retail provision and diet:

- Cummins et al. (2005a) saw access to affordable food complementing recommended dietary changes within government's "joined-up" strategy to improve public health and reduce health inequalities. They found a major new store in a disadvantaged urban area "has been positive in providing not just improved food provision, but improved food choice, increased physical and economic accessibility and wider regeneration effects" (p. 298).
- Cummins and Macintyre (2006) explored links between retail provision and obesity, and the apparent paradox of hunger and obesity coexisting in neighborhoods. They contrasted studies from North America and the United Kingdom.

Using a new food store to improve diets in deprived neighborhoods gained support, but analyses of such interventions differed, probably reflecting differing research designs. Conflicting results emerged from studies in Newcastle, Leeds and Glasgow (Cummins, Petticrew, Higgins, Findlay, & Sparks 2005b; Cummins & Macintyre, 2006), and relationships between retail-led regeneration and community health improvements became complex:

> Policymakers have suggested that improving local food shopping opportunities may improve diet and health. There is very limited evidence for the effectiveness of such interventions.
>
> Encouraging the location of large scale food retailing in deprived communities may not be the most effective method of combating poor diet. However, large scale commercial investment in deprived neighborhoods may have a psychosocial impact upon health, although the evidence presented here is not definitive. (Cummins et al., 2005b, p. 1039)

Further, while large scale retailing might have limited value in addressing dietary concerns, Guy (2004b) found convenience stores similarly inappropriate regarding such objectives.

Paralleling diet concerns was the "food desert" debate (Wrigley, 2002). What comprises a food desert is a moot point. Food deserts—areas with little or no local (healthy) retail food provision—prompted research interest (Clarke, Eyre, & Guy, 2002). Some not only accept that food deserts exist in Britain but see them manifested in diverse ways: financially, physically, and attitudinally (Shaw, 2006). Furey, Strugnell, and Milveen (2001) and Rex and Blair (2003, p. 460) found evidence of food deserts. Most significantly, government researchers found many neighborhoods had few or no food shops (Social Exclusion Unit, 2001).

Guy, Clarke, and Eyre (2004) identified two types of food desert in Cardiff. In areas of low provision but high affluence, high mobility implied little reason for concern. Areas with low incomes and low mobility that lacked good quality multiple retailers were more problematic. New food discounters had somewhat offset the closures by multiple retailers in deprived areas, and many deprived areas remained well served quantitatively at least by independent and specialist food outlets, suggesting true food deserts were not widespread in that city. Similarly Donkin, Dowler, Stevenson, and Turner (1999) found, in deprived areas of London, very few areas where someone would have to walk more than 500m to reach a food outlet. Pearson, Russell, Campbell, and Barker (2005, p. 197), from a study in deprived areas of south Yorkshire, suggest that key characteristics of food deserts (fruit and vegetable prices, socioeconomic deprivation and a lack of supermarkets) did not influence fruit or vegetable intake. Cultural influences including gender and age predominated in influencing consumption of fruit and vegetables.

Whelan, Wrigley, Warm, and Cannings (2002) suggested problems of food access needed "more nuanced analysis" at the consumer or household level to unpack interactions between factors. Hitchman, Christie, Harrison, and Lang (2002) found issues more complex than mere proximity to shop, with household circumstances impacting local accessibility. Feeding a household while coping with poverty produces resourceful responses. Piacentini, Hibbert, and Al-Dajani (2001) found that rather than being constrained to limited shopping destinations, disadvantaged Glasgow residents actually showed a greater propensity to "shop around." Those under greater disadvantage, though, relied most on "top-up" shopping away from supermarkets, due to economic, mobility and social constraints. Social aspects of shopping were important:

> An additional concern ... should, therefore be to develop a better understanding of the social and personal benefits that can be delivered through retail and other service enterprises and to appreciate the consequences of this for the broader goal of empowering consumers *who currently experience social exclusion*. (Piacentini, Hibbert, and Al-Dajani, 2001, p. 155)

A major new store in Leeds provided major inputs to the food desert debate (Wrigley, Warm, & Margetts, 2002). Treating the development as a "non-healthcare innovation" in a "low-income, socially deprived, white area" suggested such interventions could improve the diet of "at risk" groups. However, fruit and vegetable intakes remained below recommended levels, hence:

> It should not be inferred ... that an intervention-based policy focused solely on improving retail access is likely to have a profound effect on changes in diet and health—any changes are *likely to be at the margin*. (p. 178)

Research at the University of Newcastle upon Tyne (2003) explored interactions between retail provision, socioeconomic status and diet. Generally less healthy diets were associated with living in deprived areas and being poorer, if, overall, no independent relationship between healthy eating and factors relating to local retailing was demonstrable. Food deserts only existed for the most immobile consumers, and retail provision did not emerge as a primary cause of "unhealthy" diets. Wilson, Alexander, and Lumbers (2004) looked specifically at diet and food access among older people, finding no simple relationship between store usage or access to food shops and dietary variety.

Cummins and Macintyre (1999) found few areas in Glasgow lacking shops save some less well-served outlying areas. More deprived areas had greater numbers of (mainly small) food stores. Multiple outlets were distributed similarly to other food stores, and "multiple-owned retail outlets, often criticized as being inaccessible to the urban poor, are found in greater numbers in the poorest places" (p. 551). Subsequently, Cummins and Macintyre (2002a) explored spatial variations in food availability and price. Findings again ran counter to the food desert model as rather than more deprived areas having inadequate shop provision, most shops were concentrated in poorer areas—especially multiples and discounters which tend to sell basic foods at lower prices; it was shop-type, rather than location or level of deprivation, that best predicted price and availability of a satisfactory diet.

Evidence concerning food deserts, then, conflicts. Cummins and Macintyre (2002b) questioned the existence of food deserts in Britain, suggesting researches supporting the notion had been misinterpreted. They described the concept as a "factoid," an assertion reported so often to become considered true despite a lack of "hard" evidence. Cummins and Macintyre (2006) further suggest: "the term food desert, although a striking metaphor, has unintentionally led to such polarization of views by researchers, policymakers, and other interest groups so as to be of limited further use" (p. 683). Guy (2002) similarly questions the term's usefulness, suggesting many living in such areas are not reliant on local shops, and that the term may have outlived its usefulness. However some seemed convinced that introducing a superstore in a deprived area as part of a regeneration scheme might bring health benefits.

Employment Policies

Unemployment differentials dominated British regional policy from the 1930s (Hall, 1974). While unemployment is but one manifestation of complex interactions within multiple deprivation (Noble, Penhale, Smith, & Wright, 1999), it remains a major policy issue. Although impacts of enterprises in depressed areas are also multifaceted and should not be evaluated simply on jobs created (Lyon, Bertotti, Evans, Smallbone, Potts, & Ramsden, 2002), job creation by retail developments is frequently portrayed as a major benefit (Tesco, 2002).

A particular concern has been the collapse of British coal mining since the miners' strike of 1984/5. Mining employment fell from 220,000 to 7,000, and despite impressive job creation, there remained fewer jobs than formerly in coalfield areas (Beatty, Fothergill, & Powell, 2002). Attitudes to employment, though, were changing:

> whereas ex-miners themselves shunned employment they saw as "women's work", the generation of men behind them has adopted a more open-minded attitude and begun to fill the jobs that once would have been taken by women. (p. 21)

Retailing may well fall into those perceptions of "women's work."

Anti-Inflation Policies

Britain's "battle against inflation" dominated post-1960s economic policy, remaining focal to current policy. Large scale retailing potentially offers reduced prices and thus appeals to policymakers confronting inflationary pressures. Further, as previously noted, there is a widely held view that disadvantaged customers of smaller local shops tend to pay higher prices. Thus large scale retailing can claim to reinforce macroeconomic anti-inflationary policies while reducing the cost-of-living of disadvantaged consumers.

Changes in the Planning Policy Framework

The evolution of U.K. planning policy is well documented (Adams et al., 2002; Thomas & Bromley, 2002; Wrigley, Guy, & Lowe, 2002; Wood, Lowe, & Wrigley, 2006). Revisions to Planning Policy Guidance Note 6 and introduction of the "sequential test" in 1996 made permission to develop greenfield sites much harder to obtain. Wood, Lowe, and Wrigley (2006) see retailer interest in regeneration as a direct result of this tightening of planning restrictions. Regeneration sites, then, became attractive, but were not without their problems:

> The protection of greenfield land and the application of this sequential approach by planning authorities have focused company attention on brownfield sites within urban areas. These are often in need of remediation, and located in run down areas, ie, they are typically high cost/low revenue options. (Renewal.net, 2002, p. 4)

Leading retailers were described as "falling over themselves to take part in regeneration schemes designed to revitalise run-down, poverty-stricken areas". Engagement in regeneration projects could help gain speedier planning approval, but motives remained fundamentally commercial: "All this could suggest that the multiples are pursuing regeneration out of necessity, rather than the desire to help build an inclusive society" ("The Regeneration Game," 2001, p. 36).

Planning Policy Statement 6 replaced PPG6 in 2005, linking retail planning to the regeneration agenda:

> Unlike PPG6 however, PPS6 incorporates more explicitly into its wider objectives the promotion of social inclusion, investment into deprived areas in need of regeneration and the economic growth of regional, sub-regional and local economies. (GLA Economics, 2005, p. 9)

PPS6 emphasized regeneration and social inclusion benefits as important considerations in retail planning decisions (Wood, Lowe, & Wrigley, 2006). However Adams et al. (2002) suggest that appropriate sites in relation to this policy may be limited.

Property Market Pressures

Jackson and Watkins (2005, p. 1464) argue "a well-functioning property market is critical in establishing a vibrant retail sector within towns and cities and, in turn, driving economic and employment growth." From the mid-1990s, rising U.K. consumer expenditure fueled growth in retail rents, outperforming other sectors, and while peripheral areas performed strongest, central locations also showed growth. Thus the attractions of retail property investment were strong.

Recently, the property industry has become more interested in regeneration schemes. McGreal, Webb, Adair, and Berry (2006) detected a tendency in the United Kingdom to focus investment analyses on prime property markets leaving other areas "less information rich," which may perpetuate a view of regeneration areas as high risk locations where investors demand a "risk premium" and institutional investment is hard to attract. Studies across U.K. cities suggested investment in regeneration areas can equal or outperform other locations, and perceptions of regeneration areas carrying greater risk were incorrect. Similarly Adair et al. (2005) stressed that while regeneration locations may represent market failure and sources of negative externalities due to dereliction, analyses revealed good prospects for investments in regeneration areas, challenging conventional views that they typically generate low yields.

In 2003, the vice president of the British Council of Shopping Centres argued strongly for retailing's contribution to London's regeneration:

> Retail is one of the most socially inclusive forms of development and by its very nature and scale offers the pieces of jigsaw that can deliver high quality public space.... It is a pivotal time to bring together those involved in the planning for London's future to consider the opportunity for retail-led regeneration in the Capital. ("Major role," 2003, p. 130).

There was, then, increasing commercial engagement with retail-led regeneration, notwithstanding the problems of fragmented ownership that often frustrate endogenous revitalization projects in inner cities (Guy, 2005).

Changing Corporate Agendas

Retailers' concern for social responsibility is not new. Davies (1999) paralleled interest in the shopping provision for disadvantaged groups with an initiative of the early 1980s to use (then) new technologies to help disadvantaged consumers (Tesco, 1980). However recently Britain's leading retailers have become more vociferous in promoting corporate social responsibility agendas (Whysall, 2004).

Recently, urban regeneration had emerged as prominent in those agendas. In 2001, the body representing many of Britain's leading retailers put out an election brief titled *Retailing as a Positive Force in Urban Regeneration* (British Retail Consortium, 2001). Asda's statement on regeneration was quoted by Guy (2004b) with some suspicion:

> we prefer to build our stores on previously developed sites that have been identified for regeneration ... making a valuable contribution towards improving the environment ... cleaning up contaminated land, undertaking massive ground works and substantial infrastructure improvement. (p. 10)

Alongside that apparently altruistic motivation are perhaps more commercial judgements. Leading U.K. supermarket Sainsbury's opine "We recognize we've probably got an obligation to the community, particularly in inner-city areas," adding a commercial consideration when stating a key issue in any regeneration project would be "What's the project going to do for the prospects of supermarket footfall?" (Bashford, 2002, p. 19). To Ikea, regeneration has dual attractions: the opportunity to "be a good neighbor and bring something to a community" (p. 19) while also facilitating planning consent.

Retailer involvement in regeneration is clearly commercially motivated:

> the reputation a retailer gains as being a socially responsible firm is a positive externality following its decision to move into a deprived area. It is not the reason a retailer chooses to invest in the area, as this will be based solely on profitability. (GLA Economics, 2005, pp. 18-19)

Yet self-interest also permeates socially oriented initiatives. A corporate community investment strategy targeted youth populations in areas of high crime around shopping centers. The scheme sought to involve youth in crime reduction and brought them together with retailers and local agencies to improve community safety. However, the company realized benefits associated with the improvement of the areas that their properties were in and concomitant higher long term profitability. (Business in the Community, 2005a).

Tesco's Regeneration Partnership Programme—part of their social responsibility agenda—is promoted as creating sustainable new jobs, many for previously long-term unemployed people, within a wider agenda:

> How did we develop our approach to regeneration? We looked at the social exclusion agenda and at our own property programme and identified what we believed would be a win/win for communities, customers and business. (Tesco, 2002, p. 2)

McQuaid, Lindsay, and Greig (2005) found Tesco's Alloa development showed "that the negative attitudes held by many unemployed people toward service employment, and other barriers to work in sectors such as retail, can be addressed given the right job opportunities and appropriate training and support" (p. 76). As an employment generator, the initiative was no panacea, given possible displacement and substitution effects and the low pay and part-time employment typical in stores. Nevertheless it represented a useful future model. According to government documentation "Tesco want to create a virtuous cycle where other businesses invest in the area, increasing local disposable income and retail spending" (Office of the Deputy Prime Minister, 2003b, p. 24). At Leeds, an assessment of the Regeneration Partnership concluded this was "an outstanding success as judged by the key stakeholders involved, the employer, and the individuals recruited" (Walton, Hill, & Campbell, 2002, p. 45).

The Regeneration Partnership represented sound business strategy:

> In the face of a severe shortage of suitable sites for new stores and expected shortages of suitable labour, Tesco decided on a partnership approach to developing new stores in regeneration areas. (Renewal.net, 2002).

Tesco's regeneration manager accepts their motivation was "enlightened self-interest" (Wood, Lowe, & Wrigley, 2006). He argued:

> It is clearly in our interests to help local people improve their prospects, so they can spend more money with us ... we are here to make a profit for our shareholders. But we also see there is an opportunity to meet the wider objectives of the community at the same time. (West, 2002).

Nor are Tesco unique. Mitchell and Kirkup (2003) studied a Sainsbury's development to conclude that, while not without problems, retail-led regeneration benefited both the area and the retailer.

North American Influences

Retailers face particular problems in American inner cities, including the exodus of affluent residents, high operating costs, site selection problems, and community distrust of business, resulting in reduced competition (especially from larger outlets) and higher costs in the absence of economies of scale (Alwitt & Donley, 1997). Alwitt and Donley found limited choice and access was not restricted to the grocery and banking sectors, concluding that "retailers and service providers are underserving poor areas and are not responding to profit opportunities (i.e. are possibly discriminating against poor areas in site location)" (p. 162).

Ashman, de la Vega, Dohan, Fisher, Hippler, and Romain (1993) addressed food insecurity in the inner city, seeing food as a basic human right with food insecurity a crucial community concern. Their recommended responses were typically interventionist, calling for public policies, increased funding, integration with public transport policy, and more local and state support for farmers' markets and urban farms. Fisher and Gottlieb (1995) similarly saw inner city market failure creating a need for interventionist policies, given "the problematic nature of a market approach to food distribution without direct public input or the use of public policy instruments" (p. 29).

Alwitt (1995) saw marketing exchanges involving poor people unbalanced in favor of the marketer; the poor pay more for food and get less variety. In response, she explored various interventionist policy options (e.g. food stamps, regulatory interventions). Thus in the mid-1990s, the inner city retail debate in the United States seemed focused on problems of decline and calls for governmental intervention.

Porter (1995) brought a radically different perspective to the debate. Efforts to revive the inner city had failed. Those failed initiatives, not unlike Britain's, had been socially focused, while economic development programs had been fragmented:

> such programs have treated the inner city as an island, isolated from the surrounding economy and subject to its own unique laws of competition.
>
> They have encouraged and supported small, sub-scale businesses designed to serve the local community but ill equipped to attract the community's own spending power, much less to export outside it. In short, the social model has inadvertently undermined the creation of economically viable companies. (p. 55)

There are strong resonances of the "import-export" basis of economic base theory here, and Porter continued "A sustainable economic base can be created in the inner city" and "businesses should be capable not only of serving the local community but also of exporting goods and services to the surrounding economy" (pp. 55-56).

Porter dispels misconceptions of low costs and cheap labor in the inner city, arguing its key advantages are location, good communications, proximity to business centres, high density local demand characterized by growth, potential for integration with regional clusters, and human resources. These provide the basis for economic regeneration, notwithstanding problems around land availability and site assembly, high costs, security problems (real and perceived), problems of goods movement, low skills, limited capital, and some antibusiness attitudes. Primarily the inner city needed rethinking in economic rather than social terms: "The time has come to embrace a rational economic strategy and to stem the intolerable costs of outdated approaches" (p. 71).

PricewaterhouseCoopers and The Initiative for a Competitive Inner City (ICIC) (PricewaterhouseCoopers & ICIC, 1999) provided research support for Porter's claims, demonstrating an economically attractive market:

> The neglect of the inner city has created markets full of opportunities for retailers. … they represent potential growth markets that can rival those of both foreign expansion and suburban retail developments. (p. 3)

A second Initiative for a Competitive Inner City (2000) survey reinforced that message. Similarly, Allain and Ryan (1997) stressed the retail potential of U.S. inner city neighborhoods, typically ignored by retailers who tended to focus on average household income, ignoring inner areas' concentrated buying power and low competition.

Links between disadvantage and health also concerned American researchers. Bradbard, Michaels, Fleming, and Campbell (1997) suggested beneficiaries of food stamp programmes were aware of healthy eating guidelines, cognizant of shortcomings in their current diet, and sought new ways to feed their families. Yet improvements remained difficult to achieve. Morland, Wing, Roux, and Poole (2002) related locations of food outlets to the wealth and racial makeup of neighborhoods, suggesting dietary choices may be influenced by the availability of food stores. They suggested "more egalitarian local food environments will require fundamental changes in local, state, and national economic and land-use policies" (p. 28).

Studies by Lavin (2000, 2005) focused on developments in New York, particularly Harlem's Pathmark supermarket. That store featured frequently in subsequent British policy documents. Such retail development in inner cities would often face political and community relations challenges.

Alderslade (2005) reinforces Porter's perception of the inner city as a major untapped market. He contrasts the conventional data profiling of such areas, emphasizing "deficiency data" which "do much to describe social need but little to describe economic opportunity" with the "relative vacuum of market-attribute data" (p. 1). Social Compact Inc's alternative "Drilldown" methodology that presents positive information and emphasizes opportunity in such areas is advocated.

Boston Consulting Group/ICIC (1998) took Porter's initiative forward, studying six inner city markets. They reemphasized and illustrated the scale of unmet demand in American inner cities, and the opportunities provided by a concentrated consumer base of shoppers. Inner city areas possessed up to six times as much buying power per square mile as surrounding areas across retail categories. Moreover these were often fast growing markets. A model of a virtuous cycle whereby providing a competitive offering and filling unmet retail demand in the inner city leads to increased disposable income, consumer demand, local jobs, business sales, consumer traffic, improved security, and greater local spending was presented. Significant opportunities were seen for large chains and "savvy" entrepreneurs. Moreover, whereas others argued that the reentry of chain stores to inner city markets could threaten the viability of independent businesses, research here suggested inner city retailing was not a "zero-sum" game, where large retailers automatically displace smaller independents, as large retailers could increase customer flows, especially for smaller retailers in niche market positions with well-tailored offerings.

Initiative for a Competitive Inner City (2002) saw American inner city grocery retailing as "the last large domestic frontier for retail, characterized by high concentrations of income and limited competition" (p. 2). Despite many challenges and barriers, examples of thriving grocery operations demonstrated that success could result given a flexible approach to retail development, and good community relations. Independents and large chains could coexist profitably and experiences of operating with diverse populations could provide valuable transferable knowledge applicable in other national and global markets. Parallel arguments about retailing in the inner city began appearing in the American trade press (Lewis, 2000; McTaggart, 2006; Mathews, 1997; Summerour, 2002), even if some questioned the future of larger chains in inner cities (Weinstein, 2000).

American Experiences Impact the United Kingdom

American retailing has long been an important comparator for British policymakers (e.g., Distributive Trades EDC, 1971). However, in the late 1980s, British perceptions of retailing in American cities often remained primarily negative and cautionary in nature (e.g., Falk, 1998). Then U.K. bodies, notably the New Economics Foundation, started championing Porter's approach: "Recent work on inner city renewal owes a significant debt to the ideas of Harvard University Professor Michael Porter" (Ramsden et al., 2001, p. 21). While noting criticisms such as Porter's devaluing of community organizations' contributions and "laissez-faire optimism," this was clearly seen an appropriate model for Britain.

A government-endorsed report presented case studies (including Pathmark) demonstrating the merits of rebuilding inner city economies:

These neighborhoods are now being re-evaluated as missed opportunities in the US, and cases are emerging in the UK demonstrating the business benefits of entering under-served markets. (Business in the Community, 2002, p. 3).

Companies could build a new customer base, locate new suppliers, and build community relations; communities would benefit from improved retail, leisure and job opportunities, reduced crime and improved community pride. A set of British cases which recur throughout the UK regeneration literature followed, including several Tesco Regeneration Partnership stores, and a Sainsbury's store and the Merry Hill shopping centre in the West Midlands. Supportive quotations from Michael Porter made it clear how the British approach now embraced the American market-led model:

The US has taken the lead in identifying under-served markets, and there is a need here in the UK to build knowledge of the characteristics of under-served markets and where they exist. (p. 4)

A Business in the Community/Department of Trade and Industry "Under-served Markets Project" drew directly from the Harlem Pathmark, aiming to promote retail investment and investigate its potential as a catalyst for wider regeneration (Dunford, 2006). This project was seen endorsed by the deputy prime minister:

As we have seen with the Under-served Markets project ... there is significant untapped potential to create jobs—and make money—in deprived areas. (Office of the Deputy Prime Minister, 2004, p. 2)

Further American inputs to Britain's retail-led regeneration debate followed:

- Harlem again underpinned claims that "the re-instatement of a retail dimension is essential to stem the process of urban decay" (Doyle, 2004, p. 586).
- ICIC (2003) linked with the small business service to launch the "City Growth Strategy" for business-led urban regeneration in England.

- Dixon (2005) emphasized retailing's role in regeneration, locating the "intellectual roots" of the new approach in the work of Porter and studies by Boston Consulting Group and ICIC.
- The Department for Communities and Local Government (2006) argued that "US experiences demonstrate that attracting in private sector reinvestment is possible and important to the regeneration of neglected inner city areas" (p. 30).
- The Greater London Authority's researches into retail and regeneration draw directly on American sources including the ICIC and Social Compact's Drilldown approach (GLA Economics, 2005).

Thus the evidence is overwhelmingly clear that the emergence of retail-led regeneration strategies in Britain drew heavily on American theory and practice.

Britain's New Regeneration Agenda

Tony Blair's first prime ministerial speech in June 1997 prioritized the need to "tackle the desperate need for urban regeneration" (Taylor, Davies & Westall, 2004). The preferred policy would encourage entrepreneurship in deprived communities. Images of inner cities as areas of business opportunity percolated official British thought rapidly as evidenced in the forewords of a 2002 study into fast growing businesses in Britain's inner cities (McGillivray, Potts, & Raymond, 2002), where the chancellor of the exchequer, Gordon Brown, wrote that "Areas of high unemployment are not no-go areas but areas of entrepreneurial talent and business opportunity waiting to be released" (p. 2).

Retailing's centrality to the agenda was repeatedly demonstrated:

- Retail cases were prominent in an official guide for businesses locating in deprived areas. The director general of the British retail consortium, a participant in the study, provided a preface (Office of the Deputy Prime Minister, 2003b).
- The Government's principal planner stated: "Retail-led regeneration is about regenerating places—not just sites ... we're trying to focus development to promote an urban renaissance" ("Major Role," 2003).
- The Department of Trade and Industry's Retail Strategy Group (2004a) underscored retailing's importance in the new regeneration agenda. The chief executive of Wal-Mart-Asda contributed by noting retailing's economic and social significance and how it

improves living standards, increases employment opportunities, and is responsible for anchoring urban regeneration in many parts of the country. Perhaps as illuminating was the admission by a government minister that "Government and retail have not always worked together in such productive fashion" (p. 3). In a second publication, the Retail Strategy Group (2004b) specifically addressed the role of retailing in urban regeneration.

- In 2005, The deputy prime minister claimed policies had slowed out-of-town retail development, boosting urban retailing and leading to regeneration of traditional centres and location rethinks by leading retailers ("High Street Regeneration," 2005).

- The Greater London Authority saw retail-led regeneration addressing social inclusion (providing retail facilities and bringing new jobs), acting as a catalyst to economic regeneration, and bringing physical benefits, such as redeveloping brownfield sites (GLA Economics, 2005).

Lord Rooker, Minister for Regeneration, set out the government's position on regeneration clearly:

> Deprived areas can be seen as new markets with competitive advantages; their strategic locations, their often untapped retail opportunities ... and the potential of their workforce. ... the private sector plays a key role in regenerating our deprived areas. (Business in the Community, 2005b, p. 1)

Lord Rooker stressed the need to encourage innovative approaches to regeneration, and "to understand retailer thinking and to take their advice" (p. 1). Yet while business was central to neighborhood renewal policies, perceptions of neighborhood renewal had broadened to embrace sustainability, crime reduction, and health and education considerations. Nonetheless it is clear that retailing had become a central plank in British urban regeneration policies.

WHAT CHALLENGES REMAIN?

Retail-led regeneration has clearly gained widespread acceptance in Britain but issues remain to be addressed:

- Is it spatially feasible? Research in four cities suggested only one of 80 identified sites represented a prime development opportunity in a suitable location. Restricted policies toward out-of-town retailing might have to be abandoned if alternative sites, in sympathy with retail-led regeneration, are not available (Adams et al., 2002).

• Can we rely on retailer altruism? Several authors have noted that commercial self-interest drives retailers' strategies, and in America Lavin (2000) noted that "Retailers' efforts in the inner city are not altruistic; rather, they are congruent with current sociopolitical beliefs ... about the efficacy of the free market" (p. 47). If circumstances change, then, will retailer commitment to regeneration schemes atrophy, or should we expect retailers to show moral responsibilities to communities which have supported them (Davidson, 1995)?

• What is the future of British retail planning? Clarke et al. (2004) see retail policy as "a contest of strength between market policy makers ... and planning regulatory bodies" (p. 88). Carley, Kirk, and McIntosh (2001) reiterate the mantra that planning does not exist to restrict competition, protect commercial interests or prevent innovation. They see attempts to work against market forces failing and explore areas where future retail planning may need reinforcing. The "Porteresque" model is unashamedly market-led, but is that compatible with Britain's tradition of retail planning? Paradoxically planning restrictions on out-of-town sites appear critical to the success of urban retail regeneration (Jones & Hillier, 2000). Can planning and market forces be reconciled?

• Issues of interarea equity arise. A recurring theme has been of "leakages" and trade shifts between areas (Clarke, Eyre & Guy, 2002; Collis, Berkeley, & Fletcher, 2000, Cummins et al., 2005b, Dixon, 2005). In Britain inner city retailing competes most strongly with other inner city locations and the proximate central area— themselves priorities in the regeneration agenda. Is there a danger of "robbing Peter to pay Paul" in simply shifting a limited, and often declining, retail spend around between centers? How much retail-led regeneration can the inner city support?

• How will shoppers react? Clarke et al. (2004) suggest that shoppers often ignore available shopping locations, making choices that are socially and spatially contextualized. Hence making facilities available does not ensure they will be used.

• Are there unresolved conflicts between strands of policy? Guy and Bennison (2002) see potential conflict between retail-led regeneration and competition policy which seeks to avoid monopolistic tendencies. Add to that health concerns, and often conflicting concerns about the economic and employment effects of large supermarkets in local economies (Grassroots Action on Food and

Farming, 2005; Guariglia, 1999; McQuaid, Lindsay, & Greig, 2005), and the potential for policy conflict becomes significant. The whole area of food policy has been described as "a classic example of silo-based policy-making" with its various aspects separately treated by uncoordinated policies (Holden, Howland, & Jones, 2002)

- Do we have enough evidence? Initiative for a Competitive Inner City (2003) stresses the importance of evidence-based strategies and the weaknesses of much local area data. More studies into impacts in a holistic sense (i.e., across many policy strands) are unquestionably needed.

In conclusion, then, what seems clear is that retailing has moved to the centre of Britain's policy assault on poverty, disadvantage and deprivation. It did this through a series of innovations in conceptual bases, regulation and retail business policy, which represents a complex interaction of influences, agendas, and policy developments. Yet much still remains to be done, not least in putting appropriate policy frameworks in place to minimize potential conflicts and uncertainties, ensuring the continuing commitment of the retail community to regeneration regardless of other considerations, and maintaining a research infrastructure to inform and evaluate the progress of redevelopment schemes in Britain and elsewhere.

REFERENCES:

Adair, A., Berry, J., McGreal, S., Poon, J., Hutchison, N., Watkins, C., et al. (2005). Investment performance within urban regeneration locations. *Journal of Property Investment & Finance*, *23*(1), 7-21.

Adams, D., Disberry A., Hutchison, N., & Munjoma, T. (2002). Retail location, competition and urban redevelopment. *The Service Industries Journal*, *22*(3), 135-148.

Alderslade, J. (2005). *Hidden in plain sight: How different data yield different understandings of the same market.* Washington DC: Social Compact Inc./LSE Greenlining Paper.

Alexander, J. W. (1954). The basic-nonbasic concept of urban economic functions. *Economic Geography*, *30*, 246-261.

Allain, J., & Ryan, B. (1997). *Retail in the urban neighborhood. Identifying business opportunities in under-served areas* (Paper No. 17). Madison, WI: Center for Community Economic Development, University of Wisconsin—Cooperative Extension.

Alwitt, L. F. (1995). Marketing and the poor. *American Behavioral Scientist*, *38* (4), 564-577.

Alwitt, L. F., & Donley, T. D. (1997). Retail stores in poor urban neighbourhoods. *Journal of Consumer Affairs, 31*(1), 139-164.

Ashman, L., de la Vega, J., Dohan, M., Fisher, A., Hippler R., & Romain, B. (1993). *Seeds of Change: Strategies for food security for the inner city.* Los Angeles: Southern California Interfaith Hunger Coalition.

Aurousseau, M. (1921). The distribution of population: A constructive problem. *Geographical Review, 9,* 563-592.

Baldock, R. O. (1998). Ten years of the urban programme 1981-1991: The impact and implications of its assistance to small businesses. *Urban Studies, 35*(11), 2063-2083.

Ball, M. (2004). Co-operation with the community in property-led urban regeneration. *Journal of Property Research, 21*(2), 119-142.

Baron, S., Harris, K., Leaver D., & Oldfield, B. M. 2001. Beyond convenience: the future for independent food and grocery retailers in the UK. *International Review of Retail, Distribution and Consumer Research, 11*(4), 395-414.

Bashford, S. (2002). Commerce in the community. *Regeneration & Renewal, 2,* 19-21.

Beatty, C., Fothergill, S., Gore T., & Green, A. (2002). *Hidden unemployment in the East Midlands.* Sheffield, England: Centre for Regional Economic and Social Research, Sheffield Hallam University.

Beatty, C., Fothergill S., & Powell, R. (2002). *Twenty years on: Has the economy of the coalfields recovered?* Sheffield, England: Centre for Regional Economic and Social Research, Sheffield Hallam University.

Bell, R., Davies R., & Howard, E. (1997). The changing structure of food retailing in Europe: The implications for strategy. *Long Range Planning, 30,* (6), 853-861.

Blythman, J. (2005). *Shopped. The shocking power of British supermarkets.* London: Harper Perennial.

Boston Consulting Group in partnership with The Initiative for a Competitive Inner City. 1998. *The business case for pursuing retail opportunities in the inner city.* Boston: Boston Consulting Group.

Bradbard, S., Michaels, E. F., Fleming, K., & Campbell, M. (1997). *Understanding the food choices of low income families: Summary of findings.* Washington DC: Lisboa Associates.

British Retail Consortium. (2001). *Retailing as a positive force in urban regeneration.* London: British Retail Consortium.

Bromley, R., & Thomas, C. (1995). Small town shopping decline: dependence and inconvenience for the disadvantaged. *International Review of Retail, Distribution and Consumer Research, 5*(4), 433-456.

Building Design Partnership. (2002). *Urban design for retail environments.* London: British Council of Shopping Centres

Business in the Community. (2002). *Business investment in under-served markets: an opportunity for businesses and communities?* London: Business in the Community/ Department of Trade and Industry.

Business in the Community. (2005a). *The role of business in neighbourhood renewal.* London: Business in the Community.

Business in the Community. (2005b). *Under-served markets. Preliminary research findings.* London: Business in the Community.

Caraher, M., Dixon, P. Lang T., & Carr-Hill, R. (1998). Access to healthy foods: part I. Barriers to assessing healthy foods: differentials by gender, social class, income and mode of transport. *Health Education Journal*, *57*, 191-201.

Carley, M. (2000). Urban partnerships, governance and the regeneration of Britain's cities. *International Planning Studies*, *5*(3), 273-297.

Carley, M., Kirk, K., & McIntosh, S. (2001). *Retail sustainability and neighbourhood regeneration*. York, England: Joseph Rowntree Foundation.

Clarke, G., Eyre, H., & Guy, C. (2002). Deriving indicators of access to food retail provision: studies of Cardiff, Leeds and Bradford. *Urban Studies*, *39*, 2041-2062.

Clarke, I., Hallsworth, A., Jackson, P., De Kervenoael R., & Perez del Aguila, R. (2003). Real choice in food grocery shopping in Britain. *The European Retail Digest*, *39*, 7-12.

Clarke, I., Hallsworth, A., Jackson, P., De Kervenoael R., Perez del Aguila, R. et al. (2004). Retail competition and consumer choice: contextualizing the "food deserts" debate. *International Journal of Retail & Distribution Management*, *32*(2), 88-99.

Collis, C., Berkeley N., & Fletcher, D. R. (2000). Retail decline and policy responses in district shopping centres. *Town Planning Review*, *71*(2), 149-168.

Competition Commission. (2000). *Supermarkets: A report on the supply of groceries in the United Kingdom*. London: HMSO, Cm 4842.

Court, Y. (2002). Retail and renaissance. *Locum Destination Review*, *7*, 26-28.

Cummins, S., Findlay, A., Petticrew M., & Sparks, L. (2005a). Healthy cities: the impact of food retail-led regeneration on food access, choice and retail structure. *Built Environment*, *31*(4), 288-301.

Cummins, S., & Macintyre, S. (1999). The location of food stores in urban areas: a case study in Glasgow. *British Food Journal*, *101*(7), 545-553.

Cummins, S., & Macintyre, S. (2002a). A systematic study of an urban foodscape: the price and availability of food in Greater Glasgow. *Urban Studies*, *39*(11), 2115-2130.

Cummins, S., & Macintyre, S. (2002b). "Food deserts"—evidence and assumptions in health policy making. *British Medical Journal*, *325*, 436-438.

Cummins, S., & Macintyre, S. (2006.) Food environments and obesity – neighbourhood or nation? *International Journal of Epidemiology*, *35*, 100-104.

Cummins, S., Petticrew, M., Higgins, C., Findlay A., & Sparks L. (2005b). Large scale food retailing as an intervention for diet and health: quasi-experimental evaluation of a natural experiment. *Journal of Epidemiology and Community Health*, *59*, 1035-1040.

Davidson, D. K. (1995). To move or not to move out of a depressed area. *Marketing News*, *29*(2), 6.

Davies, R. L. (1999). Social equalisation in shopping. *European Retail Digest*, *21*, 39-40.

Dawson, J., & Sparks, L. (1982). Retailing developments and enterprise zones. *Retail & Distribution Management*, *10*(1), 43-46.

Department for Communities and Local Government. (2006). *The economies of deprived neighbourhoods*. London: HMSO.

Department of Health. (1999). Improving shopping access for people living in deprived neighbourhoods. London: Policy Action Team 13.

Distributive Trades EDC. (1971). *The future pattern of shopping*. London: HMSO.

Dixon, T. J. (2005). The role of retailing in urban regeneration. *Local Economy, 20*(2), 168-182.

Donkin, A. J. M., Dowler, E. A., Stevenson S. J. & Turner, S. A. (1999). Mapping access to food at a local level. *British Food Journal, 101*(7), 554-564.

Doyle, S. A. (2004). Urban regeneration in New York: gardens and grocers. *International Journal of Retail & Distribution Management, 32*(12), 582-586.

Dunford, J. (2006). Under-served markets. *Local Economy, 21*(1), 73-77.

Dunham, P., Berkeley, N., Healey, M., & Noon, D. (1994). Developing a local retail strategy: a case study of Leicester. *Local Economy, 8*(4): 352-374.

Falk, N. (1998). Resourcing the revival of town and city centres. *Built Environment, 24*(1), 6-15.

Festing, H. (1998, December). *Community food security and food poverty*. Paper presented at Local Food Systems, Lessons for Local Economies Conference, Centre for Environment and Society, University of Essex, Colchester.

Fisher, A., & Gottlieb, R. (1995). *Community food security: policies for a more sustainable food system in the context of the 1995 Farm Bill and beyond* (Working Paper 13). Los Angeles: Ralph and Goldy Lewis Center for Regional Policy Studies, University of California.

Fitch Benoy Shopping Centre Consortium. (1988). *Urban retailing and inner city regeneration* (Shopping Centre Report 11). London: Fitch Benoy.

Furey, S., Strugnell C., & Milveen, M. H. (2001). An investigation of the potential existence of "food deserts" in rural and urban areas of Northern Ireland. *Agriculture and Human Values, 18*(4), 447-457.

GLA Economics. (2005). Retail and regeneration: Retail in London (Working Paper B). London: Greater London Authority.

Grassroots Action on Food and Farming (2005). *Checkout chuckout! Addressing the supermarket's claims for the likely benefits of a new store to your town.* Retrieved August 2, 2006, from http://d=19www.gaff.org.uk/?li19

Guariglia, A. (1999). *Superstores and labour demand: Evidence from Great Britain* (Discussion Paper 99/32). Colchester, England: Institute for Labour Research, University of Essex.

Guy, C. (2002). Arid debates. *Town and Country Planning, 71*(10), 246-247.

Guy, C. M. (2004b). Neighbourhood retailing and food poverty: a case study in Cardiff. *International Journal of Retail & Distribution Management, 32*(12), 577-581.

Guy, C. M. (2005). Revival of inner-city retail areas: the potential role of property owners. *Journal of Retail & Leisure Property, 4*(2), 118-128.

Guy, C. M., & Bennison, D. (2002). Retail planning policy, superstore development and retailer competition. *International Journal of Retail & Distribution Management, 30*(9), 431-434.

Guy, C., Clarke G., & Eyre, H. (2004). Food retail change and the growth of food deserts: a case of Cardiff. *International Journal of Retail & Distribution Management, 32*(2), 72-88.

Hall, P. (1974). *Urban and Regional Planning*. Harmondsworth, Middlesex: Pelican Books.

High Street regeneration. (2005). *Cabinet Maker, 6*, 5448.

Hillman, M. (1973). The social costs of hypermarket developments. *Built Environment, 2*, 89-91.

Hitchman, C., Christie, I., Harrison M., & Lang, T. (2002). *Inconvenience food. The struggle to eat well on a low income*. London: Demos.

Holden, J., Howland L., & Jones, D. S. (2002). Closing the Loop. In *Foodstuff: Living in an age of Feast And Famine* (pp. 5-15). London: Demos.

Hoover, E .M., & Giarratani, F. (1984). *An Introduction to regional economics* (3rd ed.). New York: Alfred A. Knopf.

Initiative for a Competitive Inner City. (2000). *I* Boston: ICIC in partnership with PriceWaterhouseCoopers.

Initiative for a Competitive Inner City. (2002). *The changing models of inner city grocery retailing*. Boston: Author.

Initiative for a Competitive Inner City. (2003). *City growth strategy. A NEW agenda for business-led urban regeneration*. Boston: ICIC/Small Business Service.

Jackson, C., & Watkins, C. (2005). Planning policy and retail property markets: measuring the dimensions of planning intervention. *Urban Studies, 42*(8), 1453-1469.

Jones, P., & Hillier, D. (2000). Changing the balance—the "ins and outs" of retail development. *Property Management, 18*(2), 114-126.

Kempson, E. (1996). *Life on a low income*. York, England: Joseph Rowntree Foundation.

Lang, T. (1997). The challenge for food policy. *Resurgence*, 181.

Lavin, M. (2000). Problems and opportunities of retailing in the U.S. "Inner City." *Journal of Retailing and Consumer Services, 7*(1), 47-57.

Lavin, M. (2005). Supermarket access and consumer well-being. The case of Pathmark in Harlem. *International Journal of Retail & Distribution Management, 33*(5), 388-398.

Lavin, M., & Whysall, P. (2004). From enterprise to empowerment: the evolution of an Anglo-American approach to strategic urban economic regeneration. *Strategic Change, 13*, 219-229.

Lewis, L. (2000). Dangerous perceptions. *Progressive Grocer, 79*(3), 4.

Lloyd, M. G., McCarthy, J. McGreal S., & Berry, J. (2003). Business Improvement Districts, planning and urban regeneration. *International Planning Studies, 8*(4), 295-321.

Lowe, M. (1998). The Merry Hill regional shopping centre controversy: PPG6 and new urban geographies. *Built Environment, 24*(1), 57-69.

Lowe, M. (2005a). The regional shopping centre in the inner city: A study of retail-led urban regeneration. *Urban Studies, 42*(3), 449-470.

Lowe, M. (2005b). Revitalizing inner city retail: the impact of the West Quay development on Southampton. *International Journal of Retail & Distribution Management, 33*(9), 658-668.

Lyon, F., Bertotti, M., Evans, M., Smallbone, D., Potts G., &. Ramsden, P. (2002). *Measuring enterprise impacts in deprived areas*. London: Centre for Enterprise and Economic Development Research, Middlesex University.

Major role for retail in regeneration of London. (2003). *Estates Review,* 130.

McGillivray, A., Potts G., & Raymond, P. (2002). *Secrets of their success. Fast growing business in Britain's inner cities.* London: New Economics Foundation.

McGreal, S., Webb, J. R. Adair A., & Berry, J. (2006). Risk and diversification for regeneration/urban renewal properties: evidence from the U.K. *Journal of Real Estate Portfolio Management, 12*(1), 1-17.

McTaggart, J. (2006). Just enough for the city: Urban initiatives are growing as supermarkets make the business case and cities lift the roadblocks. *Progressive Grocer, 85*(10), 44-48.

McQuaid, R. W., Lindsay C., & Greig, M. (2005). Job guarantees, employability training and partnerships in the retail sector. *Local Economy, 20*(1), 67-78.

Mathews, R. (1997). Retailing's final frontier. *Progressive Grocer, 76*(4), 80-81.

Mitchell, A., & Kirkup, M. (2003). Retail development and urban regeneration: a case study of Castle Vale. *International Journal of Retail & Distribution Management, 31*(9), 451-458.

Morland, K., Wing, S., Roux A. D., & Poole, C. (2002). Neighborhood characteristics associated with the location of food stores and food service places. *American Journal of Preventative Medicine, 22*(1), 23-29.

Noble, M., Penhale, B., Smith, G., & Wright, G. (1999). *Measuring multiple deprivation at the local level.* Oxford, England: Department of Applied Social Studies and Social Research, University of Oxford.

Office of the Deputy Prime Minister. (2003a). *Business-led regeneration of deprived areas. A review of the evidence base* (Research Report 5). London: ODPM, Neighbourhood Renewal Unit.

Office of the Deputy Prime Minister. 2003b. *Changing Practices. A good practice guide for businesses locating in deprived areas.* Research Report 6, Neighbourhood Renewal Unit, ODPM, London.

Office of the Deputy Prime Minister. (2004). *The Private Sector Advisory Panel on neighbourhood renewal: report and government response.* London: ODPM, Neighbourhood Renewal Unit.

Pearson, T., Russell, J., Campbell M. J., & Barker, M. E. (2005). Do "food deserts" influence fruit and vegetable consumption?—a cross-sectional study. *Appetite, 45,* 195-197.

Piacentini, M., Hibbert S., & Al-Dajani, H. (2001). Diversity in deprivation: exploring the grocery shopping behaviour of disadvantaged consumers. *International Review of Retail, Distribution and Consumer Research, 11*(2), 141-158.

Piachaud, D. (1974). Do the poor pay more? (Poverty Research Series 3). London: Child Poverty Action Group.

Poole, R., Clarke G. P., & Clarke, D. B. (2002). Grocery retailers and regional monopolies. *Regional Studies, 36*(6), 643-659.

Porter, M. E. (1995). The competitive advantage of the inner city. *Harvard Business Review, 73*(3), 55-71.

PricewaterhouseCoopers & Initiative for a Competitive Inner City. (1999). *The inner city shopper: A strategic perspective.* Boston: Author.

Ramsden, P., Potts, G., Mayo E., & Raymond, P. (2001). *The competitive inner city.* London: New Economics Foundation.

Raven, H., Lang T., & Dumonteil, C. (1995). *Off our Trolleys? Food retailing and the hypermarket economy.* London: Institute for Public Policy Research.

Raynsford, N. (2000, February). *Speech to LGN/NRPF Conference on Town centres—Turning the lights on.* Retrieved June 28, 2007, from www.nrpf.org

The regeneration game. (2001). *The Grocer, 36*, 7504.

Renewal.net. (2002). *Tesco regeneration partnerships—Alloa Store.* Retrieved July 7, 2006, from http://renewal.net

Retailers face a backlash on "food miles." (2006). *Marketing, 26,* 4

Retail Strategy Group. (2004a). *Driving change.* London: Department of Trade and Industry.

Retail Strategy Group. (2004b). *The retail development process and land assembly (*Vol. 1-Report*).* London: DTI/DTZ Pieda Consulting.

Rex, D., & Blair, A. (2003). Unjust des(s)erts: Food retailing and neighbourhood health in Sandwell. *International Journal of Retail & Distribution Management, 31*(9), 459-465.

Rhodes, J., &. Bashford, S. (2002, September 16). Retail investment a major catalyst for sustainable regeneration. *RPS Group Plc News.*

Shaw H. J. (2006). Food deserts: Towards the development of a classification. *Geografiska Annaler: Series B, Human Geography, 88B,* 231–247.

Social Exclusion Unit. (2001). *National strategy for neighbourhood renewal: Policy Action Team audit.* London: Cabinet Office

Social Exclusion Unit. (2003). *Making the connections: Final report on transport and social exclusion.* London: Office of the Deputy Prime Minister.

Sparks, L. (1983). Superstores and the inner city—some reflections. *Retail & Distribution Management, 1*(1), 21-25.

Sparks, L. (1987). Retailing in enterprise zones: The example of Swansea. *Regional Studies, 21*(1), 37-42.

Summerour, J. (2002). Making it in the city: Now more than ever, opportunity knocks in the inner city for both independent and chain food retailers. *Progressive Grocer, 81*(7), 15-18.

Taylor, J., Davies , &. Westall, A. (2004). *The inner city 100. Impacts and influences.* London: New Economics Foundation.

Tesco. (1980). *Retailing and the inner city—A social study.* Cheshunt, Herts: Tesco Stores.

Tesco. (2002). *Tesco Regeneration Partnerships. The story so far.* from Retrieved July 28, 2005, from http://www.tesco.com/everyLittleHelps/downloads/TescoCR_Regeneration.pdf

Thomas, C. J., & Bromley, R. D. F. (1987). The growth and functioning of an unplanned retail park: the Swansea Enterprise Zone. *Regional Studies, 21*(4), 287-300.

Thomas, C. J., & Bromley, R. D. F. (2002). The changing competitive relationship between small town centres and out-of-town retailing: small town revival in South Wales. *Urban Studies, 39*(4), 791-817.

Tiebout, C .M. 1956. The urban economic base reconsidered. *Land Economics, 32,* 95-99.

University of Newcastle upon Tyne. (2003). *Do "foods deserts" exist? A multi-level, geographical analysis of the relationship between retail food access, socio-economic posi-*

tion and dietary intake (Project N090101, Food Standards Agency). Retrieved August 3, 2006, from http://www.food.gov.uk /science/research/researchinfo/nutritionresearch/foodacceptability/ n09programme/n09projectlist/n09010/#co

Walton, F., Hill C., &. Campbell, M. (2002). *The Tesco Job Guarantee Programme: An assessment.* Leeds:, England: Policy Research Institute, Leeds Metropolitan University.

Ward, B., & Lewis, J. (2002). *Plugging the leaks. Making the most of every pound that enters your local economy.* London: New Economics Foundation.

Weinstein, S. (2000). Too little, too late? Can chains recapture inner-city consumers? *Progressive Grocer, 79*(5), 113-117.

West, T. (2002). *Supermarket forces.* Retrieved July 30, 2006, from http://www.new-startmag.co.uk/tesco.html

Westlake, T. (1993). The disadvantaged consumer: problems and policies. In R. D. F. Bromley & C. J. Thomas (Eds.), *Retail change. Contemporary issues* (pp. 172-191). London: UCL Press.

Whelan, A., Wrigley, N., Warm D., & Cannings, E. (2002). Life in a "food desert." *Urban Studies, 39*(11), 2083-2100.

Whysall, P. 1995. Regenerating inner city shopping centres: The British experience. *Journal of Retailing and Consumer Services, 2*(1), 3-14.

Whysall, P. (2004). What can we learn from retailers' news releases? A "stakeholder engagement" perspective. *International Review of Retail, Distribution and Consumer Research, 14*(1), 31-45.

Williams, C. C. (1997). Rethinking the role of the retail sector in economic development. *The Service Industries Journal, 2*(2), 205-220.

Williams, P., & Hubbard, P. (2001). Who is disadvantaged? Retail change and social exclusion. *International Review of Retail, Distribution and Consumer Research, 11*(3), 267-286.

Wilson, L. C., Alexander A., & Lumbers, M. (2004). Food access and dietary variety among older people. *International Journal of Retail & Distribution Management, 32*(2), 109-122.

Wood, S., Lowe M., & Wrigley, N. (2006). Life after PPG6—Recent UK food retailer responses to planning regulation tightening. *International Review of Retail, Distribution and Consumer Research, 16*(1), 23-41.

Woodliffe, L. (1998). Rethinking consumer disadvantage: The importance of qualitative research. *International Journal of Retail & Distribution Management, 32*(11), 523-531.

Wrigley N. (2002). "Food deserts" in British cities: Policy context and research priorities. *Urban Studies, 39*(11), 2029-2040.

Wrigley, N., Guy C., & Lowe, M. (2002). Urban regeneration, social inclusion and large store development: The Seacroft development in context. *Urban Studies, 39*(11), 2101-2114.

Wrigley, N., Warm D., & Margetts, B. (2002). Deprivation, diet and food retail access: findings from the Leeds "Food Deserts" study. *Environment & Planning 35,* 151-188.

ABOUT THE AUTHORS

Terri Feldman Barr is an associate professor in the Department of Marketing at Miami University in Oxford, Ohio. She earned her PhD from the University of Cincinnati, an MBA from Xavier University (Cincinnati) and a BS from College of William and Mary in Virginia. Her published research spans a broad range of topics including sales team conflict, professional service failures and recovery, and effective pedagogy. Social entrepreneurship is an exciting new research area for her. An award-winning teacher, Dr. Barr teaches both an upper-level sales course for marketing majors, and a first-year course for business students.

Marcello Bertotti is a PhD research student at Middlesex University (United Kingdom). His research interests include urban and regional economic development, small firm research, cluster development and urban governance, particularly in relation to private sector involvement in policymaking. He is currently completing his thesis examining the impact of a U.S. inspired policy approach—the city growth strategies—on two inner city areas in London. Prior to the start of his PhD program, Marcello worked for 4 years as a researcher at CEEDR (Centre for Enterprise and Economic Development Research) based at Middlesex University and was involved in a variety of research projects mainly focusing on ethnic minority business and social enterprise located in areas of deprivation.

Cynthia Cycyota is an associate professor of management in the Management Department at the United States Air Force Academy in Colorado Springs, Colorado. She received her undergraduate degree in accounting from the University of Missouri, her MBA from Wright State University in

Dayton, Ohio with a concentration in finance, and completed her doctoral dissertation on biotechnology executive decision making at the University of Texas in 2003. Her current research and teaching interests include executive decision making, institutionalism, entrepreneurial strategies, international strategies, biotechnology, executive research methods, and executive ethics. She worked for Peat, Marwick, Mitchell & Co. as an audit manager, and later was a vice president for Hinsdale Federal Savings and Loan in Hinsdale, Illinois. She teaches courses in strategic management and international management.

Lisa Easterly is the project director for curriculum development for New York State schools of social work. She has 20 years of business management experience. During the last 10 years she has researched business strategies within social ventures. She is also a nonprofit organizational consultant providing training on strategic planning, fundraising, and strategy for establishing and managing social ventures. She has published several articles and papers and delivered lectures on nonprofit management, social ventures, and employment for disadvantaged individuals.

Peter S Heslam, MA, BA, DPhil FRSA, is director of Transforming Business, a research project on enterprise solutions to poverty at Cambridge University (www.transformingbusiness.net). Transforming Business is based in the Divinity Faculty, (where Peter is CARTS Fellow) and has close links with the University's Judge Business School and with international business. Peter holds degrees in social science and in theology and has an established international reputation for relating Protestant and Catholic social thought to contemporary culture, particularly business and economics. He is a senior member of Trinity College, Cambridge, a senior research associate of the London Institute for Contemporary Christianity and a fellow of the Royal Society of Arts.

Scott Hipsher earned his PhD in management science from Capella University, an MBA degree from Bangkok University, and a BSc from the University of Maryland. He is currently the general affairs manager for ZOA Refugee Care in Mae Sot, Thailand. Scott has worked in academia, including working for Bangkok University, as well as in a variety of other positions which include being member of the U.S. Navy, a horse-racing trainer, an area manager for an export company, a factory worker, and a consultant. He has authored a number of works including being the lead author of *The Nature of Asian Businesses: An Evolutionary Perspective*. He is currently working on a book on expatriates working in Asia.

Fergus Lyon is a principal consultant and professor with the Centre for Enterprise and Economic Development Research, Middlesex University. He earned his PhD from the University of Durham. Fergus is an applied researcher on economic development policy with 12 years of experience of research in economic regeneration in urban and rural areas and the role different types of enterprises can play. Fergus has particular experience in social and community enterprises, clustering and networks of enterprises, business needs assessment, institutional capacity building for enterprise support organizations, and marketing and informal finance. He is also a director of community enterprise preschool. He has written 30 substantial reports for policymakers funded by United Kindgom and international donors, published 11 papers in established international journals, written 9 book chapters, produced a number of shorter policy briefings and written a book on participatory social research methodologies.

Paul Miesing is an associate professor in the School of Business at the University at Albany, State University of New York. He earned his DBA from Colorado University. His research interests are in strategic management, and he has published dozens of articles and papers in both academic and practitioner journals including *Academy of Management Journal*, *Journal of Marketing*, and *Management Science*, among others. He has received research and teaching awards, and delivered lectures, seminars, and scholarly presentations on various management and organization issues and topics in numerous countries. He was a Fulbright lecturer at Fudan University in Shanghai during 1988-1999.

Faith Wambura Ngunjiri is an emerging scholar in leadership studies, originally from Kenya who is committed to social and economic justice issues especially as they relate to women. After graduating from Bowling Green State University with a doctorate in leadership studies, Faith taught at Indiana University-Purdue University, Fort Wayne as a visiting assistant professor for 1 year. She is currently the associate director for ethics and spirituality in the workplace at the Yale Center for Faith and Culture. Her research interests include leadership for social justice, tempered radicalism, servant leadership, and ethics and spirituality.

Neerja Raman is senior fellow at Stanford University, is an award-winning executive in innovation research. She serves on the advisory committee for Cyber-Infrastructure, National Science Foundation. Neerja was inducted into the Women in Technology Hall of Fame 2005, in recognition of her sustained leadership. At Hewlett Packard Labs as director, strategic planning and imaging systems she led a global, diverse research organization for HP's flagship printing and media businesses. She championed the cause of women in technical careers and was the first woman appointee on a 12-member Technical Career Path committee. She continues as mentor and serves in board and advisory capacities for nonprofits.

Brett R. Smith is an assistant professor of entrepreneurship and the founding director of the Center for Social Entrepreneurship at Miami University. He earned his PhD from the University of Cincinnati, his MBA from Georgia State University, and his BS from Miami University. His research interests include social entrepreneurship, entrepreneurial opportunities, and entrepreneurial teams. His work in social entrepreneurship has been quoted in *Time, Business Week, Financial Times*, CNN, MSNBC and many other media outlets. His research has been published in *Leadership Quarterly, Frontiers of Entrepreneurship Research* and the *Case Research Journal*.

James Spee is an associate professor at the University of Redlands School of Business. He earned BS degrees from Calvin College and the University of Washington, and an MBA and PhD from Claremont Graduate University. He teaches in the areas of leadership and strategy. His research focuses on management education and development through the assessment of social competencies and through focused reflection. He is the 2006-2007 past president of the Western Academy of Management, the HR/OB track chair for the North American Case Research Association, a member of the AOM membership committee, and the webmaster for the Management Education and Development Division of AOM. He was a project coordinator for the Christian Reformed World Relief Committee in Bogra, Bangladesh from 1980 to 1983.

Jim Stoner is professor of management systems and chairholder of the James A.F. Stoner Chair in Global Sustainability at Fordham University's Graduate School of Business. He earned his BS in engineering science at Antioch College in Yellow Springs, Ohio, and his MS. and PhD in industrial management at MIT, in Cambridge, Massachusetts. He has published articles in such journals and periodicals as: *Academy of Management Review, Harvard Business Review, Journal of Experimental Social Psychology, Journal of Development Studies, Personnel Psychology*, etc. and has authored and coauthored a number of books including *Management* (first-sixth editions, 1978-1995); *Fundamentals of Financial Managing* (2002 -2007) and *Modern Financial Managing: Continuity and Change* (1995 - 2007). He has consulted with a wide variety of business organizations, received a number of teaching awards, and has taught in many executive development, MBA, and executive MBA programs including ones in Ethiopia, Iran, Ireland,

Japan, Siberia. He is a past chair of the Management Education and Development Division of the Academy of Management and past board member of the Organizational Behavior Teaching Society.

Wendy Volkland is an assistant professor of management in the Management Department at the United States Air Force Academy in Colorado Springs, Colorado. She received her undergraduate degree in Engineering Sciences Astronautical Engineering from the United States Air Force Academy and her MPP in 2000 from Harvard University with a concentration in science and technology policy. Her master's thesis was on decontaminating aircraft from chemical weapons. Her current research and teaching interests include international development, social entrepreneurship, international strategies, and technology transfer. Capt Volkland worked as an engineer for the Air Force Seek Eagle Office performing stability and control flight test analysis for F-16 and F-15 fighter aircraft. She has taught courses in mechanical engineering, systems engineering, project management, management theory, and organizational behavior.

Charles Wankel is associate professor of management at St. John's University, New York. He received his doctorate from New York University. Dr. Wankel has authored and edited many books including *Rethinking Management Education for the 21st Century* (IAP, 2002), *Educating Managers with Tomorrow's Technologies* (IAP, 2003), *The Cutting-Edge of International Management Education* (IAP, 2004), *Educating Managers through Real World Projects* (IAP, 2005), *New Visions of Graduate Management Education* (IAP, 2006), and forthcoming the *Handbook of 21st Century Management* (Sage, 2008) and *Being and Becoming a Management Education Scholar* (IAP, 2008). He is the leading founder and director of scholarly virtual communities for management professors, currently directing eight with thousands of participants in more than 70 nations. Extensive foreign teaching and lecturing include in Lithuania at the Kaunas University of Technology (Fulbright Fellowship) and the University of Vilnius, (United Nations Development Program and Soros Foundation funding). Invited lectures include 2005 distinguished speaker at the E-ducation without Border Conference, Abu Dhabi, and 2004 keynote speaker at the Nippon Academy of Management, Tokyo.

Paul Whysall is professor of retailing at Nottingham Business School, Nottingham Trent University in the United Kingdom. His early background was in urban studies and planning, but for many years now he has been researching ethical and locational aspects of retailing and marketing. He was one of the first European researchers to explore retail ethics and has published widely in both retailing and ethics journals. Recently he has been especially concerned with aspects of retail employment.